SOCIOLOGY IN QUESTION

Theory, Culture & Society

Theory, Culture & Society caters for the resurgence of interest in culture within contemporary social science and the humanities. Building on the heritage of classical social theory, the book series examines ways in which this tradition has been reshaped by a new generation of theorists. It will also publish theoretically informed analyses of everyday life, popular culture, and new intellectual movements.

EDITOR: Mike Featherstone, *University of Teesside*

SERIES EDITORIAL BOARD
Roy Boyne, *University of Northumbria at Newcastle*
Mike Hepworth, *University of Aberdeen*
Scott Lash, *University of Lancaster*
Roland Robertson, *University of Pittsburgh*
Bryan S. Turner, *Deakin University*

Recent volumes include:

Changing Cultures
Feminism, Youth and Consumerism
Mica Nava

Globalization
Social Theory and Global Culture
Roland Robertson

Risk Society
Towards a New Modernity
Ulrich Beck

Max Weber and the Sociology of Culture
Ralph Schroeder

Postmodernity USA
The Crisis of Social Modernism in Postwar America
Anthony Woodiwiss

The Body and Social Theory
Chris Shilling

Symbolic Exchange and Death
Jean Baudrillard

Economies of Signs and Space
Scott Lash and John Urry

Religion and Globalization
Peter Beyer

Baroque Reason
The Aesthetics of Modernity
Christine Buci-Glucksmann

SOCIOLOGY IN QUESTION

Pierre Bourdieu

translated by

Richard Nice

SAGE Publications

London ● Thousand Oaks ● New Delhi

ISBN 0-8039-8337-9 (hbk)
ISBN 0-8039-8338-7 (pbk)
© Les Editions de Minuit, Paris 1984
First published 1984 in French as *Questions de Sociologie*
© SAGE Publications 1993 English Translation
First published in English 1993
Reprinted 1995

This translation is published with financial support from the French
Ministry of Culture

Published in association with *Theory, Culture & Society*, School of Human
Sciences, University of Teesside

SAGE Publications Ltd
1 Oliver's Yard,
55 City Road
London EC1Y 1SP

SAGE Publications Inc
2455 Teller Road
Thousand Oaks,
California 91320

SAGE Publications India Pvt Ltd
B–42 Panchsheel Enclave
PO Box 4109
New Delhi 110 017

British Library Cataloguing in Publication data
A catalogue record for this book is available from the British Library

Library of Congress Control Number: 9386215

Printed digitally and bound in Great Britain by
Lightning Source UK Ltd., Milton Keynes, Bedfordshire

301 BOU

CONTENTS

PROLOGUE

The texts that follow are all transcripts of *oral* answers and talks, addressed to non-specialists; it would be incongruous to preface them with a long written preamble. But I should at least say why it seemed both useful and legitimate to bring together some discussions of various themes that, for some readers, have already been developed elsewhere at greater length and no doubt more rigorously,[1] presenting them here in a more approachable but less thoroughly argued form.

Sociology differs in one respect at least from the other sciences: it is required to be accessible in a way that is not expected of physics or even semiology or philosophy. To deplore obscurity is perhaps *also* a way of showing that one would like to understand or to be sure of understanding things that one feels are worthy of being understood. In any case, there is probably no area in which the 'power of experts' and the monopoly of 'competence' is more dangerous and more intolerable; and sociology would not be worth an hour of anyone's time if it were to be merely an expert knowledge reserved for experts.

It should hardly need to be pointed out that no other science more obviously puts at stake the interests, sometimes the vital interests, of social groups. That is what makes it so very difficult both to produce sociological discourse and to transmit it. And one would hardly expect employers, evangelists or journalists to praise the scientific quality of research that uncovers the hidden foundations of their domination, or to strive to publicize its findings. Those who are impressed by the certificates of scientificity that the powers that be, whether temporal or spiritual, choose to award should recall that, in the 1840s, the industrialist Grandin, speaking in the French Chamber of Deputies, thanked the 'genuine scientists' who had proved that employing children was often an act of generosity. Our Grandins and our 'genuine scientists' are still with us today.

Equally, the sociologist can expect little help in his effort to make known what he has learned, from those whose job it is, day by day and week by week, to produce – on all the required subjects of our time, 'violence', 'youth', 'drugs', the 'revival of religion', and so on – the not-even-untrue discourses which become ritual essay subjects for high-school pupils.

Yet he has a great need of being helped in that task. For truth has no intrinsic capacity to prevail, and scientific discourse is itself caught up in the power relations that it uncovers. The transmission of that discourse is subject to the very laws of cultural diffusion that it sets out. Those who possess the cultural competence needed to appropriate that discourse are not those who would have most interest in doing so.

In short, in the struggle against the loudest voices in our societies – politicians, editorialists and commentators – scientific discourse has all the cards stacked against it: the difficulty and slowness of its construction, which means that it generally arrives after the battle is over; its inevitable complexity, which tends to discourage simplistic or suspicious minds or, quite simply, those who do not have the cultural capital needed to decipher it; its abstract impersonality, which discourages identification and all forms of gratifying projection; and above all its distance from received ideas and spontaneous convictions.

The only way to give some real force to that discourse is to accumulate upon it the social force that enables it to impose itself; and this, by an apparent contradiction, may require one to agree to play the social games of which it exposes the logic. The suspicion that one is compromising has to be accepted in advance. When I try to describe the mechanisms of intellectual fashion in an interview with a journal that is a beacon of intellectual fashion, or when I use the tools of intellectual marketing to make them convey exactly what they normally mask, in particular the function of those tools and of their customary users, or when I try to define the relationship between the Communist Party and French intellectuals in the pages of one of the Party journals intended for intellectuals, I am seeking to turn the weapons of intellectual power against intellectual power, by saying the thing that is least expected, most improbable, most *out of place* in the place where it is said. This represents a refusal to 'preach to the converted', which abandons the ordinary discourse that is so well received because it tells its audience only what they want to hear.

Note

1   In each case I give references at the end of the chapter, so that the reader may go further if he or she wishes.

1

THE ART OF STANDING UP
TO WORDS

Q. *Bourgeois discourse about culture tends to present interest in culture as disinterested – whereas you show that this interest, and even its apparent disinterestedness, yield profits.*

A. Paradoxically, intellectuals have an interest in *economism* since, by reducing all social phenomena, and more especially the phenomena of exchange, to their economic dimension, it enables intellectuals to avoid putting themselves on the line. That is why it needs to be pointed out that there is such a thing as cultural capital, and that this capital secures direct profits, first on the educational market, of course, but elsewhere too, and also secures profits of distinction – strangely neglected by the marginalist economists – which result *automatically* from its rarity, in other words from the fact that it is unequally distributed.

Q. *So cultural practices are always strategies for distancing oneself from what is 'common' and 'easy' – what you call 'strategies of distinction'?*

A. They may be distinctive, distinguished, without even trying to be so. The dominant definition of 'distinction' calls 'distinguished' those behaviours that distinguish themselves from what is common and vulgar, without any intention of distinction. They are the ones that consist in loving what *has* to be loved, or even 'discovering' it, at every moment, as if by accident. The profit of distinction is the profit that flows from the *difference*, the gap, that separates one from what is common. And this direct profit is accompanied by an additional profit that is both subjective and objective, the profit that comes from seeing oneself – and being seen – as totally disinterested.

Q. *If every cultural practice is a means of creating distance (you even say that Brechtian 'distanciation' is a distancing of the people), then the idea of art for all, access to art for all, has no meaning. That illusion of 'cultural communism' has to be denounced.*

Interview with Didier Eribon in *Libération*, 3–4 November 1979: 12–13, after the publication of *Distinction*

A. I have myself shared in the illusion of 'cultural (or linguistic) communism'. Intellectuals spontaneously understand the relationship to a work of art as mystical participation in a common good, without rarity. My whole book argues that access to a work of art requires instruments that are not universally distributed. And consequently that the possessors of those instruments secure profits of distinction for themselves, and the rarer these instruments are (such as those needed to appropriate avant-garde works), the greater the profits.

Q. *If all cultural practices, and all tastes, classify one as being at a particular place in the social space, then it has to be acknowledged that the counterculture is a distinguishing activity like others?*
A. We'd first have to agree on what we meant by counterculture. And that, by definition, is difficult or impossible. There are countercultures, in the plural. They are everything that is marginal, outside the 'establishment', external to official culture. At once it can be seen that this counterculture is defined negatively by what it defines itself against. I'm thinking, for example, of the cult of everything that is outside 'legitimate' culture, such as strip cartoons. But that's not all. You don't get out of culture by sparing yourself the trouble of an analysis of culture and cultural interests. For example, it would be easy to show that ecological discourse – freewheeling, rambling in sandals, barefoot theatre and so on – is full of disdainful allusions to the 'nine-to-five routine' and the 'sheep-like' holiday-making of 'the average petit-bourgeois'. (We need to use quotation marks everywhere, not to mark the prudent distance of official journalism but to signify the gap between the language of analysis and ordinary language, in which words are all instruments of struggle, weapons and stakes in the struggles of distinction.)

Q. *So don't marginal groups and protest movements shake up the established values?*
A. Of course I always start by twisting the stick the other way and pointing out that these people who see themselves as being on the fringe, outside the social space, are situated in the social world, like everyone else. What I call their 'dream of social flying'¹ is a perfect expression of an uncomfortable position in the social world – the one that characterizes the 'new autodidacts', those who stayed in the educational system until a fairly advanced age, long enough to acquire a 'cultivated' relation to culture, but without obtaining qualifications, or not all those which their initial social position promised them.

Having said that, all movements that challenge the symbolic order are important inasmuch as they call into question what seemed to go without saying – what is beyond question, unchallenged. They jostle the self-evidences. That was true of May '68. It's true of the feminist movement, which isn't disposed of by labelling it 'middle-class'. If these forms of contestation often perturb political or trade-union movements, it's perhaps because they run counter to the deep-seated dispositions and specific interests of the apparatchiks. But above all it's because the apparatchiks, who have learned that *politicization*, the political mobilization of the dominated classes, almost always has to be won against the *domestic*, the private, the psychological, etc., find it hard to understand strategies aimed at *politicizing* the *domestic*, consumption, women's work, etc. But that would require a long analysis . . . In any case, if you leave whole areas of social practice – art, home life, and so on – out of your political reflection, you risk enormous 'returns of the repressed'.

Q. *But in that case, what would a genuine counterculture be?*
A. I'm not sure I can answer that question. What I do know is that possession of the weapons necessary for defending oneself against cultural domination, the domination that is exerted through and in the name of culture, ought to be part of culture. It would have to be a culture capable of distancing culture, of analysing it, and not inverting it or, rather, imposing an inverted form of it. In that sense my book is both a cultural and a counter-cultural book. More generally, I think a genuine counterculture ought to supply weapons for use against the soft forms of domination, the advanced forms of mobilization, the gentle violence of the new professional ideologists, who often rely on a kind of quasi-scientific rationalization of the dominant ideology; against the political uses of science, the authority of science – physical science or economic science, not to mention the biology or sociology of the advanced (and highly euphemized) forms of racism. In a word, it would mean proliferating the weapons of defence against symbolic domination. It would also imply, in the light of what I was saying a moment ago, bringing many things into a necessarily political culture that the present definition of both culture and politics excludes from it. . . . And I don't think it impossible that one day a group might be able to take on such a task of reconstruction.

Q. *Shouldn't it be stressed that above all you are not trying to give intellectuals a guilt complex?*
A. Personally I have a horror of all those who try to induce a sense of 'culpability' or an 'uneasy conscience'. I think far too much play has been made, especially as regards intellectuals, with the priest's game of inducing guilt. Especially since it's very easy to shake off culpability by performing an act of contrition or a public confession. I simply want to help to produce instruments of analysis that don't make exceptions for intellectuals. I think that the sociology of the intellectuals is a preliminary to all science of the social world, which is necessarily done by intellectuals. Intellectuals who had subjected their own intellectual practice, and not their 'bourgeois souls', to sociological critique would be better armed to withstand the guilt-inducing strategies which are directed against them by all apparatuses and

which are designed to prevent them from doing what, as intellectuals, they could do for – and especially against – those apparatuses.

Q. *But aren't you afraid that your analyses (for example, of the place of the values of macho masculinity in the working-class lifestyle) might reinforce* ouvriérisme? [2]

A. You know, when I write, I fear many things, that's to say many wrong readings. That explains the complexity of my sentences, which has often been complained about. I try to discourage in advance the wrong readings that I can often predict. But the precautions that I insert in a parenthesis, an adjective or a use of quotation marks only reach those who don't need them. And in a complex analysis, everyone selects the aspect that disturbs him least.

Having said that, I think it is very important to describe the values of masculinity in the working class. It's a social fact like any other, but one that's often badly understood by intellectuals. For one thing, these values, which are inscribed in the body, in other words in the unconscious, make it possible to understand many behaviours of the working class and of some of its spokesmen. It goes without saying that I don't present the lifestyle of the working class and its system of values as a model, an ideal. I try to explain the attachment to the values of masculinity, physical strength, by pointing out for example that it's characteristic of people who have little to fall back on except their labour power, and sometimes their fighting strength. I try to show in what respect the relationship to the body that is characteristic of the working class is the basis of a whole set of attitudes, behaviours and values, and that it is the key to understanding their way of talking or laughing, eating or walking. I say that the idea of masculinity is one of the last refuges of the identity of the dominated classes. Elsewhere I try to show the political and other effects of the new therapeutic morality, which is disseminated all day long by advertisers, women's magazines, TV psychoanalysts, marriage guidance counsellors, etc., etc. That doesn't mean that I exalt the values of masculinity or the uses that are made of them, whether it's the cult of the good-hearted brute, predisposed to military services (the Jean Gabin/paratrooper side that inspires a fascinated horror in intellectuals), or the *ouvriériste* use of no-nonsense plain speaking that makes it possible to dispense with analysis, or, worse, to silence analysis.

Q. *You say that the dominated classes have only a passive role in the strategies of distinction, that they serve as a negative 'foil' for the other classes. So for you there's no such thing as popular culture?*

A. The question isn't whether *for me* there is or is not 'popular culture', but whether there is in reality something that resembles what people who talk about 'popular culture' think they are referring to. And to that question my answer is 'no'. But to find the way out of all the obfuscation that surrounds that dangerous notion would require a very long analysis. I'd rather leave the matter there for the moment. What I could say in a few sentences, like everything I've said so far, could be misunderstood. And I'd like people to read my book, I'd rather they read my book, after all. . . .

Q. *But you do point out the linkage that exists in the working class between the relation to culture and political consciousness.*
A. I think that the work of politicization is often accompanied by a process of cultural acquisition that is often experienced as a kind of rehabilitation, a restoration of personal dignity. That can be seen very clearly in the memoirs of labour activists of the old school. This liberating process seems to me to have some alienating effects, because the winning-back of a kind of cultural dignity goes hand in hand with a recognition of the culture in whose name many effects of domination are exerted. I'm not only thinking of the weight of educational qualifications in working-class organizations; I'm also thinking of some forms of unconscious and therefore unconditional recognition of legitimate culture and those who possess it. I think it might even be found that some forms of aggressive *ouvriérisme* stem from a secret recognition of culture or, quite simply, an unmastered, unanalysed cultural shame.

Q. *But aren't the changes in the relationship to the educational system that you describe in your book tending to transform not only relations to culture but also relations to politics?*
A. I think, and I show it more fully in my book, that these transformations, in particular the effects of the inflation and devaluation of educational qualifications, are among the most important factors of change, especially in the area of politics. I'm thinking in particular of the anti-hierarchical or even anti-institutional dispositions that have emerged far beyond the educational system, the exemplary bearers of which are factory workers with the baccalaureate or the new strata of office workers, the production-line workers of bureaucracy. I think that beneath the apparent oppositions – Communist Party/Trotskyists or CGT/CFDT[3] and even more, perhaps, beneath the conflicts of tendencies that now run through all organizations, you would find the effects of different relations to the educational system, which often express themselves in the form of conflicts between generations. But to give more substance to these intuitions, one would need to carry out empirical analyses that are not always possible.

Q. *How can an opposition to the imposition of the dominant values be constituted?*
A. Though it may surprise you, I'll answer by quoting Francis Ponge: 'It's then that the art of standing up to words becomes useful, the art of only saying what one wants to say. To teach everyone the art of founding his

own rhetoric is a work of public salvation.' Standing up to words, resisting them, only saying what one wants to say; speaking instead of *being spoken* by borrowed words that are charged with social meaning (as when journalists talk of a '*summit* meeting' between two trade union leaders or when the [ostentatiously nonconformist – translator] newspaper *Libération* refers to the *Normandie* or the *France* as 'our' ships). Resisting neutralized, euphemized, routinized words, in short, all the pompous platitudes of the new technocratic rhetoric, but also the threadbare words – worn down into silence – of motions, resolutions, platforms and programmes. All language that results from the compromise with internal and external censorship exercises an effect of imposition, an imposition of the unthought that discourages thought.

There has been too much use made of the excuse of realism or the demagogic concern to be 'understood by the masses' in order to substitute slogans for analysis. I think one always ends up paying for simplifications, all simplistic thinking, or making other people pay for it.

Q. *So intellectuals do have a role to play?*
A. Yes, of course – because the absence of theory, of theoretical analysis of reality, that is papered over by the language of organizations, brings forth monsters. Slogans and anathemas lead to every form of terrorism. I am not so naïve as to suppose that the existence of a rigorous, complex analysis of reality is sufficient to protect one from all forms of terroristic or totalitarian deviation. But I am sure that the absence of such an analysis leaves the door wide open. That is why, in opposition to the anti-scientism that is part of the mood of the day and is the stock-in-trade of the new ideologists, I defend science and even theory when they have the effect of providing a better understanding of the social world. It is not a question of choosing between scientism and obscurantism. 'Of two evils', Karl Kraus used to say, 'I refuse to choose the lesser.'

The realization that science has become an instrument for legitimizing power, that our new leaders govern in the name of the version of economico-political science that is taught at Sciences Po[4] and in American-style 'business schools', must not lead to a romantic and regressive anti-scientism, which always coexists, in the dominant ideology, with the professed cult of science. Rather, it is a question of producing the conditions for a new scientific and political thinking that can be liberating because it is liberated from censorships.

Q. *But isn't that liable to re-create a language barrier?*
A. My aim is to help to make it harder to speak glibly about the social world. Schoenberg once said that he composed so that people would no longer be able to write music. I write so that people, and especially those who are authorized to speak, the 'spokesmen', can no longer produce noise about the social world that sounds like music.

As for giving everyone the means of founding his own rhetoric, as Ponge put it, of being his own true spokesman, speaking instead of being spoken – that ought to be the ambition of all spokesmen, who would probably be something quite different from what they are, if they made it their aim to work themselves out of a job. . . . There's no harm in dreaming, once in a while. . . .

Notes

1 See *Distinction*, p. 370, for 'an inventory of thinly disguised expressions of a sort of dream of social flying, a desperate attempt to defy the gravity of the social field' [translator].

2 The cult of 'the workers' and their values [translator].

3 Trade union movements respectively close to and hostile to the Communist Party [translator].

4 The Paris Institut d'Études Politiques (Fondation Nationale des Sciences Politiques) [translator].

2

A SCIENCE THAT MAKES TROUBLE

Q. *Let's start with the most obvious questions. Are the social sciences, and in particular sociology, really sciences? Why do you feel the need to claim scientificity?*

A. Sociology seems to me to have all the properties that define a science. But to what extent? That's the question. And the answer that can be given will vary greatly from one sociologist to another. I would simply say that there are many people who say and believe that they are sociologists and whom I find it hard to recognize as sociologists. In any case, sociology long ago emerged from its prehistory, the age of grand theories of social philosophy, with which lay people often still identify it. All sociologists worthy of the name agree on a common heritage of concepts, methods and verification procedures. The fact remains that, for obvious sociological reasons, sociology is a very *dispersed* discipline (in the statistical sense), in several respects. That's why it gives the impression of being a divided discipline, closer to philosophy than to the other sciences. But that's not the problem. If people are so pernickety about the scientific nature of sociology, that's because it's a troublemaker.

Q. *Aren't you led to ask yourself questions that arise objectively for the other sciences although there the scientists don't have to raise them concretely for themselves?*

A. Sociology has the unfortunate privilege of being constantly confronted with the question of its status as a science. People are infinitely more demanding than they are towards history or ethnology, not to mention geography, philology or archaeology. Sociology is constantly called into question and constantly calls itself, and the other sciences, into question. And that makes people imagine there's a sociological imperialism: just what is this science, still in its infancy, that takes upon itself to question the other sciences? I'm thinking, of course, of the sociology of science. In fact, however, sociology does no more than ask the other sciences the questions that arise particularly acutely for itself. If sociology is a critical science, that's perhaps because it is itself in a *critical* position. Sociology is an awkward case, as the phrase goes. We know, for example, that it is said to have been responsible for the events of May 1968. What people object to is

Interview with Pierre Thuillier, *La Recherche*, 112, June 1980: 738–43 not just its existence as a science, but its right to exist at all – especially at the present time, when some people who unfortunately have the power to succeed in doing so, are working to destroy it, while at the same time they build up an edifying 'sociology', at the Institut Auguste Comte or Sciences Po.[1] All this is done in the name of science, with the active complicity of some 'scientists' (in the trivial sense of the word).

Q. *Why is sociology particularly a problem?*
A. Why? Because it reveals things that are hidden and sometimes *repressed*, like the correlation between educational achievement, which is identified with 'intelligence', and social origin, or more precisely, the cultural capital inherited from the family. These are truths that the epistemocrats – that's to say a good number of those who read sociology and those who finance it – don't like to hear. Another example: when you show that the scientific world is the site of a competition, oriented by the pursuit of specific profits (Nobel prizes and others, priority in discoveries, prestige, etc.), and conducted in the name of specific *interests* (interests that cannot be reduced to economic interests in their ordinary form, which are therefore perceived as 'disinterested'), you call into question a scientific hagiography which scientists often take part in and which they need in order to believe in what they do.

Q. *Right: so sociology is seen as aggressive and embarrassing. But why does sociological discourse need to be 'scientific'? Journalists ask embarrassing questions too, but they don't claim to be scientific. Why is it crucial that there should be a frontier between sociology and critical journalism?*
A. Because there is an objective difference. It's not a question of vanity. There are coherent systems of hypotheses, concepts and methods of verification, everything that is normally associated with the idea of science. And so, why not say it's a science, if it is one? And then, something very important is at stake: one of the ways of disposing of awkward truths is to say that they are not scientific, which amounts to saying that they are 'political', that is, springing from 'interest', 'passion', and are therefore relative and relativizable.

Q. *If sociology is asked the question of its own scientificity, is that also because it developed rather later than the other sciences?*
A. Certainly. But that ought to show that this 'late development' is due to the fact that sociology is an especially difficult, an especially improbable, science. One of the major difficulties lies in the fact that its objects are stakes in social struggles – things that people hide, that they censor, for which they are prepared to die. That is true of the researcher himself, who is at stake in his own objects. And the particular difficulty of doing sociology is often due

to the fact that people are afraid of what they will find. Sociology confronts its practitioner with harsh realities; it disenchants. That's why, contrary to what is commonly thought, both inside and outside the discipline, it offers none of the satisfactions that adolescents often seek in political commitment. From that point of view, it is at the opposite end of the scale from the so-called 'pure' sciences which, like art, and especially music, the 'purest' art, are no doubt to some extent refuges into which people withdraw in order to forget the world, universes purged of everything that causes problems, like sexuality or politics. That's why formal or formalistic minds generally produce wretched sociology.

Q. *You show that sociology intervenes on socially important questions. That raises the question of its 'neutrality', its 'objectivity'. Can the sociologist remain above the fray, in the position of an impartial observer?*

A. The particularity of sociology is that it takes as its object fields of struggle – not only the field of class struggles but the field of scientific struggles itself. And the sociologist occupies a position in these struggles: first as the possessor of a certain economic and cultural capital, in the field of the classes; then, as a researcher endowed with a certain specific capital in the field of cultural production and, more precisely, in the sub-field of sociology. He always has to bear this in mind, in order to try to allow for everything that his practice, what he sees and does not see, what he does and does not do (for example, the objects he chooses to study), owes to his social position. That's why, for me, the sociology of sociology is not one 'specialism' among others, but one of the primary conditions for a scientific sociology. It seems to me that one of the main causes of error in sociology lies in an unexamined relationship to the object – or, more precisely, in ignorance of all that the view of the object owes to the point of view, that is, to the viewer's *position* in the social space and the scientific field.

One's chances of contributing to the production of truth seem to me to depend on two main factors, which are linked to the position one occupies – the interest one has in knowing and making known the truth (or conversely, in hiding it, from oneself and others), and one's capacity to produce it. As Bachelard so neatly put it, 'There is no science but of the hidden.' The sociologist is better or worse equipped to dis-cover what is hidden, depending on how well armed he is scientifically – how well he uses the capital of concepts, methods and techniques accumulated by his predecessors, Marx, Durkheim, Weber and many others – and also on how 'critical' he is, the extent to which the conscious or unconscious intention that impels him is a *subversive* one, the degree of interest he has in uncovering what is censored and repressed in the social world. And if sociology does not advance more quickly than it does, like social science in general, that's perhaps partly because these two factors tend to vary in inverse ratio.

If the sociologist manages to produce any truth, he does so not *despite* the interest he has in producing that truth but *because* he has an interest in doing so – which is the exact opposite of the usual somewhat fatuous discourse about 'neutrality'. This interest may consist, as it does everywhere else, in the desire to be the first to make a discovery and to appropriate all the associated rights, or in moral indignation or revolt against certain forms of domination and against those who defend them within the scientific world. In short, there is no immaculate conception. There would not be many scientific truths if we had to condemn this or that discovery (one only has to think of the 'double helix') on the grounds that the discoverers' intentions were not very pure.

Q. *But in the case of the social sciences, can't 'interest', 'passion' and 'commitment' lead to blindness, as the advocates of 'neutrality' would argue?*

A. In fact – and this is what makes the particular difficulty of sociology – these 'interests' and 'passions', noble or ignoble, lead to scientific truth only in so far as they are accompanied by a scientific knowledge of what determines them and of the *limits* that they set on knowledge. For example, everyone knows that resentment stemming from failure produces lucidity about the social world only by inducing blindness to the very principle of that lucidity.

But that's not all: the more advanced a science is, the greater is the capital of knowledge accumulated within it and the greater the quantity of knowledge that subversive and critical strategies, whatever their 'motivations', need to mobilize in order to be effective. In physics, it is difficult to triumph over an adversary by appealing to authority or (as still happens in sociology) by denouncing the political content of his theory. There, the weapons of criticism have to be scientific in order to be effective. In sociology, on the other hand, every proposition that contradicts received ideas is open to the suspicion of ideological bias, political axe-grinding. It clashes with social interests: the interest of the dominant groups, which are bound up with silence and 'common sense' (which says that what is must be, or cannot be otherwise); the interest of the spokesmen, the 'loud speakers', who need simple, simplistic ideas, slogans. That is why sociology is asked to provide infinitely more proof (which is no bad thing, actually) than is asked of the spokesmen of 'common sense'. And every discovery of science triggers off an immense labour of conservative 'critique', which has the whole social order working for it (budgets, jobs, honours . . . and therefore belief), aimed at re-covering what has been dis-covered.

Q. *A moment ago, you cited in the same breath Marx, Durkheim and Weber. You seem to imply that their respective contributions are cumulative. But in fact their approaches are different. How can there be one single science behind that diversity?*

A. In more cases than one, to enable science to progress, one has to establish communication between opposing theories, which have often been constituted against each other. It's not a question of performing the kind of eclectic pseudo-syntheses that have been so popular in sociology. (It should be said, in passing, that the denunciation of eclecticism has often served as an excuse for ignorance – it is so easy and comfortable to wrap oneself up in a tradition. Marxism, unfortunately, has often been used to provide this kind of lazy security.) Synthesis presupposes a radical questioning that leads one to the principle of the apparent antagonism. For example, in contrast to the usual regression of Marxism towards economism, which understands the economy only in the restricted sense of the capitalist economy and which explains everything in terms of the economy defined in this way, Max Weber broadens economic analysis (in the generalized sense) to areas that are generally abandoned by economics, such as religion. Thus, in a magnificent formulation, he characterizes the Church as the holder of the monopoly of the manipulation of the goods of salvation. He opens the way to a radical materialism that seeks the economic determinants (in the broadest sense) in areas where the ideology of 'disinterestedness' prevails, such as art and religion.

The same goes for the notion of legitimacy. Marx breaks with the ordinary representation of the social world by showing that 'enchanted' relationships – such as those of paternalism – conceal power relations. Weber seems to contradict Marx radically: he points out that membership of the social world implies a degree of recognition of legitimacy. Sociology teachers – this is a typical effect of position – note the difference. They prefer contrasting authors to integrating them. It's more convenient for designing clear-cut courses: part one Marx, part two Weber, part three myself . . . But the logic of research leads one to move beyond the opposition, back to the common root. Marx evacuated from his model the subjective truth of the social world, against which he posits the objective truth of that world as a system of power relations. Now, if the social world were reduced to its objective truth as a power structure, if it were not, to some extent, recognized as legitimate, it wouldn't work. The subjective representation of the social world as legitimate is part of the complete truth of that world.

Q. *In other words, you are trying to integrate into a single conceptual system theoretical contributions that have been arbitrarily separated by history or dogmatism.*

A. Most of the time, the obstacle standing in the way of concepts, methods or techniques of communication is not logical but sociological. Those who have identified themselves with Marx (or Weber) cannot take possession of what appears to them to be its negation without having the impression of negating themselves, renouncing their identity (it shouldn't be forgotten that for many people, to call themselves Marxist is nothing more than a profession of faith – or a totemic emblem). The same is true of the relations between 'theoreticians' and 'empiricists', between the supporters of what is called 'fundamental' research and what is called 'applied' research. That is why the sociology of science can have a scientific effect.

Q. *Does it follow that a conservative sociology is bound to remain superficial?*
A. Dominant groups always take a dim view of sociologists, or the intellectuals who stand in for them when the discipline is not yet constituted, or cannot function, as in the USSR today. Their interests are bound up with silence because they have no bones to pick with the world they dominate, which consequently appears to them as self-evident, a world that goes without saying. In other words, I repeat, the type of social science that one can do depends on the relationship one has to the social world, and therefore on the position one occupies within that world.

More precisely, this relation to the world is translated into the *function* that the researcher consciously or unconsciously assigns to his practice and that governs his research strategies – the objects chosen, the methods used, and so on. You may make it your goal to understand the social world, in the sense of understanding for understanding's sake. Or you may seek techniques that make it possible to manipulate it, in which case you place sociology in the service of the *management of the established order*. A simple example will make this clear: the sociology of religion may amount to research for pastoral purposes that takes as its objects laymen, the social determinants of church-going or abstention; it then becomes a kind of market research making it possible to rationalize sacerdotal strategies for the sale of the goods of 'salvation'. Alternatively it may aim to understand the functioning of the religious field, of which the laity is only one aspect, studying for example the functioning of the Church, the strategies through which it reproduces itself and perpetuates its power – strategies that include sociological studies (initially carried out by a canon).

A good number of those who describe themselves as sociologists or economists are social *engineers* whose function is to supply recipes to the leaders of private companies and government departments. They offer a rationalization of the practical or semi-theoretical understanding that the members of the dominant class have of the social world. The governing élite today needs a science capable of (in both senses) *rationalizing* its domination, capable both of reinforcing the mechanisms that sustain it and of legitimizing it. It goes without saying that the limits of this science are set by its practical functions: neither for social engineers nor for the managers of the economy can it perform a radical questioning. For example, the science of the Managing Director of the Compagnie Bancaire, which is considerable, much greater in some ways than that of many sociologists or economists, is circumscribed by the fact that its sole and *unquestioned* goal is the maximization of the profits of that institution. Examples of this partial 'science' would be the sociology of organizations, or 'political science', as taught at the Institut Auguste Comte or Sciences Po, with their favoured instruments, such as opinion polls.

Q. *Doesn't the distinction you draw between theoreticians and social engineers put science in the position of an art for art's sake?*
A. Not at all. Nowadays, among the people on whose existence sociology depends, there are more and more who are asking what sociology is for. In fact, the likelihood that sociology will disappoint or vex the powers that be rises to the extent that it successfully fulfils its strictly scientific function. That function is not to be useful for something, that is to say, for someone. To ask sociology to be useful for something is always a way of asking it to be useful to those in power – whereas the scientific function of sociology is to understand the social world, starting with the structures of power. This operation cannot be socially neutral, and undoubtedly fulfils a social function. One reason for that is that all power owes part of its efficacy – and not the least important part – to misrecognition of the mechanisms on which it is based.

Q. *I'd now like to turn to the question of the relationship between sociology and the neighbouring sciences. Your book* Distinction *opens with the sentence: 'Sociology is rarely more akin to a social psychoanalysis than when it confronts an object like taste.' Then come statistical tables, and accounts of surveys – but also analyses of a 'literary' type, such as one finds in Balzac, Zola or Proust. How do these two aspects fit together?*
A. The book results from an effort to integrate two modes of knowledge – ethnographic observation, which can only be based on a small number of cases, and statistical analysis, which makes it possible to establish regularities and to situate the observed cases in the universe of existing cases. So you have, for example, the contrasting descriptions of a working-class meal and a bourgeois meal, each reduced to their pertinent features. On the working-class side, there is the declared primacy of *function*, which appears in all the food that is served: the food has to be 'filling', 'body-building', as sports are expected to be (weight-training, etc.), to give strength (conspicuous muscles). On the bourgeois side, there is the primacy of *form*, or formality, which implies a kind of censorship and repression of function, an aestheticization, which is found in every area, as much in eroticism, functioning as sublimated or denied pornography, as in pure art which is defined precisely by the fact that it privileges form at the expense of function. In fact, the analyses that are described as 'qualitative' or, more pejoratively, 'literary', are essential for *understanding*, that's to say fully explaining, what the statistics merely record, rather like rainfall statistics. They lead to the principle of all the practices observed, in the most varied areas.

Q. *To come back to my question, what is your relationship to psychology, social psychology, etc.?*

A. Social science has always stumbled on the problem of the individual and society. In reality, the divisions of social science into psychology, social psychology and sociology were, in my view, constituted around an initial error of definition. The self-evidence of *biological individuation* prevents people from seeing that society exists in two inseparable forms: on the one hand, institutions that may take the form of physical things, monuments, books, instruments, etc., and, on the other, acquired dispositions, the durable ways of being or doing that are incorporated in bodies (and which I call *habitus*). The socialized body (what is called the individual or the person) is not opposed to society; it is one of its forms of existence.

Q. *In other words, psychology seems to be caught between, on one side, biology (which provides the fundamental invariants) and, on the other, sociology, which studies the way these invariants develop – and which is therefore entitled to talk about everything, even what is called private life, friendship, love, sexuality, etc.*

A. Absolutely. Contrary to the common preconception that associates sociology with the collective, it has to be pointed out that the collective is deposited *in each individual* in the form of durable dispositions, such as mental structures. For example, in *Distinction*, I try to establish empirically the relationship between the social classes and the incorporated systems of classification that are produced in collective history and acquired in individual history – such as those implemented by taste (the oppositions heavy/light, hot/cold, brilliant/dull, etc.).

Q. *But then, what does the biological or the psychological represent for the sociologist?*

A. Sociology takes the biological and the psychological as a 'given'. And it tries to establish how the social world uses, transforms and transfigures it. The fact that a human being has a body, that this body is mortal, raises difficult problems of social groups. I'm thinking of the book by Kantorowicz, *The King's Two Bodies*, which analyses the socially approved subterfuges resorted to in order to assert the existence of a royalty transcending the king's real body, which suffers imbecility, sickness, weakness and death. 'The King is dead, long live the King.' Ingenious.

Q. *You yourself talk of ethnographic descriptions . . .*

A. The distinction between ethnology and sociology is a perfect example of a spurious frontier. As I try to show in my latest book, *Le Sens pratique* [*The Logic of Practice*], it's a pure product of history (colonial history) that has no kind of logical justification.

Q. *But aren't there some very marked differences of attitude? In ethnology, one has the impression that the observer remains external to his object and that he can even record appearances whose meaning he does not know – whereas the sociologist seems to adopt the point of view of the subjects he studies.*

A. In fact, the relation of externality that you describe, which I call objectivist, is more common in ethnology, probably because it corresponds to the vision of the *outsider*. But some ethnologists have also played the game – the double game – of participation in native representations: the bewitched or mystical ethnologist. Your remark could even be inverted. Because they mostly work through the intermediary of interviewers and *never* have direct contact with the respondents, some sociologists are more inclined to objectivism than ethnologists (whose first professional virtue is to be able to establish a real relationship with their respondents). To that has to be added class distance, which is no less powerful than cultural distance. That's why there is perhaps no more inhuman science than that produced in Columbia under the direction of Lazarsfeld, where the distance produced by questioning and by the buffer of the interviewer is reinforced by the formalism of blind statistics. You learn a lot about a science, its methods and its content, when, as in the sociology of work, you do a kind of job description. For example, the bureaucratic sociologist treats the people he studies as interchangeable statistical units, subjected to closed questions that are identical for all, whereas the ethnologist's informant is a person of standing, sought out for long and detailed discussions.

Q. *So you are opposed to the 'objectivist' approach that substitutes the model for the reality; but also to Michelet, who wanted to 'resurrect' the past, or Sartre, who wants to grasp meanings through a phenomenology that you see as arbitrary?*

A. Exactly. For example, since one of the functions of social rituals is to relieve the agents of everything that we put under the heading of 'subjective experience' [*le vécu*], it is particularly dangerous to put in 'subjective experience' where there is none, in ritual practices, for example. The idea that there is nothing more generous than to project one's own 'subjective experience' into the consciousness of a 'primitive', a 'witch' or a 'proletarian' has always seemed to me somewhat ethnocentric. The best the sociologist can do is to objectify the inevitable effects of the objectification techniques that he has to use – writing, diagrams, maps, calendars, models, etc. For example, in *The Logic of Practice* I try to show that, having failed to appreciate the effects of their situation as observers and of the techniques they use to grasp their object, ethnologists have constituted the 'primitive' as a 'primitive' because they have not been able to recognize in him what they themselves are as soon as they cease to think scientifically, that is, in practice. So-called 'primitive' logics are quite simply practical logics, like the logic we implement to judge a painting or a quartet.

Q. *But isn't it possible to rediscover the logic of all that and at the same time preserve 'subjective experience'?*

A. There is an objective truth of the subjective, even when it contradicts the objective truth that one has to construct in opposition to it. Illusion is not, as such, illusory. It would be a betrayal of objectivity to proceed as if social subjects had no representation, no experience of the realities that science constructs, such as social classes. So one has to rise to a higher objectivity, which makes room for that subjectivity. Agents have a subjective experience that is not the full truth of what they do but which is part of the truth of what they do. Take for example the case of a chairman who says 'The meeting is suspended' or a priest who says 'I baptize you'. Why does that language have power? It's not the words that act, through a kind of magic power. But the fact is that, in particular social conditions, certain words do have power. They derive their power from an institution that has its own logic – qualifications, ermine and robes, the professorial chair, the ritual formulae, the participants' belief, etc. Sociology points out that it is not the words, or the interchangeable person who pronounces them, that act, but the institution. It shows the objective conditions that have to be fulfilled to secure the efficacy of a particular social practice. But the analysis cannot stop there. It must not forget that, in order for it all to work, the actor has to believe that he is the source of the efficacy of his action. There are systems that run entirely on belief and there is no system, not even the economy, that does not depend to some extent on belief in order to work.

Q. *From the standpoint of science, I can see very clearly what you're doing. But the result is that you devalue people's 'lived experience'. In the name of science, you're liable to take away people's reasons for living. What gives you the right (if I can put it that way) to deprive them of their illusions?*

A. I too sometimes wonder if the completely transparent and disenchanted social universe that would be produced by a social science that was fully developed (and widely diffused, if that could ever be the case) would not be impossible to live in. I think, all the same, that social relations would be much less unhappy if people at least understood the mechanisms that lead them to contribute to their own deprivation. But perhaps the only function of sociology is to reveal, as much by its visible lacunae as through its achievements, the limits of knowledge of the social world and so to make more difficult all forms of prophetic discourse, starting, of course, with the propheticism that claims to be scientific.

Q. *Let's turn to the relationship with economics, and in particular with certain neo-classical analyses like those of the Chicago school. In fact, the confrontation is interesting because it shows how two different sciences construct the same objects – fertility, marriage and, more especially, educational investment.*

A. That would be an enormous debate. What may mislead some people is that, like the neo-marginalist economists, I refer all social behaviours to a specific form of interest, of investment. But we are only using the same *words.* The interest I am talking about has nothing to do with Adam Smith's notion of self-interest, an a-historical, natural, universal interest, which is in fact simply the unconscious universalization of the interest engendered and presupposed by the capitalist economy. It is no accident that, to escape from this naturalism, the economists have to appeal to sociobiology, as Gary Becker does in an article entitled 'Altruism, egoism and genetic fitness'. For Becker, not only 'self-interest' but also 'altruism with regard to descendants' and other durable dispositions are to be explained by the selection over time of the most adaptive features.

In fact, when I say that there is a form of interest or function that lies behind every institution or practice, I am simply asserting the *principle of sufficient reason* which is implied in the very project of 'explaining' (*rendre raison* as we say in French) and which is intrinsic to the notion of science. This principle postulates that there is a cause or reason making it possible to explain or understand why a given practice or institution *is* rather than is not, and why it is *as it is* rather than otherwise. This interest or function is in no way natural or universal, contrary to what is supposed by the neo-classical economists, whose *homo economicus* is simply a universalization of *homo capitalisticus.* Ethnology and comparative history show us that the specifically social magic of institution can constitute almost anything as an interest and as a realistic interest, i.e. as an *investment* (in both the economic and the psychoanalytic senses) that is objectively rewarded, in the more or less long term, by an *economy.* For example, the economy of honour produces and rewards economic dispositions and practices that are apparently 'ruinous' – because they are so 'disinterested' – and are consequently absurd, from the point of view of the economics of the economists. And yet, even the behaviours that are the most wildly irrational from the standpoint of capitalist economic reason are based on a form of enlightened self-interest (e.g. the interest there is in being 'above suspicion') and can therefore be studied by an economics. Investment is the disposition to act that is generated in the relationship between a space defined by a game offering certain prizes or stakes (what I call a field) and a system of dispositions attuned to that game (what I call a *habitus*) – the 'feel' for the game and the stakes, which implies both the inclination and the capacity to play the game, to take an *interest* in the game, to be taken up, taken in by the game. You only have to think of the importance, in western societies, of educational investment – which in France finds its extreme form in the classes preparing for the *grandes écoles* – to realize that the institution is capable of producing the investment and, in this case, the hyper-investment, which is the condition of the functioning of the institution. But the same could be demonstrated about any form of the sacred. The experience of the sacred presupposes, inseparably, the acquired disposition which causes sacred objects to exist as such, and the objects which objectively demand a consecrating approach (that is the role of art in our societies). In other words, investment is the historical effect of the harmony between two realizations of the social – in things, through institution, and in bodies, through incorporation.

Q. *Isn't the kind of general anthropology that you put forward a way of achieving the philosophical ambition of a system, but with the means of science?*

A. The aim is certainly not to remain eternally locked in the totalizing discourse that was expounded by social philosophy and which is still common currency nowadays, especially in France, where prophetic pronouncements still enjoy a protected market. But I think that, in trying to conform to a very one-sided representation of scientificity, sociologists have moved into premature specialization. One could cite countless cases in which artificial divisions of the object, generally following the lines of administrative demarcations, are the main obstacle to scientific under-standing. To give an example from an area I know well, there's the separation of the sociology of culture and the sociology of education; or the economics of education and the sociology of education. I also think the science of man inevitably appeals to anthropological theories; that it can make real progress only on condition that it makes explicit these theories that researchers always bring in, in a practical form, and which are generally no more than the transfigured projection of their relation to the social world.

Note

1 The Paris Institut d'Études Politiques (Fondation Nationale des Sciences Politiques) [translator].

Further reading

For further discussion see Bourdieu P. (1975) 'The specificity of the scientific field and the social conditions of the progress of reason', *Social Science Information*, 14 (6): 19–47 [also in Lemert, C. (ed.) (1981) *French Sociology, Rupture and Renewal Since 1968*, New York: Columbia University Press, 257–92; (1975) 'Le langage autorisé: note sur les conditions de l'efficacité sociale du discours rituel', *Actes de la recherche en sciences sociales*, 5–6: 183–90; (1980) 'Le mort saisit le vif: les relations entre l'histoire réifiée et l'histoire incorporée', *Actes de la recherche en sciences sociales*, 32–3: 3–14.

3

THE SOCIOLOGIST IN QUESTION

Q. *Why do you use a special jargon – an especially difficult one – that often makes your texts inaccessible to the lay reader? Isn't there a contradiction between denouncing the scientist's self-assigned monopoly and re-creating it in the text that denounces it?*

A. Often one only has to let ordinary language speak for itself, to give way to linguistic *laissez-faire*, in order to accept unwittingly a whole social philosophy. The dictionary is charged with a political mythology (I am thinking for example of all the couples of adjectives: brilliant/serious, high/low, rare/common, etc.). Devotees of 'common sense', who move in ordinary language like a fish in water and who, in language as in other things, have the objectified structures working for them, can (except for their euphemisms) speak a language that is clear as crystal and freely denounce the jargon of others. But the social sciences have to win all that they say against the received ideas that are carried along in ordinary language and have to say what they have won in a language that is predisposed to say something quite different. To try to disrupt verbal automatisms does not mean artificially creating a distinguished difference that sets the layman at a distance; it means breaking with the social philosophy that is inscribed in spontaneous discourse. Using one word in place of another often means effecting a decisive epistemological change – which may well pass unnoticed.

But it is not a question of escaping from the automatisms of common sense in order to fall into the automatisms of critical language, with all the words that have too often functioned as slogans or rallying cries, all the utterances that serve not to state the real but to paper over the gaps in knowledge. (That is often the function of concepts with capital letters and the propositions that they introduce, which are very often no more than professions of faith whereby one believer recognizes another.) I am thinking of the 'basic Marxism', as Jean-Claude Passeron calls it, that flourished recently in France: an automatic language that runs all on its own, but in neutral, and makes it possible to talk about everything with

The questions discussed in this chapter are those which seemed most important among those that were most often put to me in various discussions in the early 1980s in Paris (at the École Polytechnique), Lyon (the Université Populaire), Grenoble (the Faculté des Lettres), Troyes (the Institut Universitaire de Technologie) and Angers (Faculté des Lettres) great economy, with a very small number of simple concepts, but without much thought. The mere fact of conceptualization often exerts an effect of neutralization and even denial.

Sociological language cannot be either 'neutral' or 'clear'. The word 'class' will never be a neutral word so long as there are classes: the question of the existence or non-existence of classes is a stake in struggle between the classes. The work of writing that is necessary in order to arrive at a rigorous and controlled use of language only rarely leads to what is called clarity, in other words, the reinforcement of the self-evidences of common sense or the certainties of fanaticism.

In contrast to the search for literary quality, the pursuit of rigour always leads one to sacrifice a neat formula, which can be strong and clear because it falsifies, to a less appealing expression that is heavier but more accurate, more controlled. Thus the difficulty of a style often comes from all the nuances, all the corrections, all the warnings, not to mention the reminders of definitions and principles that are needed in order for the discourse to bear within itself all the possible defences against hijacking and misappropriations. Attention to these *critical signs* is no doubt directly proportional to the reader's vigilance and therefore his competence – which means that the warnings are most clearly seen by the reader who needs them least. At least one can hope that they discourage phrase-mongering and parroting.

But the need to resort to an *artificial language* is perhaps more compelling for sociology than for any other science. In order to break with the social philosophy that runs through everyday words and also in order to express things that ordinary language cannot express (for example, everything that lies at the level of it-goes-without-saying), the sociologist has to resort to invented words which are thereby protected, relatively at least, from the naïve projections of common sense. These words are secure against hijacking because their 'linguistic nature' predisposes them to withstand hasty readings (for example, *habitus*, which refers to acquired properties, capital) and perhaps especially because they are inserted, locked, into a network of relationships that impose their logical constraints. For example, *allodoxia*, which well expresses something that is difficult to explain or even think in a few words (the fact of taking one thing for another, of thinking that something is other than it is, etc.), is bound up in the network of words from the same root: doxa, doxosopher, orthodoxy, heterodoxy, paradox.

Having said that, the difficulty of transmitting the products of sociological research is due much less than people think to the difficulty of language. An initial cause of misunderstanding lies in the fact that even the most 'cultured' readers have only a very approximate idea of the conditions of production of the discourse that they are trying to appropriate. For example, there is a 'philosophical' or 'theoretical' reading of works in social science that consists in noting the 'theses', the 'conclusions', independently of the process of which they are the outcome (i.e. in concrete terms, the empirical analyses, the statistical tables, the indications of method, and so on). If you read like that, you are reading another book. When I 'condense' the opposition between the working class and the dominant class into the opposition between the primacy given to substance (function) and the primacy given to form, people see a philosophical disquisition, when the point I'm making is that one group eats beans while the other eats salad, that differences in consumption, which are nil or very low for *underclothes*, are very strong for *outer clothes*, etc. It is true that my analyses arise from applying very abstract schemes of thought to very concrete things, the statistics for the purchase of pyjamas, underpants or trousers. It's not easy to read statistics on pyjamas while thinking of Kant. . . Everything people learn at school tends to discourage them from thinking of Kant apropos of pyjamas or thinking of pyjamas when reading Marx (I say Marx because you will readily allow me Kant, though in this respect it's much the same thing).

Add to that the fact that many readers do not know, or reject, the very principles of the sociological mode of thought, such as the intention of 'explaining the social by the social', in Durkheim's phrase, which is often perceived as an imperialist ambition. But, more simply, ignorance of statistics or, rather, lack of familiarity with the statistical mode of thought leads people to confuse the probable (e.g. the relationship between social origin and educational achievement) and the certain, the necessary. This leads to all sorts of absurd accusations, such as the charge of fatalism, or to misplaced objections, such as the scholastic failure of a proportion of the offspring of the dominant class, which is in fact a central element in the statistical mode of reproduction. (A 'sociologist', a member of the Institute, has devoted a great deal of energy to showing that not all the sons of Polytechnicians become Polytechnicians!)

But the main source of misunderstanding lies in the fact that, ordinarily, people hardly ever talk about the social world in order to say what it is, but almost always to say what it ought to be. Discourse about the social world is almost always performative: it contains wishes, exhortations, reproaches, orders, etc. It follows that the sociologist's discourse, though it tries to be descriptive, has every likelihood of being perceived as performative. If I say that women respond less often than men to questions in opinion polls – and that the difference becomes more marked as the questions become more 'political' – there will always be someone to complain that I exclude women from politics. That's because, when I say what is, people hear 'and it's fine that way'. Similarly, if you describe the working class as it is, you're suspected of wanting to lock it into what it is, as a destiny, of trying either to push it down or to exalt it. For example, the observation that, most of the time, men (and even more so, women) in the culturally most deprived classes entrust their political choices to the party of their choice, and, as it happens, to the Communist Party, has been understood as an exhortation to abandon oneself to the Party. In fact, in ordinary life, people will describe a working-class meal only in order to express wonderment or disgust, never in order to understand its logic, to explain it, in other words to secure the means of *taking it for what it is.* Readers read sociology through the spectacles of their *habitus.* And some people will find a reinforcement of their class racism in the same realist description that others will suspect of being inspired by class contempt.

In that lies the principle of a *structural misunderstanding* in the communication between the sociologist and his reader.

Q.   *Don't you think that, given the way in which you express yourself, your only possible readers are intellectuals? Isn't that a limit on the effectiveness of your work?*

A.   The sociologist's misfortune is that, most of the time, the people who have the technical means of appropriating what he says have no wish to appropriate it, no *interest* in appropriating it, and even have powerful interests in refusing it (so that some people who are very competent in other respects may reveal themselves to be quite obtuse as regards sociology), whereas those who would have an interest in appropriating it do not have the instruments for appropriation (theoretical culture, etc.). Sociological discourse arouses *resistances* that are quite analogous in their logic and their manifestations to those encountered by psychoanalytical discourse. The people who read that there is a very strong correlation between educational level and museum-going have every likelihood of being museum-goers, of being art lovers ready to die for the love of art, experiencing their encounter with art as a pure love, a love at first sight, and of setting countless systems of defence in the way of scientific object-ification.

In short, the laws of diffusion of scientific discourse mean that, despite the existence of relays and mediators, scientific truth is very likely to reach those who are least disposed to accept it and very unlikely to reach those who would have most interest in receiving it. Yet one may think that one would only have to provide the latter with a language in which they recognized themselves, or rather, in which they felt *recognized,* that's to say accepted, justified in existing as they exist (which they are necessarily offered by all good sociology, a science that, as such, *explains* things), in order to induce a transformation of their relationship to what they are.

What needs to be made available to people is the scientific gaze, a gaze that is at once objectifying and understanding, and which, when turned back on oneself, makes it possible to accept oneself and even, so to speak, lay claim to oneself, claim the right to be what one is. I'm thinking of slogans like the American blacks' 'Black is beautiful' and the feminists' assertion of the right to the 'natural look'. I have been accused of sometimes writing pejoratively about those who impose new needs and of thereby putting forward an ideal image of humanity that is reminiscent of the 'noble savage' but in a socialized version. In fact, it's not a question of locking agents into an 'original social being' treated as a destiny, a nature, but of offering them the *possibility* of taking on their *habitus* without guilt or suffering. That can be seen clearly in the area of culture, where the sense of inadequacy often comes from a dispossession that cannot recognize itself as such. What probably emerges through my way of speaking about beauticians, dietitians, marriage guidance counsellors and other purveyors of needs is indignation against that form of exploitation of people's deprivation which consists of imposing impossible norms and then selling the means – generally ineffective ones - of bridging the gap between these norms and the real possibilities of achieving them.

In that area, which is completely ignored by political analysis, although it is the site of objectively political action, the dominated groups are left to their own weapons; they are absolutely bereft of weapons of collective defence in order to confront the dominant groups and their 'poor man's psychoanalysts'. Yet it would be easy to show that the most typically political kind of political domination also runs through these channels. For example, in *Distinction*, I wanted to start the chapter on the relationship between culture and politics with a photograph – which, in the end, I didn't use, fearing that it might be misread – in which two trade union leaders are seen sitting on Louis XV chairs facing Giscard d'Estaing, who is himself seated on a Louis XV sofa. That picture pointed out, in the clearest possible way, through the ways of sitting, of placing the hands, in short, all the body language, which participant has on his side not only all the culture, that's to say the furniture, the décor, the Louis XV chairs, but also the ways of using it, inhabiting it – which one is the possessor of that objectified culture, and which ones are possessed by that culture, in the name of that culture. If, when face to face with the managing director, the trade-unionist 'feels small', that's at least partly because he only has instruments of analysis, and self-analysis, that are too general and too abstract, which give him no possibility of understanding and controlling his relation to language and the body. And this state of abandonment in which the available theories and analyses leave him is particularly serious – although the state of abandonment of his wife, in the kitchen of their council flat, faced with the simpering condescension of the presenters on the commercial radio stations, is not unimportant – because lots of people speak through him, because the speech of a whole group passes through his mouth and his body, and because his reactions, generalized in this way, may have been determined, without his realizing it, by his horror of long-haired hippies or intellectuals wearing spectacles.

Q. *Doesn't your sociology imply a deterministic view of man? What role, if any, is left for human freedom?*
A. Like every science, sociology accepts the principle of determinism understood as a form of the principle of sufficient reason. The science which must give the reasons for that which is thereby postulates that nothing is

without a reason for being. The sociologist adds: 'social reason' – nothing is without a specifically social reason for being. Faced with a statistical table, he postulates that there is a social factor that explains that distribution, and if, having found it, there is a residue, then he postulates the existence of another social factor, and so on. (That's what makes people sometimes imagine a sociological imperialism: but it's fair enough – every science has to use its own means to account for the greatest number of things possible, including things that are apparently or really explained by other sciences. It's on that condition that it can put real questions to the other sciences – and to itself – and destroy apparent reasons or raise clearly the problem of overdetermination.)

Having said that, people are often referring to two quite different things under the term 'determinism' – objective necessity, implied in reality itself, and 'experiential', apparent, subjective necessity, the *sense* of necessity or freedom. The degree to which the social world *seems* to us to be determined depends on the knowledge we have of it. On the other hand, the degree to which the world is *really* determined is not a question of opinion; as a sociologist, it's not for me to be 'for determinism' or 'for freedom', but to discover necessity, if it exists, in the places where it is. Because all progress in the knowledge of the laws of the social world increases the degree of perceived necessity, it is natural that social science is increasingly accused of 'determinism' the further it advances.

But, contrary to appearances, it's by raising the degree of perceived necessity and giving a better knowledge of the laws of the social world that social science gives more freedom. All progress in knowledge of necessity is a progress in *possible* freedom. Whereas misrecognition of necessity contains a form of recognition of necessity, and probably the most absolute, the most total form, since it is unaware of itself as such, knowledge of necessity does not at all imply the necessity of that recognition. On the contrary, it brings to light the possibility of choice that is implied in every relationship of the type '*if* X, *then* Y'. The freedom that consists in choosing to accept or refuse the 'if' has no meaning so long as one is unaware of the relationship that links it to a 'then . . .'. By bringing to light the laws that presuppose non-intervention (that's to say, unconscious acceptance of the conditions of realization of the expected effects), one extends the scope of freedom. A law that is unknown is a nature, a destiny (that's true, for example, of the relationship between inherited cultural capital and educational achievement); a law that is known appears as a possibility of freedom.

Q. *Isn't it dangerous to speak of laws?*
A. Yes, undoubtedly. And, as far as possible, I avoid doing so. Those who have an interest in things taking their course (that's to say in the 'if' remaining unchanged) see the 'law' (when they see it at all) as a destiny, an inevitability inscribed in social nature (which gives the iron laws of the

oligarchies of the neo-Machiavellians, such as Michels or Mosca). In fact, a social law is a historical law, which perpetuates itself so long as it is allowed to operate, that's to say as long as those whose interests it serves (sometimes unknown to them) are able to perpetuate the conditions of its efficacy.

What we have to ask is what we are doing when we state a social law that was previously unknown (such as the law of the transmission of cultural capital). One may claim to be fixing an eternal law, as the conservative sociologists do with the tendency towards the concentration of power. In reality, science needs to know that it merely records, in the form of tendential laws, the logic that is characteristic of a *particular game, at a particular moment*, and which plays to the advantage of those who dominate the game and are able, *de facto* or *de jure*, to define the rules of the game.

Having said that, as soon as the law has been stated, it may become a stake in struggles – the struggle to conserve, by conserving the conditions of the functioning of the law, the struggle to transform, by changing these conditions. Bringing the tendential laws to light is a precondition for the success of actions aimed at frustrating them. The dominant groups have an interest in the law, and therefore in a physicalist interpretation of the law, which pushes it back to the state of an infra-conscious mechanism. By contrast, the dominated groups have an interest in the discovery of the law as such, that is, as a historical law, which could be abolished if the conditions of its functioning were removed. Knowledge of the law gives them a chance, a possibility of countering the effects of the law, a possibility that does not exist so long as the law is unknown and operates unbeknown to those who undergo it. In short, just as it de-naturalizes, so sociology de-fatalizes.

Q. *Isn't an ever more developed knowledge of the social world likely to discourage all political action aimed at transforming the social world?*

A. Knowledge of the most probable outcome is what makes it possible, by reference to other ends, to bring about the least probable. By consciously playing with the logic of the social world one can bring about possible outcomes that did not seem to be implied by that logic.

True political action consists in making use of knowledge of the probable so as to strengthen the chances of the possible. It differs from utopianism which, like magic, attempts to act on the world through performative discourse. Political action, often more unconsciously than consciously, expresses and exploits the potentialities inscribed in the social world, in its contradictions or immanent tendencies. The sociologist – and this is why people sometimes deplore the absence of the political in his discourse – describes the conditions that political action has to take account of and on which it depends for its success or failure (for example, nowadays, the collective disenchantment of young people). In so doing, he warns against the error that leads one to take the effect for the cause and to see effects of political action in the historical conditions of its efficacy – though one should not ignore the effect that political action can have when it accompanies dispositions that it does not produce and that pre-date it, and intensifies them by expressing them and orchestrating their manifestation.

Q. *I am rather worried about the conclusions that might be drawn, perhaps based on a misreading, from what you demonstrate about the nature of opinion. Isn't that analysis liable to be somewhat demobilizing?*

A. Let me clarify. Sociology reveals that the idea of personal opinion (like the idea of personal taste) is an illusion. From this it is concluded that sociology is reductive, that it disenchants, that it demobilizes people by taking away all their illusions.

Does that mean that one can only mobilize on the basis of illusions? If it is true that the idea of personal opinion itself is socially determined, that it is a product of history reproduced by education, that our opinions are determined, then it is better to know this; and if we have some chance of having personal opinions, it's perhaps on condition that we know our opinions are not spontaneously so.

Q. *Sociology is both an academic activity and a critical, even a political, activity. Isn't there a contradiction there?*

A. Sociology as we know it was born, in France at least, from a contradiction or a misunderstanding. Durkheim was the one who did all that needed to be done to make sociology exist as a universally recognized science. When an activity is constituted as a university discipline, the question of its function and the function of those who practise it no longer arises. One only has to think of the archaeologists, philologists, medieval historians, historians of China or classical philosophy, who are never asked what use they are, what their work is for, who they work for or who needs it. No one calls them into question and they consequently feel completely justified in doing what they do. Sociology is not so lucky . . . The question of its *raison d'être* is asked increasingly the more it moves away from the definition of scientific practice that the founders had to accept and impose, that of a pure science, pure as the purest, most 'useless' and 'gratuitous' of the academic sciences (papyrology or Homeric studies), those that the most repressive regimes allow to survive and that serve as a refuge for specialists from the 'hot' sciences. You know how much work Durkheim had to do to give sociology this 'pure', purely scientific, 'neutral' image – ostentatious borrowings from the natural sciences, countless signs of a break with external functions and politics, such as preliminary definition, etc.

In other words, from the very beginning, sociology has been an ambiguous, dual, masked science; one that had to conceal and renounce its own nature as a *political* science in order to gain acceptance as an academic science. It's no accident that ethnology raises many fewer problems than sociology.

But sociology can also use its autonomy to produce a truth that no one – among those who are in position to command or commission it – asks of it. Through skilful use of the institutional autonomy that it has as a university discipline, it can find the conditions for epistemological autonomy and try to offer what *no one* really asks of it, truth about the social world. It's not surprising that this socio-logically impossible science, capable of revealing what ought socio-logically to remain masked, could only arise from false pretences as to its ends, and that anyone who wants to perform sociology as a science must constantly reproduce this initial misrepresentation. *Larvatus prodeo.*

Truly scientific sociology is a social practice that, socio-logically, ought not to exist. The best proof of this is that as soon as social science refuses to be locked into the forced choice between pure science, which can scientifically analyse objects that have no social importance, and false science, which manages and caresses the established order, its very social existence is threatened.

Q. *Can't scientific sociology count on the solidarity of the other sciences?*

A. Indeed it can. But sociology, the newcomer among the sciences, is a critical science, critical of itself and the other sciences and also critical of the powers that be, including the powers of science. It's a science that strives to understand the laws of production of science; it provides not means of domination but, perhaps, the means of dominating domination.

Q. *Doesn't sociology try to give a scientific answer to the traditional problems of philosophy and, to some extent, to eclipse them by a dictatorship of reason?*

A. I think this was true at the beginning. The founders of sociology explicitly made that their objective. For example, it's no accident that the first object of sociology was religion. The Durkheimians immediately attacked what was (at a particular time) the primary instrument for constructing the world, and especially the social world. I also think that some traditional questions of philosophy can be re-posed in scientific terms (that's what I tried to do in *Distinction*). Sociology as I conceive it consists in transforming metaphysical problems into problems that can be treated scientifically and therefore politically. On the other hand, sociology, like all sciences, constructs itself in opposition to the totalizing ambition of philosophy, or rather of prophecies, discourses which, as Weber indicates, claim to offer total answers to total questions, especially on 'life and death' questions. In other words, sociology was built up with the ambition of stealing some of the problems of philosophy, but without the prophetic project that philosophy often set for itself. It broke with social philosophy and all the ultimate questions in which the latter indulged itself, such as the questions of the meaning of history, progress and decadence, the role of great men in history, and so on. The fact remains that sociologists encounter those problems in the most elementary operations of practice, through the way a question is asked, by presupposing, in the very form and content of their enquiry, that practices are determined by the immediate conditions of existence or by the whole previous history, and so on. Only if they are aware of them, and direct their practice appropriately, will they avoid slipping unawares into the philosophy of history. For example, if you question someone directly about the social class to which he belongs, or alternatively if you try to determine his place 'objectively' by questioning him about his income, his job, his level of education, etc., you are making a decisive choice between two opposing philosophies of practice and history. This choice cannot be settled, if it is not addressed as such, by asking both questions at the same time.

Q. *Why are you so harsh on theory, which you almost always seem to identify with philosophy? You yourself theorize, even if you deny it.*
A. What is called theory is generally verbiage fit for manuals. Theorization is often just a kind of 'manualization', as Raymond Queneau once put it. To make the play on words clearer I can quote Marx by way of commentary: 'Philosophy is to the study of the world as onanism is to sexual intercourse.' If everyone in France knew that, social science would make a 'great leap forward', as someone once said. As for whether I theorize, it depends what one means by the word. A theoretical problem that is converted into a *machine for research* is set in motion, it becomes in a sense self-propelling, it is driven as much by the difficulties it brings up as by the solutions it provides.

One of the secrets of the craft of sociology is to know how to find empirical objects about which one can really raise general problems. For example, the question of realism and formalism in art, which, at certain times and in certain contexts, has become a political question, can be raised, empirically, in connection with the relation of the working class to photography, or through analysis of reactions to various types of television programmes, and so on. But it can equally well be raised, and simul- taneously too, in connection with frontality in Byzantine mosaics or the depiction of the Sun King in paintings or historiography. Having said that, the theoretical problems raised in that way are so profoundly transformed that the friends of theory would no longer recognize their offspring in them.

The logic of research is this *intermeshing of problems* in which the researcher is caught up and which drags him along, often despite himself. Leibniz constantly complained to Descartes in his *Animadversiones* that he expected too much of intuition, insight and intelligence and did not rely enough on the automatisms of 'blind thought' (he was thinking of algebra, which would make up for the intermissions of intelligence). What is not

understood in France, the land of the brilliant essay, the cult of originality
and intelligence, is that method and the collective organization of research
work can produce intelligence, intermeshings of problems and methods
that are more intelligent than the researchers (and also, in a world in which
everyone seeks originality, the only true originality, the one that is not
looked for – I am thinking for example of the extraordinary exception
represented by the Durkheimian school). To be scientifically intelligent is to
place oneself in a situation that generates real problems and real difficulties.
That is what I have tried to do with the research group that I run. A research
group that works is a socially instituted interlocking of problems and ways
of solving them, a network of cross-checks, and, at the same time, a whole
set of productions which, without any imposition of norms or any
theoretical or political orthodoxy, have a family resemblance.

Q. *What is the relevance of the distinction between sociology and
ethnology?*

A. That distinction is unfortunately inscribed, and probably irreversibly
so, in university structures, that's to say in the social organization of the
university and the mental organization of academics. My work would not
have been possible if I had not tried to hold together some problematics
traditionally regarded as ethnological and other problems traditionally
regarded as sociological. For example, for a number of years ethnologists
have addressed the problem of taxonomies, classifications, a problem that
arises at the crossroads of several traditions in ethnology. Some are
interested in the taxonomies applied in classifying plants, or diseases, etc.
Others are interested in the taxonomies used to organize the social world,
the taxonomy *par excellence* being the one that defines kinship relations.
This tradition has developed in areas where, because of the relatively
undifferentiated nature of the societies in question, the problem of classes
does not arise. Sociologists, on the other hand, deal with the problem of
classes but without addressing the problem of the systems of classification
used by the agents and their relationship to the objective division of classes.
My work has consisted in bringing together, in a non-scholastic way – I say
that because otherwise it could sound like one of the academic cross-
fertilizations that are performed in lectures – the problem of social classes
and the problem of classification systems, and in asking questions such as
this: don't the taxonomies that we use to classify things and people, to judge
a work of art, a pupil, a hairstyle, clothes, etc. – and thereby to produce
social classes – have some connection with the objective classifications, the
social classes understood (crudely speaking) as classes of individuals linked
to classes of material conditions of existence?

What I am talking about is a typical effect of the division of scientific
labour: there are objective divisions (the division into disciplines, for
example) which, having become mental divisions, function in such a way as
to make certain thoughts impossible. This analysis is an illustration of the

theoretical problematic that I have just outlined. Institutional divisions, which are a product of history, function in objective reality (for example, if I put three sociologists on an examining board it must be a sociology thesis, etc.) in the form of legally sanctioned objective divisions, inscribed in career paths, etc., and also in people's heads, in the form of mental divisions, logical principles of division. The obstacles to knowledge are often sociological obstacles. Having crossed the frontier between ethnology and sociology, I have been led to ask ethnology all sorts of questions that ethnology does not ask, and vice versa.

Q. *You define social class in terms of volume and structure of capital. How do you define the kinds of capital? For economic capital, it seems that you depend entirely on the statistics provided by INSEE,[1] and for educational capital on qualifications. Can you really construct classes on that basis?*

A. It's a long-standing debate. I explain my position in *Distinction*. You are faced with a choice between either a pure (and simple) theory of social classes, which is based on no empirical data (position in the relations of production) and which has practically no capacity to describe the state of the social structure or its transformations; or empirical studies, like those of INSEE, which are based on no theory but which provide the only available data for analysing the division into classes. Personally I have tried to move beyond what has been treated as a *theological* opposition between theories of social classes and theories of social stratification, an opposition that goes down well in lectures and in 'dialectical materialist' thinking, but which is in fact merely the reflection of a state of the division of sociological labour. So I have tried to put forward a theory that is both more complex (taking into account states of capital that are ignored in classical theory) and empirically better grounded, but which is obliged to resort to imperfect indicators such as those provided by INSEE. I am not so naïve as to be unaware that the indicators provided by INSEE, even for example concerning share ownership, are not good indicators of the economic capital possessed. That is clear to everyone. But there are cases where theoretical purism is an alibi for ignorance or the abdication of practice. Science consists in doing what one does while knowing and saying that it is all one can do, making clear the *limits* of validity of what one does.

Having said that, the question you have asked me in fact conceals another problem. What do people *mean* when they say, or write, as they often do: 'What *ultimately* are social classes in so-and-so's theory?' In asking a question like that, one is sure of winning the approval of all those who are convinced that the problem of social classes is resolved and that one only has to consult the canonical texts (which is very convenient and economical, when you think about it), and who cast *suspicion* on all those who, by continuing to look, *betray* that they think that not everything has been found. This strategy of suspicion, which is particularly likely to be generated by certain class *habitus*), is an unbeatable one, and gives much satisfaction to those who practise it, because it comforts them in their self-satisfaction. For that reason it seems to me scientifically and politically obnoxious.

It is true that I have constantly insisted on going back to basics on things that were regarded as settled. Capital, for example: we all know what that is . . . . You only have to read *Capital* or, better, to read *Reading Capital* [2] (and so on). Fine, if it were true, but in my view it isn't, and if there has always been this gulf between theoretical theory and empirical descriptions (a gulf that means that people who have only their Marxist spectacles to aid them are totally helpless when it comes to understanding the historical originality of the new forms of social conflict, for example those that are linked to the contradictions resulting from the functioning of the educational system), if this gulf has always existed, perhaps it is because the analysis of the different kinds of capital still remained to be done. To get beyond it, it was necessary to shake up some self-evidences, and not for the pleasure of performing heretical, and therefore distinctive, readings.

To return to the question of the kinds of capital, I think it's a very difficult question and I realize, when I tackle it, that I am moving outside the charted area of established truths, where one is sure of immediately attracting approval, esteem, and so on. (At the same time, I think that the scientifically most fruitful positions are often the most risky ones, and therefore the socially most improbable.) As regards economic capital, I leave that to others; it's not my area. What concerns me is what is abandoned by others, because they lack the interest or the theoretical tools for these things, cultural capital and social capital. Very recently I've tried to set out in simple terms for didactic purposes what I mean by these notions. I try to construct rigorous definitions that are not only descriptive concepts, but means of *construction*, which make it possible to produce things that one could not see previously. Take social capital, for example: one can give an intuitive idea of it by saying that it is what ordinary language calls 'connections'. (It often happens that ordinary language designates very important social facts; but it masks them at the same time, by the effect of familiarity, which leads one to imagine that one already knows, that one has understood everything, and which stops research in its tracks. Part of the work of social science consists in dis-covering what is both unveiled and veiled by ordinary language. This means running the risk of being accused of stating the self-evident, or, worse, of laboriously translating, into a heavily conceptual language, the basic verities of common sense or the more subtle and more agreeable intuitions of moralists and novelists. When, that is, people do not accuse the sociologist of saying things that are simultaneously banal and untrue, which just goes to show the extra-ordinary resistances that sociological analysis arouses.)

To return to social capital: by constructing this concept, one acquires the means of analysing the logic whereby this particular kind of capital is accumulated, transmitted and reproduced, the means of understanding how it turns into economic capital and, conversely, what work is required to convert economic capital into social capital, the means of grasping the function of institutions such as clubs or, quite simply, the *family*, the main site of the accumulation and transmission of that kind of capital, and so on. We are a long way, it seems to me, from common-sense 'connections', which are only one manifestation among others of social capital. The 'social round' and all that is related in the high-society gossip columns of *Le Figaro*, *Vogue* or *Jours de France* cease to be, as is generally thought, exemplary manifestations of the idle life of the 'leisure class' or the 'conspicuous consumption' of the wealthy, and can be seen instead as a particular form of social labour, which presupposes expenditure of money, time and a specific competence and which tends to ensure the (simple or expanded) reproduction of social capital. (It can be seen, incidentally, that some ostensibly very critical discourses miss what is essential, because intellectuals are not very 'sensitive' to the form of social capital that accumulates and circulates in 'society' gatherings and tend to sneer, with a mixture of fascination and resentment, rather than analyse.)

So it was necessary to construct the object that I call social capital – which immediately brings to light that publishers' cocktail parties or reciprocal reviewing are the equivalent, in the intellectual field, of the 'social work' of the aristocracy – to see that high-society socializing is, for certain people, whose power and authority are based on social capital, their principal occupation. An enterprise based on social capital has to ensure its own reproduction through a specific form of labour (inaugurating monuments, chairing charities, etc.) that presupposes professional skills, and therefore an apprenticeship, and an expenditure of time and energy. As soon as this object is constructed, one can carry out genuine comparative studies, talk to historians about the nobility in the Middle Ages, reread Saint-Simon and Proust, or, of course, the work of the ethnologists.

At the same time, you are quite right to ask the question. Since what I do is not at all theoretical work, but scientific work that mobilizes all the theoretical resources for the purposes of empirical analysis, my concepts are not always what they ought to be. For example, I constantly raise the problem of the conversion of one kind of capital into another, in terms that do not completely satisfy even me. It's an example of a problem that could not be posed explicitly – it posed itself before one knew it – until the notion of kinds of capital had been constructed. Practice is familiar with this problem. In certain games (in the intellectual field, for example, in order to win a literary prize or the esteem of one's peers), economic capital is inoperative. To become operational it has to undergo a transmutation. That's the function, for example, of the 'social work' that made it possible to transmute economic capital – always at the root in the last analysis – into nobility. But that's not all. What are the laws governing that conversion? What defines the exchange rate at which one kind of capital is converted into another? In every epoch there is a constant struggle over the rate of exchange between the different kinds of capital, a struggle among the different fractions of the dominant class, whose overall capital is composed in differing proportions of the various kinds of capital. Those who in nineteenth-century France were called the 'capacities' have a constant interest in the revaluing of cultural capital with respect to economic capital. It can be seen – and this is what makes sociological analysis so difficult – that these things that we take as our object – cultural capital, economic capital, etc. – are themselves at stake in struggles within the reality that we are studying and that what we say about them will itself become a stake in struggles.

Analysis of these laws of conversion is not complete – far from it – and if there is one person for whom it's a problem, it's myself. Which is fine. There's a host of questions, very fertile ones I think, that I ask myself or that are put to me, objections that are raised and that were only made possible because these distinctions had been made. Research is perhaps the art of creating fruitful problems for oneself – and creating them for other people. Where things were simple, you bring out problems. And then you find yourself facing a much more sticky reality. Of course, I could have produced one of those courses of Marxism-without-tears on the social classes that have sold so well in the last few years, under the name of theory, or even science. Or even sociology – you find yourself dealing with things that are both suggestive and worrying (I know the effect that what I do has on the guardians of orthodoxy and I think I also have some idea why it has that effect, and I'm delighted that it does). The idea of being both suggestive and worrying is one that suits me fine.

Q. *But isn't there something static about the theory of the social classes that you put forward? You describe a state of the structure without saying how it changes.*
A. What statistical analysis can grasp is a moment, a state of a game with two, three, four or six players, or whatever. It gives a photograph of the piles of tokens of various colours that they have won in the previous rounds and which they will play in the rounds to come. Capital apprehended instantaneously is a product of history that will produce more history. I'll simply say that the strategies of the different players will depend on their resources in tokens, and more specifically on the overall volume of their capital (the number of tokens) and the structure of this capital, that's to say the composition of the piles (those who have lots of red tokens and few yellow ones, that is, a lot of economic capital and little cultural capital, will not play in the same way as those who have many yellow tokens and few red ones). The bigger their pile, the more audacious they can be (bluff), and the more yellow tokens (cultural capital) they have, the more they will stake on the yellow squares (the educational system). Each player sees the play of the others, that is, their way of playing, their style, and he derives clues from

this regarding their hand, tacitly hypothesizing that the former is a manifestation of the latter. He may even have direct knowledge of part or all of the capital of the others (educational qualifications play the role of calls in bridge). In any case, he uses his knowledge of the properties of the other players, that is, their strategy, to guide his own play. But the principle of his anticipations is nothing other than the sense of the game, that is, the practical mastery of the relationship between tokens and play (what we express when we say of a property – a garment or a piece of furniture, for example – that it's 'petit-bourgeois'). This sense of the game is the product of the progressive internalization of the immanent laws of the game. It's what Thibaut and Riecken grasp, for example, when their respondents, questioned about two people who give blood, spontaneously assume that the person of higher class is free, the person of lower class forced (although we do not know, and it would be very interesting to know how the proportion of those who make this assumption varies between upper- and lower-class respondents).

Obviously the image I have just used is only valid as a didactic device. But I think it gives an idea of the real logic of social change and gives a sense of how artificial it is to oppose the static to the dynamic.

Notes

1   Institut National de la Statistique et des Études Économiques [translator].
2   By Louis Althusser [translator].

4

ARE INTELLECTUALS OUT OF PLAY?

Q. *When you were studying the educational system, your analysis of social relations in the cultural field referred back to an analysis of cultural institutions. Now, when you analyse discourse, it seems that you short-circuit institutions; and yet you are explicitly interested in political discourse and political culture.*

A. Although this is of purely biographical interest, I would remind you that my earliest work was on the Algerian people and dealt, among other things, with the forms of political consciousness and the foundations of political struggles. If, subsequently, I have concerned myself with culture, this is not because I gave culture some kind of 'ontological' priority, and certainly not because I made it a privileged explanatory factor for understanding the social world. In fact, the area had been abandoned. Those who did touch on it oscillated between a reductive economism and an idealism or spiritualism, and that operated as a perfect 'epistemological couple'. I think I am not one of those who transpose economic concepts uncritically into the area of culture, but I wanted – and not just metaphorically – to establish an economy of symbolic phenomena and to study the specific logic of the production and circulation of cultural goods. There was a kind of split thinking which meant that in many people's heads a materialism applicable to the movement of material goods could coexist with a idealism applied to the movement of cultural goods. People were content with a meagre stock of formulae: 'The dominant culture is the culture of the dominant classes,' etc.

And that enabled a good many intellectuals to live out their contradictions without too much discomfort. As soon as one studies cultural phenomena as obeying an economic logic, as determined by specific interests, irreducible to economic interests in the narrow sense, and consequently the pursuit of specific profits, even intellectuals are forced to see themselves as determined by these interests which may determine the positions they take, instead of situating themselves in the universe of pure disinterestedness, free 'commitment', etc. And it becomes clearer why, for example, it is, at bottom, much easier for an intellectual to be progressive in the area of general politics than in the area of cultural politics or, more precisely, of university politics, etc.

Extract from an interview with François Hincker, *La nouvelle critique*, 111–12, 1978: 56–61

If you like, I brought back into play what was out of play: intellectuals always agree among themselves to leave out of play their own game and their own stakes.

So I came back to politics on the basis of the observation that the production of representations of the social world, which is a fundamental dimension of political struggle, is the virtual monopoly of intellectuals. The struggle over social classifications is a crucial dimension of the class struggle, and it is the route through which symbolic production intervenes in the political struggle. Classes exist twice over, once objectively, and a second time in the more or less explicit social representation that agents form of them, which is a stake in struggles. If you say to someone 'What's happening to you is because you have an unhappy relation with your father', or if you say to him 'What's happening to you is because you're a proletarian from whom surplus value is stolen', it isn't at all the same thing.

The terrain where people struggle for the appropriate, just, legitimate way of speaking the social world cannot be eternally excluded from the analysis – even if the claim to legitimate discourse tacitly or explicitly implies the refusal of that objectification. Those who claim the monopoly of thought about the social world do not expect to be thought sociologically.

Yet it seems to me to be all the more important to pose the question of what is at stake in this game because those who would have an interest in posing it, that's to say those who delegate the defence of their interests to intellectuals, to spokesmen, do not have the means of posing it, and those who benefit from this delegation do not have an interest in posing it. One has to take seriously the fact that intellectuals are the object of a *de facto* delegation, a comprehensive, tacit delegation, which in the case of party leaders becomes conscious and explicit but no less comprehensive, and one has to analyse the social conditions in which this delegation is received and used.

Q. *But can one speak of this delegation, which to some extent is undeniable, in the same way in the case of a worker close to the Communist Party and in that of a worker who entrusts himself to a reactionary party or politician?*

A. Delegation often takes place on the basis of indices that are not the ones that people imagine. A worker may 'identify' with the 'style', the accent, the manner, the relation to language, of a Communist activist, much more than with his discourse, which sometimes seems designed to turn him off. He says to himself: 'That one wouldn't back down in front of a boss.' This elementary 'class sense' is not infallible. So, in this respect, and even when the delegation has no other basis than a kind of 'class affinity', the difference exists. The fact remains that, as regards the control of the contract of delegation, power over the words and actions of the delegates, the difference is not as radical as one might suppose. People suffer from this dispossession, and when they swing into indifference or towards conservative positions, it's often because, rightly or wrongly, they feel themselves cut off from the universe of delegates: 'they're all the same', 'all tarred with the same brush'.

Q. *At the same time, although what you observe is fast disappearing, the Communist, even when silent, acts; his relationship to politics is not that of language.*

A. Action depends to a large extent on the words with which one speaks. For example, the differences between the struggles of 'first-generation' factory workers, the sons of peasants, and those of factory workers whose fathers were factory workers, rooted in a tradition, are related to differences in political consciousness and therefore in language. The spokesmen's problem is to offer a language that enables the individuals concerned to universalize their experiences without thereby effectively excluding them from the expression of their own experience, which amounts to dispossessing them. As I have tried to show, the work of the activist consists precisely in transforming the personal, individual misfortune ('I've been made redundant') into a particular case of a more general social relation ('you've been made redundant because . . .'). This universalization necessarily moves through concepts; it therefore contains the danger of the ready-made formula, automatic, autonomous language, the ritual word in which those of whom one speaks and for whom one speaks no longer 'recognize themselves'. This dead language (I'm thinking of all the grand phrases of political language that make it possible to speak without thinking) blocks thought, as much in those who pronounce it as in those to whom it is addressed and whom it ought to mobilize, first of all intellectually; whom it ought to prepare for critique (including self-critique) and not only for adherence.

Q. *It's true that there is an intellectual in every activist, but an activist is no ordinary intellectual, especially when his cultural heritage is not that of an intellectual.*

A. One of the conditions required in order for him not to be an ordinary intellectual – one condition among others, which has to be added to everything that is generally relied on, such as 'monitoring by the masses' (of which it has to be asked in what conditions it could be exercised, etc.) – is also that he should be able to monitor himself (or be monitored by his competitors, which is even more reliable) in the name of an analysis of what it means to be an 'intellectual', to have the monopoly of production of discourse on the social world, to be involved in a field of play, the political space, which has its own logic, in which a particular type of interests are invested, etc. The sociology of intellectuals is a contribution to the socio-analysis of intellectuals. Its function is to make more difficult the too often triumphant relation that intellectuals and leaders have with themselves; to point out that we are manipulated in our categories of thought, in everything that enables us to think and speak the world. It also has to point out that positions taken on the social world perhaps owe something to the conditions in which they are produced, the specific logic of political apparatuses and the political 'game', of co-option, the circulation of ideas, and so on.

Q. *What worries me is that your assumption of the identity between the political activist and the intellectual prevents one from adequately addressing the question of the relationship between action and theory, consciousness and practice, 'base' and 'summit', especially between activists of working-class origin and activists of intellectual origin, not to mention the relations between classes – the working class and the intellectual strata.*

A. In fact, there are two very different forms of discourse on the social world. That can be seen clearly in relation to prediction: if an ordinary intellectual makes a wrong prediction, it's of no great consequence because he only commits himself, he only leads himself astray. A political leader, on the other hand, is someone who has the power to make what he says come into existence; that's the mark of a 'watchword'. The language of a political leader is an authorized language, which exercises a power, which can bring into existence what it states. In that case, an error can be a blunder. That's probably what explains – without, in my view, ever justifying it – why political language so often indulges in anathemas, excommunications, and so on ('traitor', turncoat, etc.). The 'committed' intellectual who makes a mistake leads into error those who follow him, because his word has power in so far as it is believed. It may happen that something good for those for whom he speaks ('for' being taken in the dual sense of 'in favour of' and 'in place of'), something that could happen, does not happen, or that something that might not happen does happen. His words help to make history, to change history.

There are several competing ways of producing the truth, and they each have their biases and their limits. In the name of his 'political responsibilities', the 'committed' intellectual tends to reduce his thought to activist thought, and it may happen – it often does – that what was a provisional strategy becomes a *habitus*, a permanent way of being. The 'free' intellectual has a propensity to terrorism: he would gladly bring into the political field the kind of fight to the death that takes place in the battles over truth in the intellectual field ('if I'm right, you're wrong') – but these battles take a totally different form when what is at stake is more than symbolic life and death.

It seems to me essential both for politics and for science that the two competing modes of production of representations of the social world should have an equal right to exist, and that, in any case, the second should not abdicate before the first, adding terrorism to simplism, as has often happened in certain periods in relations between the intellectuals and the

Communist Party. You will tell me that that goes without saying, and in principle no one disagrees, but at the same time I know that sociologically it is not self-evident.

In my jargon, I'll say that it is important that the space in which discourse on the social world is produced continues to function as a field of struggle in which the dominant pole, orthodoxy, does not crush the dominated pole of heresy – because, in that area, so long as there is struggle there is history, and therefore hope.

5

HOW CAN 'FREE-FLOATING INTELLECTUALS' BE SET FREE?

Q. *You are sometimes accused of a polemical violence towards intellectuals, verging on anti-intellectualism. In your latest book,* Le Sens pratique,[1] *you reoffend. You call into question the very function of intellectuals, their claim to objective knowledge and their capacity to give a scientific account of practice . . .*

A. It's remarkable that people who, day after day, or week after week, quite arbitrarily impose the verdicts of a small mutual admiration society should complain of violence, when the mechanisms of that violence are for once brought out into the open. It's also curious that these profoundly conformist people should thereby give themselves, by an extraordinary reversal, airs of intellectual audacity, and even political courage (one might almost think they risked the Gulag). What the sociologist can't be forgiven for is that he reveals secrets reserved for initiates to every Tom, Dick and Harriet. The efficacy of symbolic violence is proportionate to the mis-recognition of the conditions and instruments of its exercise. It's surely no accident that the production of cultural goods has not given rise to cultural consumers' associations. Just think of all the economic and symbolic interests linked to the production of books, paintings, plays, ballets and films that would be threatened if the *production of value* of cultural products were suddenly completely revealed to all the consumers. I'm thinking, for example, of processes like the circular circulation of flattering reviews among a small number of producers (of works but also of reviews), high-level academics who accredit and consecrate, journalists who accredit themselves and celebrate. The reactions provoked by unveiling the mechanisms of cultural production are reminiscent of the legal actions some firms have brought against consumers' associations. What is at stake is the whole set of operations that make it possible to pass off a Golden Delicious as an apple, or the products of marketing, rewriting and editorial publicity as intellectual works.

Q. *You think that intellectuals – or at least, those of them who have most to lose – are up in arms when someone unmasks their profits and*

Interview with Didier Eribon, *Le Monde Dimanche*, 4 May 1980, pp. I and XVII

the more or less admissible means they use to secure them?
A.   Absolutely. What makes the charges against me particularly absurd is that I have constantly denounced the tendency of social science to think in terms of the logic of the trial, or the tendency of the readers of works of social science to make them operate in terms of that logic. Where science seeks to state tendential laws, transcending the persons through which they are realized or manifested, resentment, which can take all kinds of masks, not least that of science, sees the *denunciation* of persons.

These warnings seem to me especially necessary since, in reality, social science, whose vocation is to understand, has sometimes been used to condemn. But there is a certain bad faith in reducing sociology, as the conservative tradition always has done, to its caricature as a policing activity – and especially in exploiting the fact that a rudimentary sociology of intellectuals has been used as a means of repression against intellectuals, in order to denounce the questions that a real sociology of intellectuals puts to intellectuals.

Q.   *Could you give an example of those questions?*
A.   It's clear, for example, that Zhdanovism provided some second-rank intellectuals (classified as such by the criteria prevailing in the intellectual field) with an opportunity to take their revenge, in the name of a self-interested representation of popular demands, on the intellectuals who had enough specific capital to be able to claim autonomy *vis-à-vis* the political authorities. That is not enough in itself to disqualify all enquiry into the functions of intellectuals and what their way of performing those functions derives from the social conditions in which they perform them. So when I point out that distance from ordinary necessities is the condition of theoretical perception of the social world, I don't do so in order to denounce intellectuals as 'parasites', but to point to the limits imposed on all theoretical knowledge by the social conditions of its performance. If there is one thing that the men of academic leisure find hard to understand, it's practice as such, even the most banal, whether it's that of a football player or a Kabyle woman performing a ritual or a Béarn family marrying off its children.

Q.   *We've come back to one of the fundamental theses of* The Logic of Practice. *One has to analyse the social situation of those who analyse practice, the presuppositions they engage in their analysis . . .*
A.   The subject of science is part of the object of science; he has a place within it. It is not possible to understand practice without having mastered – through theoretical analysis – the effects of the relation to practice that is inscribed in the social conditions of every theoretical analysis of practice. (I do indeed say 'through theoretical analysis', and not, as people often think, through some form of practical or mystical participation in practice – 'participant observation', 'intervention' or whatever.) Thus, rituals,

which are perhaps the most practical of practices, since they are made up of manipulations and gesticulations, a whole gymnastics, are very likely to be misunderstood by people who, being in no way dancers or gymnasts themselves, are inclined to see in them a kind of logic or algebraic calculation.

Q. *For you, situating intellectuals means pointing out that they belong to the dominant class and derive profits from their position, even if those profits are not strictly economic?*
A. Contrary to the illusion of the 'free-floating intellectual', which is in a sense the professional ideology of intellectuals, I point out that, as holders of cultural capital, intellectuals are a (dominated) fraction of the dominant class and that a number of the stances they take up, in politics for example, derive from the ambiguity of their dominated–dominant position. I also point out that having a place in the intellectual field implies specific interests, not only, in Paris as in Moscow, Academy posts or publishing contracts, university positions or book reviewing, but also signs of recognition and gratifications that are often imperceptible for someone who is not part of that world but which expose intellectuals to all sorts of subtle constraints and censorship.

Q. *And you think that a sociology of the intellectuals offers intellectuals freedom from the determinisms they undergo?*
A. It offers at least the possibility of some freedom. Those who give the illusion of dominating their epoch are often dominated by it, and, growing terribly dated, they disappear with it. Sociology gives a chance of breaking the charm, of denouncing the possessed–possessor relationship through which those who are always up to the minute are bound to their time. There is something desperate in the docility with which 'free intellectuals' rush to hand in their essays on the required subjects of the moment, currently desire, the body or seduction. And there is no more dismal reading, twenty years on, than these obligatory exercises brought together, in perfect harmony, by the special issues of the major 'intellectual' magazines.

Q. *It might be retorted that at least these intellectuals have the merit of living with their time . . .*
A. Yes, if living with their time means being carried along by the current of intellectual history, swept this way and that by changing fashions. No, if the intellectual's task is not to 'know what to think' about everything that fashion and its agents designate as worthy of being thought, but to try to discover everything that the history and logic of the intellectual field require him to think, at a given moment, with the illusion of freedom. More than any other intellectual, a sociologist who does his job immerses himself in history, and in the present (which, for other intellectuals, is the object of an optional interest, external to their professional tasks as philosophers,

philologists or historians, but which is for him the main, essential, even exclusive object). But his ambition is to extract from the present the laws that make it possible to dominate it, to break free of it.

Q. *You mention somewhere, in one of those notes which are, as it were, the 'Inferno' of your texts, the 'imperceptible slippages that have led in thirty years from a state of the intellectual field in which it was so necessary to be a Communist that one hardly needed to be a Marxist, to a state in which it was so smart to be Marxist that one even "read" Marx, ending up with a state in which the latest "must" of fashion is to have seen through everything, starting with Marxism'.*

A. It's not a polemical formulation but a shorthand description of the evolution of a good number of French intellectuals. I think it stands up to criticism. And I think it needs to be said, at a time when those who have allowed themselves to be carried along like silt in the eddies of the intellectual field seek to impose their latest conversion on those who have not followed them in their successive enthusiasms. There's no fun in observing terrorism practised in the name of anti-terrorism, witch-hunting in the name of liberalism, often by the same people who once applied the same self-interested conviction in imposing the Stalinist order. Especially at a time when the Communist Party and its intellectuals are regressing towards practices and discourses worthy of the halcyon days of Stalinism and, more precisely, towards mechanical thought and language, produced by the apparatus and solely concerned with conserving the apparatus.

Q. *But doesn't this reminder of the social determinisms that bear on intellectuals lead to a disqualifying of intellectuals and a discrediting of their productions?*

A. I think that the intellectual has the privilege of being placed in conditions that enable him to strive to understand his generic and specific conditions. In so doing, he can hope to free himself (in part at least) and to offer others the means of liberation. The critique of intellectuals, if there is a critique, is the opposite of a demand or an expectation. It seems to me that an intellectual can fulfil the liberating function that he claims for himself, often in an entirely usurped way, only on condition that he understands and masters what determines him. Intellectuals who are shocked by the very intention of classifying the 'unclassifiable' intellectual thereby demonstrate how remote they are from awareness of their true position and of the freedom it could give them. The sociologist's privilege, if he has one, is not that of trying to remain suspended above those whom he classifies, but that of knowing he is classified and knowing roughly where he stands in the classifications. When people who think they will win an easy revenge ask me what are my tastes in paintings or music, I reply, quite seriously: those that correspond to my place in the classification. Bringing the subject of science into history and into society does not mean condemning oneself to relativism; it means preparing the conditions for a critical knowledge of the limits of knowledge which is the precondition for true knowledge.

Q. *Is that what leads you to denounce the usurpation of speech by intellectuals?*

A.   In fact, it is very common for intellectuals to use the *competence* (in the quasi-legal sense of the word) that is socially conferred on them as a pretext for speaking with authority far beyond the limits of their technical competence, especially in the area of politics. This usurpation which is the very essence of the ambition of the old-style intellectual, engaged on all the fronts of thought, the supplier of all the answers, reappears in another guise in the *apparatchik* or the technocrat who invokes dialectical materialism or economic science in order to dominate.

Intellectuals take upon themselves the usurped right to legislate in all matters in the name of a social competence that is often quite independent of the technical competence that it seems to guarantee. I'm thinking here of what is, in my view, one of the hereditary vices of French intellectual life, the 'essay' style that is so deeply rooted in our institutions and our traditions that it would take hours to spell out its social conditions of possibility (let me just mention that kind of cultural protectionism, linked to the ignorance of foreign languages, which allows outmoded enterprises of cultural production to survive; or the habits of the *lycée* classes preparing for the exams for the grandes écoles, or the traditions of philosophy classes). But I would add that errors come in couples and support each other: on one side there is the 'essayism' of those who are ready to write, at the drop of a hat, *de omni re scibili*, 'about everything that can be known', and on the other the inflated dissertations that theses often amount to. In short, I'm talking about the complementary traditions of pedantry and futility, the leaden thesis and the journalistic squib, which render major scientific works entirely improbable, and which, when they do arise, condemn them to oblivion or popular simplification.

Q. *In a recent article[2] you attack the kind of philosophy that is written in capital letters . . .*

A.   Yes. It's one of the most typical manifestations of the lofty mode of thought that often passes for theoretical elevation. To talk about Apparatuses with a big A, or The State, or Law, or The School, to make 'Concepts' the subjects of historical action, is to refuse to sully one's hands in empirical research by reducing history to a kind of battle of the giants, in which The State is challenged by The Proletariat, or even by 'The Struggles' – the Furies of our day.

Q. *You denounce a phantasmagorical philosophy of history. But don't your own analyses sometimes forget history, as some of your critics have claimed?*

A. In fact, I endeavour to show that what is called the social *is* history, through and through. History is inscribed in things – in institutions (machines, instruments, law, scientific theories, etc.) and also in bodies. My whole effort aims to discover history where it is best hidden, in people's heads and in the postures of their bodies. The unconscious is history. That's true, for example, of the categories of thought and perception that we spontaneously apply to the social world.

Q. *And sociological analysis is a snapshot of the encounter between these two histories: history-in-things and history-in-bodies?*

A. Panofsky points out that when a man raises his hat in greeting, he unwittingly reproduces the gesture whereby, in the Middle Ages, knights would raise their helmets as a sign of their peaceful intentions. We are doing such things all the time. When the history in things and the history in bodies are perfectly attuned to each other, when, for a footballer, for example, the rules of the game and the sense of the game fit together perfectly, then the actor does exactly what he has to, the 'only thing there was to do', as we say, without even needing to know what he is doing. He's neither an automaton nor a rational calculator, but rather like 'blind Orion moving towards the rising sun', in Poussin's *Landscape with Orion*, the painting that so fascinates Claude Simon.

Q. *Does that imply that, underpinning your sociology, there is an anthropological theory, or, more simply, a certain image of man?*

A. Yes. This theory of practice, or rather, of the 'practical sense', defines itself, above all, in opposition to the philosophy of the subject and of the world as representation. Between the socialized body and the social fields, two products of the same history that are generally attuned to each other, there develops an infra-conscious, corporeal complicity. But my theory is also defined in opposition to behaviourism. Action is not a response that can be fully explained by reference to the triggering stimulus; and it has as its principle a system of dispositions, what I call the *habitus*, which is the product of all biographical experience (so that, just as no two individual histories are identical, so no two individual *habitus* are identical, although there are classes of experiences and therefore classes of *habitus* – the *habitus* of classes). These *habitus*, functioning, so to speak, as historically assembled programs (in the computing sense), are in a sense the principle of the efficacy of the stimuli that trigger them, since these conventional and conditional stimulations can only work on organisms disposed to perceive them.

Q. *Is this theory opposed to psychoanalysis?*

A.   There, the answer is rather more complicated. I'll simply say here that individual history, in its most individual aspects, and even in its sexual dimension, is socially determined. Carl Schorske put it very well when he said: 'Freud forgets that Oedipus was a king.' But though the sociologist is entitled to remind the psychoanalyst that the father–son relation is also a relationship of succession, the sociologist himself must try not to forget that the specifically psychological dimension of the father–son relation can be an obstacle to a 'trouble-free' succession, in which the heritage inherits the inheritor.

Q.   *But when internalized history is in perfect harmony with the history contained in things, there's a tacit complicity of the dominated with domination . . .*
A.   Some people have wondered why the dominated have not revolted more often. You only have to bear in mind the social conditions of the production of the agents and the durable effects that they exercise by inscribing themselves in dispositions, to understand that people who are the product of revolting social conditions are not necessarily as revolted as they would be if they were the product of less revolting conditions (like most intellectuals) and were *then* placed in those conditions. That doesn't amount to saying that they make themselves the accomplices of power, through some kind of bad faith. And then one shouldn't forget all the mismatches between embodied history and reified history, all the people who 'feel out of place' – in the wrong place, the wrong job. These out-of-place people, *déclassé* upwards or downwards, are the troublemakers who often make history.

Q.   *You often say that you have a sense of being out of place . . .*
A.   People who are sociologically improbable are often said to be 'impossible' . . . Most of the questions that I ask, and that I put first of all to intellectuals, who have so many answers and, at bottom, so few questions, no doubt stem from the sense of being an *outsider* in the intellectual world. I question that world because it calls me into question, and in a very deep way that goes beyond the simple sense of social exclusion. I never feel myself fully justified in being an intellectual, I don't feel 'at home', I have the feeling of having to justify (to whom? I have no idea) what seems to me an unjustifiable privilege. This experience, which I think I recognize in many socially stigmatized people (and in Kafka, for example), does not incline one to an immediate fellow-feeling with all those – and they are no less numerous among intellectuals than elsewhere – who feel fully justified in existing as they exist. The most elementary sociology of sociology confirms that the greatest contributions to social science have been made by people who were not perfectly in their element in the social world as it is.

Q. *This sense of not being 'at home' perhaps explains the pessimistic image that is sometimes stuck on you – an image that you reject . . .*

A. Nor would I want people to find nothing to praise in my work except its optimism. My optimism, if that is what it is, consists in thinking that one has to make the best of the whole historical evolution that has led many intellectuals into a disabused conservatism – whether it is that deplorable 'end of history' that is celebrated by theories of 'convergence' (of 'socialist' and 'capitalist' regimes) and the 'end of ideology', or, closer to home, the competitive games which divide the parties of the left, showing that the specific interests of professional politicians can take precedence over the interests of their electors. When there is no longer much left to lose, especially in the way of illusions, it's time to ask all the questions that have long been censored in the name of voluntaristic optimism, often identified with progressive dispositions. It's also time to turn one's gaze towards the blind spot of all philosophies of history, that's to say the point of view from which they are developed; to question, for example (as Marc Ferro does in his latest book on the Russian revolution), the interests that the ruling intellectuals may have in some forms of 'voluntarism' that can be used to justify 'democratic centralism', in other words the domination of the party officials, and more generally the tendency towards bureaucratic hijacking of the subversive spirit, a tendency inherent in the logic of representation and delegation, etc.

'He who increases his knowledge increases his pain,' said Descartes. And the spontaneist optimism of the sociologists of liberty is often merely an effect of ignorance. Social science destroys many impostures, but also many illusions. However, I doubt whether there is any other real freedom than that made possible by knowledge of necessity. Social science would not have too badly fulfilled its contract if it were able to raise itself against both irresponsible voluntarism and fatalistic scientism; if it were able to contribute in any degree to defining a *rational utopianism* that can play on knowledge of the probable in order to bring about the possible.

Notes

1   Translated as (1990) *The Logic of Practice*, Oxford: Polity Press.
2   Bourdieu, P. (1980) 'Le mort saisit le vif: les relations entre l'histoire réifiée et l'histoire incorporée', *Actes de la recherche en sciences sociales*, 32–3: 3–14.

Further reading

For further discussion see Bourdieu, P. (1980) 'Le mort saisit le vif ', *Actes de la recherche en sciences sociales*, 32–3: 3–14.

6

FOR A SOCIOLOGY OF SOCIOLOGISTS

I want to try to pose a very general question – the question of the social conditions of possibility and the scientific functions of a social science of social science – in relation to a specific case, that of the social science of the colonized and decolonized countries. The improvised nature of what I have to say may imply a certain number of somewhat risky positions . . . It's a risk I have to take.

First question: you decided to talk here about the social history of social science, and so on. Now, does that have any interest? That's the type of question that people never ask. If we've met here to talk about it, that's because we think it's interesting. But to say we are interested in a problem is a euphemistic way of naming the fundamental fact that we have vital stakes in our scientific productions. Those interests are not directly economic or political; we experience them as disinterested. The distinguishing feature of intellectuals is that they have disinterested interests, that they have an interest in disinterestedness. We have an interest in the problems that seem to us to be interesting. That means that at a particular moment, a particular academic group – without any one person deciding it – defines a problem as interesting. A conference is held, journals are created, people write articles, books and reviews. That means that it's 'worthwhile' to write on that theme, it brings in profits, not so much in royalties (though that may count) as in the form of prestige, symbolic gratifications, and so on. All that is just a preamble to say that one should make it a rule never to embark on sociology, and especially the sociology of sociology, without first, or simultaneously, undertaking a self-socio-analysis (in so far as that is ever completely possible). What use is the sociology of science? What is the sociology of colonial science for? The subject of scientific discourse needs to be asked the same questions that are put to the object of that discourse. How and by what right can the researcher ask, about researchers of the past, questions that he does not put to himself (and vice versa)?

Contribution to a colloquium on Ethnology and Politics in the Maghreb, Paris, June 1975, reprinted as 'Les conditions sociales de la production sociologique: sociologie coloniale et décolonisation de la sociologie' in *Le Mal de voir*, Cahiers Jussieu no. 2, Paris: Union Générale d'Éditions, 1976: 416–27

It is impossible to have a proper understanding of the stakes of the scientific games of the past unless one realizes that the past of science is a stake in present-day scientific struggles. Strategies of rehabilitation often mask strategies of symbolic *speculation*: if you manage to discredit the lineage at the end of which your intellectual adversary is situated, then the value of his shares collapses. That's really what people are saying when they say that Marxism or structuralism or structural Marxism are 'outmoded'. In a word, one needs to ask what interest people have in doing the sociology of sociology, or the sociology of other sociologists. For example, it would not be hard to show that the sociology of right-wing intellectuals is almost always done by left-wing intellectuals, and vice versa. These objectifications owe their partial truth to the fact that one has an interest in seeing the truth about one's opponents, seeing what determines them (right-wing intellectuals are generally materialists when explaining left-wing intellectuals). Except that what is never seen, because that would oblige the analyst to ask what he is doing there, what interest he has there, and so on, is the system of positions from which these antagonistic strategies are generated.

Unless it is assumed that the social history of social science has no other function than to give social science researchers reasons for existing, and that it needs no other justification, we have to ask whether it has any importance for today's scientific practice. Is the science of the social science of the past the precondition for the work that the social science of today has to perform? And, more precisely, is the social science of 'colonial' 'science' one of the preconditions for a genuine decolonization of the social science of a recently decolonized society? I would be tempted to accept that the past of social science is always one of the main obstacles to social science, and especially in the case which concerns us. As Durkheim said in *L'Évolution pédagogique en France*, the unconscious is the forgetting of history. I think that the unconscious of a discipline is its history; its unconscious is made up of its social conditions of production, masked and forgotten. The product, separated from its social conditions of production, changes its meaning and exerts an ideological effect. Knowing what one is doing when one does science – that's a simple definition of epistemology – presupposes knowing how the problems, tools, methods and concepts that one uses have been historically formed. (In that light, nothing is more urgent than to make a social history of the marxist tradition, in order to resituate modes of thought or expression, which have been fixed and fetishized by the forgetting of history, in the historical context of their production and their successive uses.)

What the social history of 'colonial' 'science' could offer – from the only standpoint that seems to me to be of interest, namely the progress of the science of present-day Algerian society – would be a contribution to knowledge of the categories of thought through which we look at that society. The papers given this morning have shown that the colonizers, in a sense dominated by their domination, were the first victims of their own intellectual instruments; and those instruments can still 'trap' those who merely 'react' against them without understanding the social conditions of their work, since they can easily simply fall into the opposite errors and in any case will deprive themselves of the only information available on some objects. So, in order to understand what has been left to us – corpuses, data, theories – we have to make a sociological study of the social conditions of production of that object. What does that mean?

One cannot do a sociology of the social conditions of production of 'colonial' 'science' without first studying the appearance of a relatively autonomous scientific field and the social conditions of the autonomization of this field. A field is a universe in which the producers' characteristics are defined by their position in relations of production, the place they occupy in a particular space of objective relationships. Contrary to what is presupposed by the study of isolated individuals – for example, in literary history of the type 'the author and his works' the most important properties of each producer are in the objective relationships with the others, that's to say, outside him, in the relationship of objective competition, etc.

We first need to determine what were the specific properties of the field in which the 'colonial' 'science' of people like Masqueray, Desparmet or Maunier produced its discourse on the colonial world, and how these properties varied at different times. In other words, we need to analyse the relationship this relatively autonomous scientific field had with, on the one hand, the colonial power, and, on the other, the central intellectual power, that's to say the metropolitan science of the day. There is indeed a *double dependence*, and one of them may cancel out the other. This relatively autonomous field seems to me to have been generally characterized (with exceptions such as Doutté, Maunier, etc.) by very strong dependence on the colonial power and very strong independence *vis-à-vis* the national (and international) scientific field. A whole set of properties of its 'scientific' production flow from this. Then one would have to analyse the variations in the relationship of this field with national and international science and with the local political field, and how these changes were translated in its production.

One of the important properties of a field lies in the fact that it implicitly defines 'unthinkable' things, things that are not even discussed. There's orthodoxy and heterodoxy, but there is also doxa, everything that goes without saying, and in particular the systems of classification determining what is judged interesting or uninteresting, the things that no one thinks worthy of being mentioned, because there is no *demand*. We talked about these self-evidences this morning, and Charles-André Julien described some intellectual contexts that are quite astonishing for us. What is most hidden is what everyone agrees about, agreeing so much that they don't even mention them, the things that are beyond question, that go without saying. That's just what historical documents are likely to mask most completely, because it doesn't occur to anyone to write out what is self-evident; and it is what informants don't say, or say only by omission, in their silences. It's important to wonder about these things that no one says, when one wants to do the social history of social science, if one wants to do something more than distribute praise and blame. It's not a question of setting oneself up as a judge, but of understanding why these people could not understand certain things, could not raise certain problems; of determining what are the social conditions of error – necessary error, inasmuch as it is the product of historical conditions, determinations. In the 'goes-without-saying' of a particular period, there is the *de jure* unthinkable (the politically unthinkable, for example), what is unnameable, taboo, the problems that cannot be dealt with – and also the *de facto* unthinkable, the things that the intellectual tools of the day do not make it possible to think. (And that's why error is not distributed on the basis of good or bad intentions, and why good intentions can make very bad sociology.)

This would lead one to pose quite differently the problem of the privileged relation to the object – native or external, 'sympathetic' or hostile, etc. – in which discussion of colonial sociology and the possibility of a decolonized sociology is normally trapped. I think that the question of the privileged viewpoint needs to be replaced by the question of scientific control of the relation to the object of science, which in my view is one of the fundamental conditions of the construction of a genuine object of science. Whatever object the sociologist or the historian chooses, this object, his way of constructing the object, raises the question not of the historian or sociologist as an individual subject, but of the objective relationship between the pertinent social characteristics of the sociologist and the social characteristics of the object. The objects of social science and the way they are treated always have an intelligible relationship with the researcher as he or she is sociologically defined, that is, by a certain social origin, a certain position within the university system, a certain discipline, etc. I think, for example, that one of the mediations through which the domination of the dominant values is exerted within the framework of science is the social hierarchy of the disciplines, which places philosophical theory at the top and geography right at the bottom (that's not a value judgement but an empirical observation – the social origin of students declines as one moves from philosophy to geography or from mathematics to geology). At every moment, there is a hierarchy of the objects of research and a hierarchy of the subjects of research (the researchers), which make a decisive contribution to the distribution of the objects among the subjects. No one ever says (or only rarely), 'Given who you are, you deserve this subject and not that one, this approach – "theoretical" or "empirical", "fundamental" or "applied" – rather than that one, this way – "brilliant" or "serious" – rather than that way of presenting the results.' Such reminders are quite superfluous, most of the time, because all one has to do is to give free rein to the internal censorships, which are simply internalized social and academic censorships ('I'm not a theorist', 'I can't write'). So nothing is less socially neutral than the relationship between subject and object.

The important thing is to be able to objectify one's relation to the object so that discourse on the object is not the simple projection of an unconscious relation to the object. Among the techniques that make this objectification possible, there is, of course, all the equipment of science; so long as it is understood that this equipment must itself be subjected to historical critique, because at every moment it is inherited from previous science.

To conclude, I will say that the problem of the outsider's or the native's privilege no doubt conceals a very real problem, which arises just as much whether one is analysing Kabyle rites, or what goes on in this room, or in a student demonstration, or in a car factory: it's the question of what it means to be an observer or an agent, in a word the question of what practice is.

Further reading

For further discussion see Bourdieu, P. (1975) 'The specificity of the scientific field and the social conditions of the progress of reason', *Social Science Information*, 14(6): 19–47 [also in Lemert, C. (1981) *French Sociology, Rupture and Renewal since 1968*, New York: Columbia University Press, 257–92].

7

THE PARADOX OF THE SOCIOLOGIST

The central idea that I would like to put forward today is that theory of knowledge and political theory are inseparable: every political theory contains, in implicit form at least, a theory of perception of the social world, and theories of perception of the social world are organized in accordance with oppositions very analogous to those found in the theory of the perception of the natural world. In the latter case, there is a traditional contrast between an empiricist theory, according to which perception borrows its structures from reality, and a constructivist theory which says that objects are only perceived through an act of construction. It is no accident that, in relation to a problem which concerns perception of the social world, that of the social classes, we find the same type of oppositions. Again we find two antagonistic positions which are not expressed with the rather brutal simplicity that I am going to give them: for some people, social classes exist in reality, and social science merely registers and records them; for others, social classes, social divisions, are constructions performed by sociologists or by social agents. Those who want to deny the existence of social classes often point out that social classes are the product of sociological construction. In their view, social classes only exist because sociologists construct them.

(I should say straight away that one of the fundamental problems raised by the theory of the perception of the social world is that of the relationship between scientific consciousness and everyday consciousness. Is the act of construction the work of the scientist or the native? Does the native have categories of perception and where does he get them from, and what is the relationship between the categories constructed by science and the categories that ordinary agents implement in their practice?)

To return to my initial question: how is the social world perceived and what is the theory of knowledge that accounts for the fact that we perceive the world as organized? The realist theory will say that social classes exist in reality, that they can be measured by objective indices. The main objection to the realist theory lies in the fact that, in reality, there is never any discontinuity. Incomes are distributed continuously, as are most of the social properties that can be attached to individuals. Now, scientific

Presentation given at Arras in October 1977, published in *Noroit*, 222, 1977 construction and even ordinary perception see discontinuity where the observer sees continuity. For example, it is clear that from a strictly statistical point of view, it is impossible to say where poor people end and rich people start. Yet the ordinary consciousness thinks that there are rich and poor people. It's the same for young and old. When does youth end? Where does old age begin? Where does a city end, where do the suburbs begin? It's said that towns of more than 20,000 people are more left-wing than towns of under 20,000. Why 20,000? One is perfectly justified in questioning the division. That's a first opposition: are divisions constructed or discovered?

Having presented the first opposition in terms of the sociology of knowledge (do we know the social world by construction or by recording?), I want to re-present it in political terms. (A parenthesis on terms ending in 'ism': most of these concepts, in the history of art, literature or philosophy as much as in political theory, are historical concepts that were invented for particular polemical purposes – and therefore in a quite precise historical context – and are then used outside and beyond that context and so come to be invested with a trans-historical value. That is true of the rather reckless use that I am going to make of a whole series of 'ism' concepts.) To return to the second, more obviously political opposition, the one that can be established between a scientistic or theoreticist objectivism and a subjectivism or spontaneism: this is one of the problems that haunted social thought in the late nineteeth century and which the marxist tradition called the problem of the final catastrophe. This problem can be formulated, in crude terms, as follows: will the revolution be the product of an inevitable process, inscribed in the logic of history, or will it be the product of a historical action? Those who think that it is possible to know the immanent laws of the social world and can count on them to produce the 'final catastrophe' are opposed to those who call the historical laws into question and assert the primacy of praxis, the primacy of the subject, the primacy of historical action over the invariant laws of history.

This opposition – reduced in this way to its most basic expression – between deterministic scientism and subjectivism or spontaneism is perfectly clear as regards the social classes. If I take the example of social classes, this is no accident. It's both something that sociologists need in order to conceptualize reality and something which 'exists' in reality, that's to say both in the objective distribution of properties and in the heads of the people who are part of social reality. It's the most complicated problem there is to think about, because you're trying to think about what you think with, something that is no doubt at least partly determined by what you want to think; and so – I admit this in all sincerity – I am very likely to speak of it less than satisfactorily.

In politics, the problem of knowledge is posed in the form of the relationship between the parties and the masses. Many questions that have been raised on this subject are conscious or unconscious transpositions of the classic questions of the sociology of knowledge concerning the relationship between subject and object. The sociologist Sartori develops the ultra-subjectivist thesis with a great deal of logic and rigour: he asks whether the principle of the differences observed in the situation of the working class in Britain, France and Italy lies in the relatively autonomous history of the parties, that's to say collective subjects, capable of constructing social reality through their *representations*, or in the corresponding social realities. At present, the problem arises in a particularly acute way. Do the parties express differences, or do they produce them? According to the theory intermediate between ultra-subjectivism and ultra-objectivism that is expressed by Lukács, the party simply reveals the proletariat to itself, an idea expressed in the metaphor of the midwife.

Can't these two oppositions – the opposition in terms of the theory of knowledge and the opposition in terms of political action – be superimposed? If one had to distribute the various thinkers of the social world in a kind of theoretical space according to the position they adopt on these two problems, one would see that the answers are not independent of each other. In the area of anthropology, where the directly political question does not arise, the main division is the opposition between subjectivism and objectivism. The objectivist tradition conceives the social world as a universe of objective regularities independent of the agents and constructed from the standpoint of an impartial observer who is outside the action, looking down from above on the world he observes. The ethnologist is someone who reconstitutes a kind of unwritten score which lies behind the actions of the agents, who think they are improvising their own melody when, in reality, whether in matrimonial exchanges or linguistic exchanges, they are acting out a system of transcendent rules, etc. On the opposite side, Sartre, in his *Critique of Dialectical Reason*, explicitly takes issue with Lévi-Strauss and with the reification effect that objectivism produces. A disciple of Husserl, Schutz, devised a phenomenology of the ordinary experience of the social world. He tried to describe how social agents experience the social world in the naïve state, and this tradition has been carried on in the United States in the current known as 'ethnomethodology', which is a kind of rigorous phenomenology of the subjective experience of the world. It's the absolute antithesis of objectivist description. In its extreme form, as some of Goffman's texts suggest, the social world is the product of individual actions. Far from people behaving respectfully because there are hierarchies, it's the infinity of individual actions of respect, deference, etc., that ultimately produces hierarchy. The political implications of that are immediately clear. On the one hand, there is the language of the objective structures of domination, the objective power relations; on the other hand, there's a cumulation of infinitesimal acts of respect which engenders the objectivity of social relations. On one side, determinism, on the other freedom and spontaneity. ('If everyone ceased to salute great men, there would be no great men . . .' [Pascal].) It is clearly a major issue. It is also clear that in sociology, and when dealing with societies divided into classes, it is more difficult than it is in anthropology (though people almost always do it) to separate the problem of knowledge from the political problem.

In the Marxist tradition, there is a permanent struggle between an objectivist tendency which tries to find classes in reality (hence the eternal problem: 'How many classes are there?') and a voluntarist or spontaneist theory in which classes are something that people make. On one side, the talk is of class condition; on the other, of class consciousness. On one side, talk of position in the relations of production; on the other, of 'class struggle', action and mobilization. The objectivist vision is more that of the academic; the spontaneist vision more that of the militant. In fact, I think that the position one takes on the question of classes depends on the position one occupies in the class structure.

In a paper I wrote a while ago[1] I raised some of the questions that I want to consider this evening. A polling organization asked a sample of people to associate a number of politicians with a selection of objects, as in the party game ('If he was a tree, what tree would he be?'). If the politician in question were a tree, would he be a plane tree, or an oak, etc.? If he were a car, would he be a Rolls-Royce, or a Porsche, or a 2 CV, etc.? On the face of it, it was a trivial game of no consequence. And yet, when they were invited to connect two series of things about which they manifestly had no concept, on the one hand a series of politicians and on the other a series of objects, the subjects produced a series of coherent attributions. For Jean-Jacques Servan-Schreiber, for example, they gave: if he were a tree, it would be a palm tree; a piece of furniture – furniture from Knoll; a car – a Porsche; a relative – a son-in-law. You can find in that the idea that Servan-Schreiber is a flashy parvenu, and a whole aspect of the identity of the new bourgeoisie that he belongs to. (In fact the newspapers tell us he does have Knoll furniture in his Paris home.) In other words, there's an overall intuition of the person in so far as he is the bearer of the 'style' of a whole class fraction.

The natural objects (trees, flowers and so on), not being socially preconstituted, are constituted by the application of social schemes of perception. But hats (bowler, top hat, cap, beret, etc.), or games (bridge, *belote*, etc.), are objects that are already classified, in reality itself, since by the mere fact of putting on a beret, or a cap, or no hat at all, people classify themselves and know what they are doing. So the classifications that the sociologist applies are second-degree classifications. You could say that the attributions that people make are performed by a social sense that is a quasi-sociology, a practical and well-grounded intuition of the correspondence between social positions and tastes.

I'm starting to answer the question that I raised at the beginning: is the representation of the social world the simple recording of divisions that are in reality or is it a construction performed by the application of classificatory schemes? Agents spend their lives classifying themselves by the mere fact of appropriating objects that are themselves classified (because they are associated with classes of agents); and also classifying the other people who classify themselves by appropriating the objects that they classify. So the classification of the object is part of the object itself. All agents in a society have roughly the same system of classification in their heads. Consequently, one could say that there are two orders of objectivity: the objective classes that I can construct on the basis of income, qualifications, number of children and so on; and the objective classes as they exist in the minds of all the agents who are subject to the scientific classification. These classifications are something the agents fight over. In other words, there is a classification struggle that is one dimension of the class struggle. In one of his *Theses on Feuerbach*, Marx says, roughly, that the trouble with materialism is that it abandoned to idealism the idea that the object is the product of our constructions, that it identified materialism with a theory of knowledge as a reflection of the world, when in fact knowledge is a production, a collective labour. Now, as I've said, this production is antagonistic. Classification systems are social products and, as such, they are fought over in a permanent struggle. All that is very abstract, but I can come back to some extremely concrete things. To take an example: collective agreements are records of industrial struggles between employers, trade unions, etc. Struggles over what? Over words, classifications, differentials. Most of the words available to us to express the social world lie in the space between euphemism and insult. There's *plouc* ['clod, yokel'], an insult, and *agriculteur*, a euphemism; and between the two, *paysan*. There are never any neutral words to describe the social world, and the same word has different meanings in different people's mouths. Take the word *petit-bourgeois*: that word, which concentrates a certain number of properties quite characteristic of that category, has so often been used as an insult in philosophical or literary battles ('petty-bourgeois', 'grocer', etc.), that whatever one does, it will function as a polemical weapon.

In everyday life, we are constantly objectifying other people. An insult is an objectification ('You're just . . .'). It reduces the other to one of his properties, preferably a hidden one; it reduces him, as the phrase goes, to his objective truth. Someone says: 'I'm generous, disinterested, etc.' The answer comes: 'You're there to make a living.' It's a reduction, degree zero. (Materialism has a particular propensity to fall into the economism which corresponds to the spontaneous tendency of the everyday classification struggle, which consists in reducing the other to his objective truth. And the most elementary reduction is reduction to economic interest.)

In everyday practice, the struggle between objectivism and subjectivism is a permanent one. Everyone seeks to impose his subjective representation of himself as an objective representation. A dominant agent is one who has the means to force the dominated agent to see him as he wants to be seen. In political life, each person is objectivist against his adversaries. Indeed, we are all objectivist towards others.

There's a complicity between objectivist scientism and a form of terrorism. The propensity towards objectivism that is inherent in the scientistic posture is linked to certain positions in the social universe, and more especially to the position of a researcher who dominates the world in thought, who has the impression of having a thought of the world that is quite inaccessible to those who are immersed in action. Economism is the temptation of people who know more economics. On the other hand, those who are more involved in action are inclined to spontaneism. The opposition between objectivism and subjectivism is part of the nature of things; it is the historical struggle itself. Marx is more likely to possess the truth of Bakunin than Bakunin, and Bakunin is more likely to possess the truth of Marx than Marx. In any case one cannot be Marx and Bakunin at the same time. You can't be in two places in social space at the same time. The fact that one is at a point in social space is linked to probable errors: the subjectivist error, the objectivist error. As soon as there is a social space, there is struggle, there is a struggle for domination, there is a dominant pole and a dominated pole, and from that moment there are antagonistic truths. Whatever one does, the truth is antagonistic. If one thing is true, it is that truth is a stake in struggles.

I think that in the labour movement, there's always a struggle between a centralizing, scientistic tendency and a more spontaneist tendency, and each of these tendencies relies, for the sake of the struggle within the party, on real oppositions within the working class itself: the former appeals to the sub-proletariat, the underclass; the latter to the working-class élite. This opposition is history itself, and the monistic pretension which tries to cancel it out is anti-historical and therefore terroristic.

I don't know if I have argued correctly. What I said at the end is not a credo. I think it flows from the analysis.

Note

1 See Bourdieu, P. (1985) *Distinction*, London: Routledge & Kegan Paul, pp. 546–59 [translator].

8

WHAT TALKING MEANS

If the sociologist has a role to play, it's more to give weapons than to give lessons.

I have come here to contribute to your discussions and to try to provide people who have practical experience of a certain number of educational problems with the instruments that sociological research offers for interpreting and understanding those problems.

So if what I have to say is disappointing, sometimes even depressing, it's not because I take any pleasure in discouraging people; on the contrary. It is because knowledge of realities inclines one to realism. One of the temptations of the craft of sociology is what the sociologists themselves have called sociologism, that's to say the temptation to transform historical laws or historical regularities into eternal laws. That is what makes it so difficult to communicate the products of sociological research. One constantly has to situate oneself between two roles – on the one hand that of the wet blanket, the Cassandra, and on the other that of the accomplice of utopian thinking.

Here, today, I would like to take as my starting-point the questionnaire that some of you drew up for this meeting. I want to start from there because I wish to speak as concretely as possible and (since this seems to me to be one of the practical conditions of all genuine communication) to avoid a situation in which the speaker, the one who has the effective monopoly of speech, completely imposes the arbitrary character of his own enquiry, the arbitrariness of his own interests. Awareness of the arbitrariness of the imposition of speech is increasingly widespread nowadays, both among those who have the monopoly of discourse and those who suffer it. Why is it that in certain historical circumstances, in certain social situations, we feel anxiety or unease at the imposition that is always implicit in 'taking the floor' in a situation of authority, or, one might say, an *authorized situation* (the model of this situation being that of the teacher)?

So, to dissolve this anxiety in my own eyes, I have taken as my starting-point some questions that have *really* arisen for a group of you and which may arise for all of you.

Paper given at the conference of the AFEF (Association Française des Enseignants de Français), Limoges, 30 October 1977, published in *Le Français aujourd'hui*, 41, 1978: 4–20, 51–7

The questions revolve around the relationship between written and oral expression, and could be formulated as follows: 'Can oral expression be taught?'

This question is a reformulation for modern tastes of a centuries-old problem that was already being raised by Plato: 'Can excellence be taught?' It's a quite central question. Can one teach something? Can one teach something that cannot be learned? Can one teach what one teaches with, that's to say, the spoken word?

Such questions do not arise at all times in history. If, for example, it arises in Plato's dialogues, it seems to me that it's because the question of teaching arises for teaching when teaching is called into question. Critical enquiry into what it means to teach is something that emerges when teaching is in crisis. In normal times, in what might be called the organic phases, education does not question itself. One of the properties of an educational system that is working too well – or too badly – is that it is sure of itself, that it has the kind of self-assurance (it's no accident that in French we talk about 'assurance' in language) that springs from the certainty of being not only *heard* but *listened to*, a certainty that is characteristic of all authoritative or authorized discourse. So this questioning is not a-temporal but historically situated. That historical situation is what I want to reflect on. It is linked to a state of the teaching relationship, a state of the relationship between the educational system and society as a whole, that is, the structure of social classes, a state of the language, and a state of the educational institution. I would like to try to show that, starting from the concrete questions that arise from the use of language in education, one can address the most fundamental questions in the sociology of language (or sociolinguistics) and also in the sociology of the educational institution. For it seems to me that sociolinguistics would have emerged from abstraction more quickly if it had taken as the site for its reflection and its constitution that very particular but quite exemplary space, the classroom, and if it had taken as its object that very particular use of language, the language of the classroom.

I turn to the first set of questions: 'Do you try to teach oral expression? What difficulties do you encounter? Do you encounter resistance? Do you encounter passivity on the part of your pupils . . .?'

I immediately want to ask: 'Teach oral expression? But *which* oral expression?'

There's a hidden agenda here, as in all oral and even written discourse. There's a set of presuppositions that everyone brings in when raising this question. Given that mental structures are internalized social structures, there is every likelihood that with the opposition between written and oral expression, one will bring in a quite classic opposition between the distinguished and the vulgar, the formal and the popular, 'elaborated' and 'restricted' codes and so on, so that oral teaching is very likely to be accompanied by a whole populist aura. Teaching oral expression would then mean teaching the language that is learned in the street, which already leads us to a paradox. In other words, doesn't the question of the very nature of the language taught itself raise a question? Or, to put it another way, isn't this oral expression that one wants to teach something that is already taught, and very unequally so, from one educational establishment to another? We know, for example, that the various institutions of higher education train students very unequally for oral tests. Institutions that prepare students for politics, like Sciences Po or the École Nationale d'Administration, teach oral performance much more and give it much more importance in their assessment than institutions that train students for teaching, or for engineering. For example, at the École Polytechnique, they do what they call the *grand oral*, which is exactly like drawing-room conversation, requiring a certain type of relation to language, a certain type of culture. Talking about 'teaching oral expression', just like that, is not new at all; there's already a lot of it going on. This 'spoken language' may be the language of bourgeois dinner parties, the language of international symposiums, and so on.

So it is not sufficient to ask 'Should we teach spoken language?' and 'Which spoken language shall we teach?' We also have to ask *who* is going to define which oral language to teach. One of the laws of sociolinguistics is that the language used in a particular situation depends not only, as internal linguistics supposes, on the speaker's competence in the Chomskian sense, but also on what I call the linguistic market. The speech that we produce, according to the model that I am suggesting, is a 'resultant' of the speaker's competence and the market on which his speech is offered; speech depends in part – this would need to be assessed more rigorously – on the conditions of reception.

So every linguistic situation functions as a market on which the speaker places his products, and the product he produces for this market depends on his anticipation of the price his products will receive. Willy-nilly, we enter the educational market with an expectation of the profits and sanctions we shall receive. One of the great mysteries that sociolinguistics has to solve is this kind of sense of acceptability. We never learn language without learning *at the same time* the conditions of acceptability of this language. In other words, learning a language means learning at the same time that this language will be profitable in this or that situation.

We learn inseparably to speak and to evaluate in advance the price that our speech will receive; on the educational market – and in this respect the educational market offers an ideal situation for analysis – this price is the grade awarded, a grade that very often implies a material prize (if you don't get a good grade in your passing-out exam at the École Polytechnique you will end up as an administrator at INSEE[1] and earn two-thirds less . . .). So every language situation functions as a market on which something is exchanged. These things are words, of course, but these words are not uttered solely to be understood; the relation of communication is never just a relation of communication, it is also an economic relation in which the speaker's value is at stake: did he speak well or poorly? Is he brilliant or not? Could one marry him? . . .

Pupils who enter the educational market have an anticipation of the chances of reward, or the sanctions, that await this or that type of language. In other words, the scholastic situation, as a linguistic situation of a particular type, exerts an enormous censorship on those who knowingly and accurately anticipate the chances of profit or loss that they have, given the linguistic competence they possess. And some people's silence is simply enlightened self-interest.

One of the problems raised by this questionnaire is knowing *who* controls the classroom situation. Is the teacher really in charge? Does he really have the initiative in defining acceptability? Does he have control over the laws of the market?

All the contradictions that will be encountered by those who embark on the experience of teaching oral expression stem from the following proposition: when it comes to defining the laws of the specific market of his classroom, the teacher's freedom is limited, because he will never manage to create 'an empire within an empire', a sub-space in which the laws of the dominant market are suspended. Before going any further, we need to recall the very special character of the scholastic market. It is dominated by the imperative demands of the teacher of French, who is legitimized to teach what would not need to be taught if everyone had equal chances of having that capacity, and who has the right of correction in both senses – linguistic 'correctness' ('refined' language) is the product of correction. The teacher is a kind of juvenile magistrate in linguistic matters: he has a right to correct and sanction his pupils' language.

Let's imagine, for example, a populist teacher who refuses this right of correction and says 'Anyone who wants to speak should just speak; the most beautiful French is street French.' In fact, whatever his intentions, this teacher remains in a space that does not normally obey this logic, because it's very likely that there will be a teacher who demands rigour, correctness, spelling . . . . But even if we suppose, all the same, that a whole educational establishment is transformed in this way, then the anticipations of the chances that the pupils bring on to the market will lead them to exercise a censorship in advance, and it will take a long time for them to abandon the correctness and hypercorrectness that appear in all situations that are linguistically – that is, socially – asymmetrical (and especially in the survey situation). All of Labov's work was only made possible by a whole set of tricks designed to destroy the linguistic artefact that is produced by the mere fact of bringing face to face a 'competent' speaker, one who feels authorized, and an 'incompetent' speaker, who does not feel authorized. In the same way, all the work we've done on culture involved us in trying to overcome the legitimacy-imposing effect that stems from the mere fact of asking questions about culture. Putting questions about culture in a survey situation (which resembles a scholastic situation) to people who do not think they are cultured excludes from their discourse everything that really interests them. Then they search for everything that might resemble culture. So when you ask 'Do you like music?', you never get the answer 'I like Dalida', but rather 'I like Strauss waltzes' because, for popular competence, that is what best resembles the idea people have of what the bourgeoisie likes. In all revolutionary situations, populists have always come up against this kind of revenge of the laws of the market, which seem to assert themselves most strongly when one thinks one is violating them.

To return to the starting-point of this digression: who defines acceptability?

The teacher is free to abdicate his role as a 'talking master' who – by producing a certain type of linguistic situation or simply allowing the logic of things (the podium, the chair, the microphone, the distance, the pupils' *habitus*) to take its course, or allowing the laws that produce a certain type of discourse to work their effects – produces a certain type of language, not only in himself, but in his interlocutors. But to what extent can the teacher manipulate the laws of acceptability without entering into extraordinary contradictions, so long as the general laws of acceptability are not changed? That's what makes the experiment of teaching oral French so fascinating. One cannot touch such a central and yet so self-evident a thing without raising the most revolutionary questions about the educational system. Can one change the language in the educational system without changing all the laws that define the value of the linguistic products of the different classes on the market; without changing the relations of domination in the realm of language, that's to say without changing the relations of domination?

I now come to an analogy that I hesitate to formulate, although it seems to me necessary: the analogy between the crisis of the teaching of French and the crisis of religious liturgy. Liturgy is a ritualized language which is entirely codified (both in its actions and its words) and whose sequence is entirely predictable. The liturgy in Latin is the extreme form of a language which, while not understood, is *authorized*, and functions none the less, in certain conditions, as a language, to the satisfaction of its emitters and receivers. In a crisis situation, this language ceases to function; it no longer produces its principal effect, which is to induce belief, induce respect, acceptance – and to get *itself* accepted even if it is not understood.

The question raised by the crisis of liturgy, of this language that no longer functions, that is no longer heard, that no one believes in any more, is the question of the relationship between the language and the institution. When a language is in crisis and the question arises of what language to speak, it's because the institution is in crisis and the question of the delegating authority has been opened up – the authority that lays down how to speak and that gives authority and authorization to speak.

With that detour through the Church, I wanted to raise the following question: is the linguistic crisis separable from the crisis of the educational institution? Isn't the crisis of the linguistic institution simply the manifestation of the crisis of the educational institution? In its traditional definition, in the organic phase of the French educational system, the teaching of French was not a problem, the teacher of French was sure of his role. He knew what had to be taught and how to teach it, and he encountered pupils ready to listen to him and understand him, and understanding parents who understood that understanding. In that situation, the teacher of French was a celebrant. He celebrated a cult of the French language, he defended and illustrated the language; and strengthened its sacred values. In doing so, he defended his own sacred value. That's very important, because morale and belief are an awareness, which one hides from oneself, of one's own interests. If the crisis of the French language provokes such dramatic personal crises, as violent as those we saw in May 1968 and afterwards, it's because, through the value of the French language as a commodity on the market, a certain number of people, with their backs to the wall, are defending their own value, their own capital. They are ready to die for French . . . or for its spelling! Just as people who've spent fifteen years of their lives learning Latin, when their language is suddenly devalued, are like holders of Imperial Russian bonds . . .

One of the effects of the crisis is that it opens up questions about the tacit conditions, the presuppositions, of the educational system. When the crisis brings to light a certain number of presuppositions, it's possible to raise the systematic question of the presuppositions and ask what a scholastic linguistic situation *has* to be in order for the problems that arise in a crisis situation not to arise. The most advanced linguistics is now joining up with sociology on this point, that the prime object of research on language is to define the presuppositions of communication. The essential part of what happens in communication is not in the communication. For example, the essential part of what happens in a communication like pedagogic communication lies in the social conditions of possibility of the communication. In the case of religion, in order for the Roman liturgy to function, a certain type of emitters and a certain type of receivers have to be produced. The receivers have to be predisposed to recognize the authority of the emitters; the emitters have to be able to speak not in their own right but always as delegates, mandated priests, and must never take it upon themselves to define what is and what is not to be said.

The same is true in education. In order for the teacher's ordinary discourse, uttered and received as self-evident, to function, there has to be a relationship of authority and belief, a relation between an authorized emitter and a receiver ready to receive, and it is not the pedagogic situation that produces this.

To recapitulate quickly in rather abstract terms, communication in a situation of pedagogic authority presupposes legitimate emitters, legitimate receivers, a legitimate situation and a legitimate language.

It needs a legitimate emitter, that's to say someone who recognizes the implicit laws of the system and who is, by virtue of that, recognized and co-opted. It needs addressees recognized by the emitter as worthy of receiving, which presupposes that the emitter has a power of elimination, that he is able to exclude those who 'should not be there'. But that is not all: it needs pupils who are ready to recognize the teacher as a teacher, and parents who give a kind of credit, an open cheque, to the teacher. It also requires that, ideally, the receivers should be relatively homogeneous linguistically (that's to say socially), homogeneous in knowledge of the language and *recognition* of the language, and that the structure of the group should not function as a system of censorship capable of forbidding the language that has to be used.

In some classroom groups with a working-class majority, the working-class children may be able to impose the linguistic norm of their milieu and to depreciate the language of Labov's 'wimps', who have a language for the teachers, that's to say effeminate and somewhat ingratiating. So it can happen that the scholastic linguistic norm clashes within some social structures with a counter-norm. (Conversely, in structures with a bourgeois majority, peer-group censorship runs in the same direction as the censorship imposed by the teacher: language that is not 'correct' is self-censored and cannot be produced in the educational situation.)

The legitimate situation is something that brings in both the structure of the group and the institutional space within which the group functions. For example, there's the whole set of institutional signs of importance, in particular the language of importance (the language of importance has a rhetoric of its own, the function of which is to say how important what is being said is). This language of importance is that much more effective when one occupies an eminent position, on a dais, in a consecrated place, etc. Among the strategies for manipulating a group, there is manipulation of the spatial structures and the institutional signs of importance.

A legitimate language is a language with legitimate phonological and syntactic forms, that's to say a language meeting the usual criteria of grammaticality, and a language which constantly says, together with what it says, that it says it well. And in so doing, it implies that what it says is true – which is one of the fundamental ways of passing off the false in place of the true. One of the political effects of the dominant language is this: 'He says it so well, it must be true.'

This set of properties, which *constitute a system* and which are brought together in the organic state of an educational system, defines social acceptability, the state in which language 'gets across': it is listened to (i.e. believed), obeyed, heard (understood). Communication can take place even through hints and winks. One of the properties of organic situations is that language itself – the strictly linguistic part of the communication – tends to become secondary.

In the role of celebrant which often fell to teachers of art or literature, language was little more than a series of interjections. The discourse of celebration, that of art critics for example, does not say much more than an 'exclamation'. Exclamation is the fundamental religious experience.

In a crisis situation, this mutual credit system breaks down. It's like a monetary crisis: people begin to question the value of the tokens they are offered.

The best illustration of the extraordinary freedom that the emitter is given by a conjunction of favourable factors is *hypocorrectness*. Hypocorrection – the opposite of the *hypercorrection* that characterizes petit-bourgeois speech – is only possible because the person who transgresses the rule (Giscard d'Estaing, for example, when he fails to make his past participles agree) manifests in other ways, through other aspects of his speech, such as pronunciation, and also by everything that he is, everything he does, that he could speak correctly if he wanted to.

A linguistic situation is never purely linguistic, and the questions asked by the questionnaire, taken as a starting-point, in fact raised the most fundamental questions of sociolinguistics (What does it mean to speak with authority? What are the social conditions of possibility of communication?) and also the fundamental questions of the sociology of the educational system, which are all organized around the ultimate question of *delegation*.

Whether he knows it or not, whether he wants it or not, and more especially when he thinks he is being radical, the teacher remains the holder of a mandate, a delegated authority, who cannot redefine his task without entering into contradictions or putting his receivers into contradictions, so long as there is no change in the laws of the market in relation to which he negatively or positively defines the relatively autonomous rules of the little market he sets up in his classroom. For example, a teacher who refuses to correct his pupils' speech is perfectly entitled to do so, but in doing so he may compromise his pupils' chances on the matrimonial market or the economic market, where the laws of the dominant linguistic market still prevail. All of which should not lead to a surrender.

The idea of producing an autonomous space isolated from the laws of the market is a dangerous utopia so long as one does not simultaneously pose the question of the political conditions of possibility of the generalization of that utopia.

Q. *It's certainly useful to push further the notion of linguistic competence in order to move beyond the Chomskian model of an ideal emitter and speaker. But your analyses of competence in the sense of everything that makes an utterance legitimate are sometimes rather fluid, especially the idea of the market. Sometimes you seem to mean a* *market in the economic sense, sometimes you identify the market with exchange in the macro-situation, and it seems to me that there's an ambiguity there. Apart from that, you don't take enough account of the fact that the crisis you refer to is a kind of sub-crisis that is linked more essentially to the crisis of a system in which we're all involved. One would need to refine the analysis of all the conditions of situations of linguistic exchange in the scholastic sphere or in the educational sphere in the broad sense.*

A.   I referred here to the model of competence and the market after some hesitation, because it's clear that to defend it properly I would need much more time and I would have to spell out some very abstract analyses which might not interest everybody. I'm glad that your question gives me a chance to clarify a few points.

I do give a very broad sense to the word *market*. It seems to me quite legitimate to use the term *linguistic market* to describe the relationship between two housewives talking in the street, or the educational sphere, or the interview situation in which executives are recruited.

As soon as two speakers exchange utterances, there's an objective relationship between their competences, not only their linguistic competence (their more or less complete command of the legitimate language) but also their whole social competence, their right to speak, which depends objectively on their sex, their age, their religion, their economic and social status, all of which is information that might be known in advance or anticipated through imperceptible cues (he's polite, wearing an insignia, etc.). This relationship gives the market its structure and defines a certain type of law of price formation. There's a micro-economics and a macro-economics of linguistic products, though of course the micro-economy is never autonomous with respect to the macro-economic laws. For example, in a situation of bilingualism, speakers will change their language in a way that has nothing random about it. I've been able to observe both in Algeria and in a Béarn village that people change language according to the subject, but also according to the market, the structure of the relationship between the speakers. The propensity to adopt the dominant language rises with the interlocutor's position in the anticipated hierarchy of linguistic competences. A speaker will try to address someone he regards as important in the best possible French. The dominant language is that much more dominant, the more the dominant speakers dominate that particular market. The probability that the speaker will adopt French in order to express himself rises with the domination of the market by the dominant speakers, in official situations, for example. And the educational situation belongs to the series of official markets. There's no economism in that analysis. I'm not saying that every market is an economic market. But nor should one say that there is not a linguistic market which involves economic stakes, at a greater or lesser distance.

As for the second part of the question, it raises the problem of the scientific right to abstraction. You abstract out a certain number of problems and you work in the space that you've defined for yourself.

Q. *In the educational system as you have defined it by that set of properties, do you think that the teacher has any room for manoeuvre? And if so, what is it?*

A. That's a very difficult question, but I think the answer is 'Yes'. If I were not convinced that there is some room for manoeuvre, I wouldn't be here now.

More seriously, at the level of analysis, I think that one of the practical consequences of what I've said is that awareness and knowledge of the specific laws of the linguistic market of which a particular class is the site can completely transform the way of teaching, whatever the objective one is pursuing (preparing pupils for the baccalaureate, introducing modern literature or linguistics, etc.).

It's important to know that a linguistic production owes a major part of its properties to the structure of its audience of receivers. You only have to consult the record cards of the pupils in a class to see that structure. In a class where three-quarters of the pupils are the children of manual workers, you have to be aware of the need to spell out your presuppositions. Any communication which wants to be effective also presupposes a knowledge of what sociologists call the peer group. Every teacher has had the experience in a classroom, his teaching may come up against a counter-teaching, a counterculture. Given what he wants to transmit, he may try (it's another choice) to combat that counterculture, within certain limits, which presupposes that he knows it. Knowing it means knowing, for example, the *relative weight* of the different forms of competence. Among the very profound changes that have occurred in the French school system, there are qualitative effects of quantitative transformations. Beyond a certain threshold in the representation of working-class children in a school class, the overall atmosphere of the classroom changes, the forms of disorder change, the type of relationships with teachers changes. These are all things that can be observed and taken into account practically.

But all that only concerns the means. And indeed the sociologist cannot answer the question of the ultimate ends (what should one teach?). They are defined by the structure of relations between the social classes. The changes in the definition of the content of education and even the freedom that teachers are allowed in going through their crisis stem from the fact that there is also a crisis in the dominant definition of the legitimate content and that the dominant class is currently the site of conflicts about what deserves to be taught.

I cannot define the project of education (to try to do so would be a usurpation – I'd be acting like a prophet); I can simply say that teachers need to know that they are delegated, mandated, and that their prophetic effects themselves still presuppose the support of the institution. Which does not mean that they should not fight in order to have their say in the definition of what they have to teach.

Q. *You have presented the teacher of French as the legitimate dispenser of legitimate discourse which is the reflection of a dominant ideology and of dominant classes, through a tool – language – very largely 'impregnated' with that dominant ideology.*

Don't you think that that definition is also very reductive? Moreover, there's a contradiction between the beginning of your talk and the end, when you were saying that the French class and oral exercises could also be the site of a raising of awareness, and that this same language, which could be the vehicle of dominant class models, could also provide those in front of us, and ourselves, with a means of access to the use of tools which are indispensable tools.

I'm here, in the AFEF, because I think that language is also a tool which only works if one learns how to make it work. It's because we are convinced of that that we demand a more scientific approach to the study of our discipline. What do you think?

Do you think that oral exchange in the classroom is merely the image of a legality that is also social and political legality? Isn't the school classroom also the object of a contradiction that exists in society – political struggle?

A. But you are putting words into my mouth! I have never said that language was the dominant ideology. I don't even think I have once used here the expression 'dominant ideology' . . . For me that's one of the very regrettable misunderstandings. In fact, my whole effort is aimed at destroying verbal and mental automatisms like the linkage dominant class/dominant ideology.

What does *legitimate* mean? The word is a technical term in sociological vocabulary that I use quite deliberately, because technical words make it possible to say, and to think, difficult things, and to think them rigorously. An institution, or an action, or a usage is legitimate when it is dominant but not recognized as such, in other words tacitly recognized. The language that teachers use, the language you use to speak to me. . . [A voice: You use it too . . .!] Of course I use it, but I never stop explaining that I use it! . . . the language that *we* use in this space is a dominant language unrecognized as such, and so tacitly recognized as legitimate. It's a language that produces the essential part of its effects by seeming not to be what it is. Which leads to the question: if it is true that we speak a legitimate language, isn't everything that we can say in that language affected by that, even if we apply this instrument in the service of the transmission of contents which seek to be critical?

Here's another fundamental question: this dominant language, unrecognized as such, and therefore recognized as legitimate – doesn't it have an affinity with certain contents? Doesn't it exercise effects of censorship? Doesn't it make certain things difficult or impossible to say? Isn't this legitimate language designed, among other things, to prevent plain speaking? (But I shouldn't have said 'designed to' [*fait pour*]. One of the principles of sociology is to challenge that kind of negative functionalism. Social mechanisms are not the product of a Machiavellian intention. They are much more intelligent than the most intelligent of the dominant agents.)

Let's take an indisputable example. In the educational system, I think that the legitimate language has an affinity with a certain type of relation to the text that denies (in the psychoanalytic sense) the relation to the social reality that the text is talking about. If texts are read by people who read them in such a way that they don't read them, it's largely because people are trained to speak a language in which one speaks to say that one is not saying what one is saying. One of the properties of legitimate language is precisely that it *de-realizes* what it says. Jean-Claude Chevalier put it very pungently when he said: 'Is a school that teaches oral French still a school? Is the oral language taught in a school still oral?'

I'll take a very specific example, from politics. I've been struck by the fact that the very same interlocutors who, in casual conversation, would produce very complex political analyses of the relations between management and workforce, unions and their local branches, were completely disarmed, had little more than banalities to offer, as soon as I asked them questions of the type that are asked in opinion polls and also in school dissertations. That's to say, questions that require one to adopt a style such that the question of true or false does not arise. The educational system teaches not only a language but a relation to language that is bound up with a relation to things, to beings, to the world, that is completely de-realized.

Notes

1   The Institut National de la Statistique et des Études Économiques [translator].

Further reading

For further discussion see Bourdieu, P. (1975) 'Le fétichisme de la langue', *Actes de la recherche en sciences sociales*, 4: 2–32; (1977) 'The economics of linguistic exchanges', *Social Science Information*, 16 (6): 645–8; (1975) 'Le langage autorisé: note sur les conditions sociales de l'efficacité du discours rituel', *Actes de la recherche en sciences sociales*, 5–6: 183–90.

9

SOME PROPERTIES OF FIELDS

Fields present themselves synchronically as structured spaces of positions (or posts) whose properties depend on their position within these spaces and which can be analysed independently of the characteristics of their occupants (which are partly determined by them). There are *general laws of fields*: fields as different as the field of politics, the field of philosophy or the field of religion have invariant laws of functioning. (That is why the project of a general theory is not unreasonable and why, even now, we can use what we learn about the functioning of each particular field to question and interpret other fields, so moving beyond the deadly antinomy of monographic idiography and formal, empty theory.) Whenever one studies a new field, whether it be the field of philology in the nineteenth century, contemporary fashion, or religion in the Middle Ages, one discovers specific properties that are peculiar to that field, at the same time as one pushes forward our knowledge of the universal mechanisms of fields, which are specified in terms of secondary variables. For example, national variables mean that generic mechanisms such as the struggle between the challengers and the established dominant actors take different forms. But we know that in every field we shall find a struggle, the specific forms of which have to be looked for each time, between the newcomer who tries to break through the entry barrier and the dominant agent who will try to defend the monopoly and keep out competition.

A field – even the scientific field – defines itself by (among other things) defining specific stakes and interests, which are irreducible to the stakes and interests specific to other fields (you can't make a philosopher compete for the prizes that interest a geographer) and which are not perceived by someone who has not been shaped to enter that field (every category of interests implies indifference to other interests, other investments, which are therefore bound to be perceived as absurd, irrational, or sublime and disinterested). In order for a field to function, there have to be stakes and people prepared to play the game, endowed with the *habitus* that implies knowledge and recognition of the immanent laws of the field, the stakes, and so on.

The *habitus* of a philologist is all at once a 'craft', a collection of techniques, references, and a set of 'beliefs', such as the propensity to give as

Talk given at the École Normale Supérieure, Paris, in November 1976, to a group of philologists and literary historians much importance to the notes as to the text. These are properties that derive from the history (national and international) of the discipline and its (intermediate) position in the hierarchy of disciplines, and which are both the condition of the functioning of the field and the product of its functioning (but not entirely: a field may simply receive and consecrate a particular type of *habitus* that is more or less fully constituted).

The structure of the field is a *state* of the power relations among the agents or institutions engaged in the struggle, or, to put it another way, a state of the distribution of the specific capital which has been accumulated in the course of previous struggles and which orients subsequent strategies. This structure, which governs the strategies aimed at transforming it, is itself always at stake. The struggles which take place within the field are about the monopoly of the legitimate violence (specific authority) which is characteristic of the field in question, which means, ultimately, the conservation or subversion of the structure of the distribution of the specific capital. (When one speaks of specific capital, this means to say that this capital is effective *in relation to* a particular field, and therefore within the limits of that field, and that it is only convertible into another kind of capital on certain conditions. You only have to think, for example, of the failure of Pierre Cardin when he tried to transfer capital accumulated in *haute couture* into high culture. Every last art critic felt called upon to assert his structural superiority as a member of a structurally more legitimate field by saying that everything Cardin did in legitimate art was contemptible, thus imposing the most unfavourable conversion rate on Cardin's capital.)

Those who, in a determinate state of the power relations, more or less completely monopolize the specific capital, the basis of the specific power or authority characteristic of a field, are inclined to conservation strategies – those which, in the fields of production of cultural goods, tend to defend *orthodoxy* – whereas those least endowed with capital (who are often also the newcomers, and therefore generally the youngest) are inclined towards subversion strategies, the strategies of *heresy*. Heresy, heterodoxy, functioning as a critical break with doxa (and often associated with a crisis), is what brings the dominant agents out of their silence and forces them to produce the defensive discourse of orthodoxy, the right-thinking, right-wing thought that is aimed at restoring the equivalent of silent assent to doxa.

Another property of fields, a less visible one, is that all the agents that are involved in a field share a certain number of fundamental interests, namely everything that is linked to the very existence of the field. This leads to an objective complicity which underlies all the antagonisms. It tends to be forgotten that a fight presupposes agreement between the antagonists about what it is that is worth fighting about; those points of agreement are held at the level of what 'goes without saying', they are left in the state of doxa, in other words everything that makes the field itself, the game, the stakes, all the presuppositions that one tacitly and even unwittingly accepts by the mere fact of playing, of entering into the game. Those who take part in the struggle help to reproduce the game by helping – more or less completely, depending on the field – to produce belief in the value of the stakes. The new players have to pay an entry fee which consists in recognition of the value of the game (selection and co-option always pay great attention to the indices of commitment to the game, investment in it) and in (practical) knowledge of the principles of the functioning of the game. They are condemned to use the strategies of subversion, but, if they are not to incur exclusion from the game, these strategies have to remain within certain limits. The *partial revolutions* which constantly occur in fields do not call into question the very foundations of the game, its fundamental axioms, the bedrock of ultimate beliefs on which the whole game is based. On the contrary, in the fields of production of cultural goods – religion, literature or art – heretical subversion claims to be returning to the sources, the origin, the spirit, the authentic essence of the game, in opposition to the banalization and degradation which it has suffered. (One of the factors protecting the various games from total revolutions, which could destroy not only the dominant agents and their domination, but the game itself, is the very size of the investment, in time, effort and so on, presupposed by entry into the game. Like the ordeals in rites of passage, this investment helps to make the pure and simple destruction of the game *unthinkable* in practical terms. Thus whole sectors of culture – with an audience of philologists, I can't help thinking of philology – are saved by the cost entailed in acquiring the knowledge needed even to destroy them with due form.)

Through the practical knowledge of the principles of the game that is tacitly required of new entrants, the whole history of the game, the whole past of the game, is present in each act of the game. It is no accident that, together with the presence in each work of traces of the objective (and sometimes even conscious) relationship to other works, one of the surest indices of the constitution of a field is the appearance of a corps of conservators of lives – the biographers – and of works – the philologists, the historians of art and literature, who start to archive the sketches, the drafts, the manuscripts, to 'correct' them (the right to 'correct' is the legitimate violence of the philologist), to decipher them, etc. These agents' interests lie in conserving what is produced in the field, and in so doing to conserve themselves. And another index that an area has started to function as a field is the trace of the history of the field in the individual work (and even in the life of the producer). For a proof of this, *a contrario*, one could analyse the history of the relations between a so-called 'naïve' painter (one who almost stumbles into the field, without paying the entry fee, the toll) such as Douanier Rousseau, and the contemporary artists, like Jarry, Apollinaire or Picasso, who play (in the literal sense, with all kinds of more or less charitable hoaxes) with someone who does not know how to play the game, who wants to paint like Bouguereau or Bonnat in the age of futurism and cubism, and who breaks the game, but unwittingly, in contrast to people like Duchamp, or even Satie, who understand the logic of the game well enough to defy it and exploit it at the same time. And then one would also have to analyse the history of the subsequent interpretation of the *œuvre*, which, through over-interpretation, pushes it back into the ranks, into the history, and endeavours to turn this weekend painter (the aesthetic principles of his painting, such as the uncompromising frontality of his portraits, are those which working-class people put into their photography) into a conscious, inspired revolutionary.

There is a field effect when it is no longer possible to understand a work (and the *value*, i.e. the belief, that it is granted) without knowing the history of the field of production of the work. That is how the exegetes, commentators, interpreters, historians, semiologists and philologists, come to be justified in existing, as the only people capable of accounting for the work and the recognition of value that it enjoys. The sociology of art or literature that *directly* relates works of art to the producers' or clients' position in social space (their social class) without considering their position in the field of production (a 'reduction' which is, strictly, only valid for 'naïve' artists) sweeps aside everything that the work owes to the field and its history – that is to say, precisely that which makes it a work of art, or science, or philosophy. A philosophical (or scientific, etc.) problem is a problem that philosophers (or scientists) recognize (in both senses) as such (because it is inscribed in the logic of the history of the field and in their dispositions, which are historically constituted by and for membership of the field) and which, by virtue of the specific authority they are recognized as having, has every chance of being very widely recognized as legitimate. Here too, the example of 'naïve' producers is very enlightening. They are people who have had the status of painters or writers (revolutionary ones, to boot) thrust upon them in the name of a problematic of which they were quite unaware. The verbal associations of Jean-Pierre Brisset, his long sequences of word equations, alliterations and incongruities, which he intended for learned societies and academic conferences, making a 'field mistake' which testifies to his innocence, would have remained the ramblings of a madman for which they were first taken, if Jarry's 'pataphysics', Apollinaire's and Duchamp's puns, or the automatic writing of the surrealists had not created the problematic in relation to which they could take on a meaning. These object-poets and object-painters, these 'objective revolutionaries', enable us to observe, in isolation, the transmuting power of the field. This power equally operates, albeit in a less striking and better grounded way, on the works of the professionals who know the game and the problematic, who know what they are doing (which does not in the least mean that they are cynical), so that the *necessity* that a consecrating reading finds in them does not appear so obviously as the product of an objective accident (which it also is, inasmuch as it presupposes a miraculous harmony between a philosophical disposition and a state of the expectations inscribed in the field). Heidegger is often Spengler or Jünger transposed into the philosophical field. He has some very simple things to say: 'technique' is the decline of the West; everything has gone downhill since Descartes, and so on. The field, or, more precisely, the *habitus* of a professional, adjusted in advance to the demands of the field (for example, to the prevailing definition of the legitimate problematic), will function as a translating machine: being a 'revolutionary conservative' in philosophy means revolutionizing the image of Kantian philosophy by showing that at the root of this philosophy which presents itself as the critique of metaphysics, there is more metaphysics. This systematic transformation of problems and themes is not the product of a conscious (and cynically calculated) endeavour, but an automatic effect of belonging to the field and the mastery of the specific history of the field that it implies. Being a philosopher means knowing what one needs to know of the history of philosophy in order to be able to behave as a philosopher within a philosophical field.

I want to re-emphasize that the principle of philosophical (or literary) strategies is not cynical calculation, the conscious pursuit of maximum specific profit, but an unconscious relationship between a *habitus* and a field. The strategies I am talking about are actions objectively oriented towards goals that may not be the goals subjectively pursued. And the theory of the *habitus* is aimed at establishing the possibility of a science of practices that escapes the forced choice between finalism and mechanism. (The word *interest*, which I have used several times, is also very dangerous, because it is liable to suggest a utilitarianism that is the degree zero of sociology. That said, sociology cannot dispense with the axiom of interest, understood as the *specific investment* in the stakes, which is both the condition and the product of membership of a field.) The *habitus*, a system of dispositions acquired by implicit or explicit learning which functions as a system of generative schemes, generates strategies which can be objectively consistent with the objective interests of their authors without having been expressly designed to that end. We have to learn to escape from the forced choice between naïve teleology (according to which, for example, the 'revolution' which led Apollinaire to the audacities of *Lundi rue Christine* and other poetic 'ready-mades' was motivated by the aim of placing himself at the head of the movement pioneered by Cendrars, the futurists or Delaunay) and mechanistic explanation (which would see this trans-formation as a direct and simple effect of social determinations). When people only have to let their *habitus* follow its natural bent in order to comply with the immanent necessity of the field and satisfy the demands contained within in it (which, in every field, is the very definition of excellence), they are not at all aware of fulfilling a duty, still less of seeking to maximize their (specific) profit. So they enjoy the additional profit of seeing themselves and being seen as totally disinterested.

Further reading

For further discussion, see Bourdieu, P. (1975) 'Le couturier et sa griffe: contribution à une théorie de la magie', *Actes de la recherche en sciences sociales*, 1: 7–36; (1988) *L'Ontologie politique de Martin Heidegger*, Paris: Éditions de Minuit; (1988) *The Logic of Practice*, Oxford: Polity Press.

10

THE LINGUISTIC MARKET

I shall try to set out what I have to say step by step, taking account of the diversity of the audience, which could indeed scarcely be more varied, given the range of disciplines represented, the levels of competence in those disciplines, and so on. Some may find what I have to say somewhat simplistic; for others it may be too rapid and too allusive. I shall first put forward a number of concepts and principles which I regard as fundamental, hoping that in the course of the day we shall be able to clarify, discuss and go back to points that I may have touched on too rapidly.

What I basically want to do is to spell out a very simple model that could be formulated as follows: linguistic *habitus* + linguistic market = linguistic expression, speech. I shall explain the successive terms of this very general formula, starting with the notion of the *habitus*. As ever, I want to warn against the tendency to fetishize concepts. One needs to take concepts seriously, keep a check on them, and above all make them work under supervision, under control, in research. That is how they gradually improve, and not through pure logical control, which fossilizes them. A good concept – and the *habitus* is one of them, I believe – destroys many false problems (the dilemma of mechanism or finalism, for example), and brings up other, real problems. When it is well constructed and well controlled, it tends to defend itself against reductions.

The linguistic *habitus*, crudely defined, can be distinguished from competence as the term is used by Chomsky, in that it is the product of social conditions and is not a simple production of utterances but the production of utterances adapted to a 'situation' or, rather, adapted to a market or a field. The idea of 'situation' was brought in at a very early stage – I am thinking for example of Prieto, who in his *Principes de noologie* stressed the fact that a whole host of linguistic behaviours cannot be understood independently of implicit reference to the *situation* (when I say 'I', it needs to be known that I'm the one saying 'I'; otherwise it might be someone else; and think of the confusions between 'I' and 'you' that are used in jokes, and so on) – as a corrective to all the theories that exclusively stressed competence and forgot about the conditions of the implementation of competence. It has been used, in particular, to question the implicit presuppositions of the Saussurian model, in which *parole* (like Chomsky's *performance*) is reduced to an act of *execution*, like performing

Talk given at the University of Geneva in December 1978

a musical score – or executing an order. The notion of situation reminds us that there is a specific logic of execution; that what happens at the level of execution cannot be simply deduced from knowledge of competence. But then I was led to wonder whether, in conserving the still very abstract notion of situation, one was not doing what Sartre complained of in the theory of tendencies: reproducing the concrete by crossing two abstractions, in this case situation and competence.

The Sophists used to bring in an idea that seems to me very important, that of *kairos*. As teachers of speech, they knew it was not sufficient to teach people how to talk – they also had to be taught to talk to the point. In other words, the art of speaking, of speaking well, of producing figures of speech or thought, manipulating language, mastering it, is nothing without the art of using that art to the point. *Kairos* is, originally, the bull's-eye. When you speak to the point, you score a bull's-eye, you hit the nail on the head. In order to do that, in order for your words to *count*, to 'go home', you must not only say the grammatically correct words, but the socially acceptable words.

In my article in *Langue française*, I tried to show that the notion of acceptability that has been reintroduced by the Chomskians remains quite inadequate because it reduces acceptability to grammaticality. In fact, sociologically defined acceptability does consist solely in speaking a language correctly. In some cases, if one wants, for example, to appear relaxed, a too impeccable French may be unacceptable. In its full definition, acceptability presupposes the conformity of words not only to the immanent rules of the language, but also to the intuitively grasped rules that are immanent in a 'situation', or rather a certain linguistic market.

What is this *linguistic market*? I'll give a first, provisional definition, which I shall have to complicate later. There is a linguistic market whenever someone produces an utterance for receivers capable of assessing it, evaluating it and setting a price on it. Knowledge of linguistic competence alone does not enable one to predict what the value of a linguistic performance will be on a market. The price that the products of a given competence will receive on a given market depends on the laws of price formation specific to that market. For example, on the educational market, the imperfect subjunctive had a high value in the days of my teachers, who identified their professorial identity with using it – at least in the third person singular. Nowadays, that would provoke smiles and can't be done in front of a student audience, unless you emit a metalinguistic sign to show that although you're doing it you could equally well not do it. Similarly, the tendency to controlled hypocorrection among present-day intellectuals is explained by the fear of over-doing things, and, like the open collar, it is one of the controlled forms of non-control that are linked to effects of the market. The linguistic market is something that is both very concrete and very abstract. Concretely, it's a particular social situation, more or less official and ritualized, a particular set of interlocutors, situated at a particular level in the social hierarchy – all properties that are perceived and appreciated in an infra-conscious way and unconsciously orient linguistic production. Defined in abstract terms, it is a particular type of (variable) laws of the formation of the prices of linguistic products. When I say that there are laws of price formation, I am making the point that the value of a given competence depends on the particular market in which it is implemented and, more precisely, on the state of the relationships within which the values set on the linguistic products of the various producers are defined.

This leads me to replace the notion of competence with that of *linguistic capital*. The notion of linguistic capital implies that there are linguistic profits: someone who lives in the 7th *arrondissement* of Paris – as most of the people who now govern France do – receives a linguistic profit as soon as he opens his mouth, and there is nothing fictitious or illusory about this profit, as one might be led to think by the kind of economism that a rudimentary Marxism has imposed on us. The very nature of his speech (which can be analysed phonetically, etc.) says that he is authorized to speak, so much so that it hardly matters what he says. What linguists present as the primary function of language, the communication function, may be not fulfilled at all, while its real – social – function may continue unabated. Situations of linguistic power relations are situations in which there is speech without communication, the extreme case being the Mass. That is why I have been interested in liturgy. They are cases in which the authorized speaker has so much authority, has the institution, the laws of the market and the whole social space so much on his side, that he can speak and yet say nothing; it is the voice of authority.

Linguistic capital is power over the mechanisms of linguistic price formation, the power to make the laws of price formation operate to one's advantage and to extract the specific surplus value. Every act of interaction, every linguistic communication, even between two people, two friends, boy and girl, all linguistic interactions, are in a sense micro-markets which always remain dominated by the overall structures.

As can be seen in national struggles where language is an important stake (in Quebec, for example), there is a very clear relation of dependence between the mechanisms of political domination and the mechanisms of linguistic price formation that characterize a given social situation. For example, the struggles between French-speakers and Arabic-speakers in a number of Arab countries formerly colonized by France always have an economic dimension, in the sense in which I use the word, that is, in the sense that, through the defence of a market for their own linguistic products, the holders of a given competence are defending their own value as linguistic producers. Faced with nationalist struggles, analysis hesitates between economism and mysticism. The theory that I am putting forward makes it possible to understand that linguistic struggles may not have obvious linguistic bases, or only transposed ones, and yet involve interests as vital, sometimes more vital, than economic interests in the narrow sense.

So, when I bring in the notion of the market, I underline the simple fact that a competence has value only so long as it has a market. That's why the people who are currently trying to defend their value as possessors of Latin are obliged to defend the existence of the market in Latin, which means, in particular, the reproduction, through the school system, of the consumers of Latin. A certain type of conservatism, which is sometimes pathological, within the educational system, can only be understood in terms of the simple law that a competence without a market becomes worthless, or rather, ceases to be linguistic capital and becomes a mere competence in the linguists' sense.

So a capital can exist and function as such, and bring in profits, only on a certain market. Now I must flesh out this notion of the market and try to describe the objective relations that give the market its structure. What is the market? There are individual producers (this is the marginalist view of the market) who offer their products, and then the judgements of all the actors come into play and a market price emerges. This liberal theory of the market is as inaccurate for the linguistic market as it for the market in economic goods. Just as, in the economic market, there are monopolies, objective power relations which mean that all the producers and their products do not start out equal, so too in the linguistic market there are power relations. So the linguistic market has laws of price formation which are such that the producers of linguistic products, of utterances, are not equal.

The power relations which dominate this market, and mean that certain producers and certain products start out with a privilege, presuppose that the linguistic market is relatively unified. Consider the document taken from a Béarn newspaper which I reproduced in my article on 'The illusion of linguistic communism'. Reporting that, in the course of a ceremony in honour of a Béarn poet, the Mayor of Pau addressed his audience in Béarnais, the journalist notes: 'This gesture was much appreciated [*Cette attention touche l'assistance*].' The audience consisted of people whose first language was Béarnais, and they are 'touched' by the fact that a Béarn mayor speaks to them in Béarnais. They are touched by a gesture that is a form of condescension. In order for there to be condescension, there has to be an objective gap: condescension is the demagogic use of an objective power relation, since the person who condescends makes use of the hierarchy in order to deny it. At the very moment when he denies it, he exploits it ('the common touch'). These are cases where a relation of interaction in a small group suddenly reveals transcendent power relations. What happens between the Béarn mayor and those Béarnais is not reducible to what happens in the interaction between them. If the Mayor can be seen as showing a mark of attention to his Béarnais fellow citizens, it is because he is playing on the objective relationship between French and

Béarnais. And if French were not a dominant language, if there were not a unified linguistic market, if French were not the legitimate language, the one to be spoken in legitimate situations – in *official situations*, the Army, at the post office, the tax office, at school, in speeches, etc. – the fact of speaking Béarnais would not have this 'touching' effect.

That is what I mean by linguistic power relations: they are relations that transcend the situation, irreducible to the relations of interaction as they can be grasped in the situation. This is important because, when one talks about the situation, one thinks one is bringing back in the social because one is bringing back interaction. Interactionist description of social relations, which is very interesting in itself, becomes dangerous if it is forgotten that these relations of interaction are not 'an empire within an empire'; if it is forgotten that in what happens between two persons – an employer and her domestic servant, or two colleagues, or a French-speaker and a German-speaking colleague – these relations between two persons are always dominated by the objective relationship between the corresponding languages, that is to say, the relationship between the groups speaking those languages. When a German-speaking Swiss talks with a French-speaking Swiss, it's German Switzerland and Francophone Switzerland that are talking.

But to return to the anecdote from which I started: the Béarn mayor can produce this effect of condescendence only because he is an *agrégé*.[1] If he were not an *agrégé*, his Béarnais would be a peasant's Béarnais, and therefore worthless, and the peasants to whom this 'quality Béarnais' is anyway not addressed (they rarely attend official gatherings) want nothing better than to speak French. 'Quality Béarnais' is rehabilitated at the very moment when the peasants are increasingly abandoning it for French. One has to ask who has an interest in restoring Béarnais at the very time that the peasants feel obliged to speak French to their children so they can do well at school.

The Béarnais peasant who explained why he had never thought of becoming Mayor of his village, although he had won most votes in the elections, by saying that he 'didn't know to talk' had a perfectly realistic, entirely sociological definition of legitimate competence; the dominant definition of legitimate competence is indeed such that his real competence is illegitimate. (That ought to be the starting-point for analysis of a phenomenon such as that of the 'spokesman' [*le porte-parole*], an interesting word for those who talk about *langue* and *parole*.) In order for the effects of capital and linguistic domination to occur, the linguistic market has to be relatively unified, that is, the totality of speakers has to be subject to the same law of linguistic product price formation. That means, concretely, that the humblest of Béarn peasants, whether he knows it or not (and he does know it, since he says he does not know how to talk), is objectively measured against a norm which is that of 'standard Parisian French'. And even if he has never heard 'standard Parisian French' (in fact he is hearing it more and more, 'thanks' to television), the Béarn speaker is dominated by the Paris speaker and, in all his interactions, at the post office, at school, etc., he is in objective relationship with him. That is what is meant by *unification of the market* or *relation of linguistic domination*. The linguistic market is the site of forms of domination which have a specific logic and, as in every market in symbolic goods, there are specific forms of domination which are not at all reducible to strictly economic domination either in the way they work or in the profits they secure.

One of the consequences of this analysis concerns the survey situation itself. Being an interaction, it is one of the sites in which linguistic and cultural power relations, cultural domination, is actualized. It is impossible to imagine a survey situation that is 'purged' of any effect of domination (as some sociologists sometimes suppose). If one is not to take artefacts for facts, the best one can do is to bring into analysis of the 'data' analysis of the social determinations of the situation in which the data have been produced – analysis of the linguistic market in which the facts being analysed have been established.

About fifteen years ago, I carried out a survey of people's preferences, tastes in the broadest sense, in food, music, paintings, clothes, sexual partner, and so on. The greater part of the material was collected in verbal interactions. After a whole series of analyses, I was led to consider the relative weight, in the determination of preferences, of cultural capital, as measured by qualifications, and social origin; and how the relative weights of these two factors vary according to the particular area of practice – for example, tastes seem to be more closely linked to social origin as regards cinema and more closely linked to education as regards theatre. I could have carried on endlessly calculating coefficients of correlation but methodological hypercorrection would have prevented me from questioning the situation in which I had collected the material. Might it not be that, among the explanatory variables, the most important, hidden behind the material itself, is the *effect of the very characteristics of the survey situation*? From the start of the survey, I had been aware that the legitimacy effect, which also plays a major role in matters of language, caused members of the working classes, when questioned about their culture, to tend, consciously or unconsciously, in the survey situation, to select what seemed to them to correspond best to the image they had of the dominant culture, so that it was impossible to get them to say simply what they really liked. It is to Labov's credit that he has emphasized that one of the variables that a rigorous sociolinguistic analysis needs to vary is the survey situation. One of the most original features of his studies of speech in Harlem is that he takes note of the effect of the survey situation to see what was obtained when the surveyor was not a WASP but one member of the ghetto speaking to another. If the survey situation is varied, it can be seen that the more the tension of control is relaxed, and the further one moves from the most controlled areas of culture, the more performance is linked to social origin.

Conversely, the tighter the control, the more it is linked to educational capital. In other words, the problem of the relative weight of the two variables cannot be resolved in the absolute, by reference to some sort of neutral, constant situation. It can only be resolved if one introduces a variable to be treated as a factor of these two variables: the nature of the market on which these linguistic or cultural products are going to be offered. (Parenthesis: epistemology is often perceived as a kind of meta-discourse outside of scientific practice; in my view, it is a reflection which really changes practice and leads one to avoid errors, not to measure the efficacy of a factor while forgetting the factor of factors, namely the situation in which one measures the factors. Saussure said, 'One needs to know what the linguist does.' Epistemology is the effort to find out what one is doing.)

What a cultural or linguistic survey records is not a direct manifestation of competence, but a complex product of the relationship between a competence and a market, a product which does not exist outside that relationship. It is a *competence in a situation*, a competence for a particular market (very often the sociolinguist tends to ignore the effects of the market because his data have been gathered in a situation that is constant from his point of view, i.e. the relationship with himself, the interviewer). The only way to control the relationship is to *vary it by varying the market situations*, instead of privileging one market situation among others (as Labov does, for example, with the speech of a Harlem black for other Harlem blacks) and seeing the *truth* of speech, authentic popular speech, in the language produced in those conditions.

The effects of domination, the objective power relations of the linguistic market, are exerted in all linguistic situations. In the relationship with a Parisian, a bourgeois from the southern provinces is 'at a loss'; his capital collapses. Labov has discovered that what is grasped under the name of popular speech in a survey is popular speech as it appears in a market situation dominated by the dominant values, that's to say a disrupted language. The situations in which relations of linguistic domination take effect, that is, official, formal situations, are situations in which the relations actually established, the interactions, are perfectly in accordance with the objective laws of the market. We come back to the Béarn peasant saying, 'I don't know how to talk.' He means: 'I don't know how to talk as one has to talk in formal situations; if I became Mayor, I would become an official, required to make formal speeches and therefore subject to the official rules of formal French. Because I can't talk like Giscard d'Estaing, I can't talk.' The more formal a situation is, the more the speaker himself has to be authorized. He has to have qualifications, he has to have the right accent, so he has to have been born in the right place. The more formal the situation, the more it is ruled by the general laws of price formation.

By contrast, when people say 'no, but frankly . . .', they can let themselves go, as in a village bar. They are saying: 'We're going to create a haven of freedom outside the laws of speech, which continue to operate, we know, but we shall take liberties.' They feel free to speak freely. This 'plain talking' is popular speech in the popular situation, when the laws of the market are bracketed off. But it would be a mistake to say that the 'truth' of popular speech is this 'plain talking'. It is no more 'true' than the other: the full truth of popular competence is *also* the fact that, when it is confronted with an official market, it breaks down, whereas when it is on its own territory, at home, in a familiar relationship, among its own, it is plain speaking. It is important to know that plain speaking exists but as an island set apart from the laws of the market – a island that people define by *licensing* themselves to speak out (there are markers to say that one is setting up a special game, that one can speak freely). The effects of the market continue to operate, on working-class people too; they can always potentially be called to account by the laws of the market. That is what I call legitimacy. The phrase *linguistic legitimacy* serves to remind us that ignorance of the law of language is no defence. That doesn't mean that working-class people recognize the beauty of Giscard's style. It means that when they find themselves face to face with someone like Giscard, they are at a loss for words; *de facto* their speech will be fractured and they will shut up, condemned to silence, the silence that is called respectful. The laws of the market exert a very important effect of *censorship* on those who can only talk in situations of plain talking (i.e. when they can make it clear that the ordinary demands have to be momentarily suspended) and who are condemned to silence in the formal situations in which major political, social and cultural stakes are involved. (The matrimonial market, for example, is a market on which linguistic capital plays a decisive role: I think it is one of the mediations through which class homogeneity is maintained.) The market effect which censors plain speaking is a particular case of a more general censorship effect which leads to euphemization: each specialized field – religious, literary, philosophical, etc. – has its own laws and tends to censor utterances that do not conform to those laws.

Relations to language seem to me to be closely associated with relations to the body. For example, and to put it schematically, the bourgeois relation to the body or to language is the easy relation of those who are in their element, who have the laws of the market on their side. The experience of ease is a quasi-divine experience. To feel oneself *comme il faut*, exemplary, 'just so', is the experience of absoluteness, the very one which people expect of religions. The sense of being what one ought to be is one of the most absolute profits reaped by dominant groups. By contrast, the petit-bourgeois relation to the body and to language is a relation that is described as timidity, tension, hypertension; they always do too much or too little, they are ill at ease with themselves.

Q. *What relationship do you establish between* ethos *and* habitus, *and other concepts, such as* hexis, *that you use?*

A. I've used the word *ethos*, after many others, in opposition to *ethic*, to designate an objectively systematic set of dispositions with an ethical dimension, a set of practical principles (an ethic being an intentionally coherent system of explicit principles). It's a useful distinction, especially for controlling practical errors. For example, if one forgets that we may have principles in the practical state, without having a systematic morality, an ethic, one forgets that simply by asking questions, interrogating, one forces people to move from ethos to ethic; in inviting a judgement on constituted, verbalized norms, one assumes that this shift has been made. Or, in another sense, one forgets that people may prove incapable of responding to ethical problems while being quite capable of responding *in practice* to situations raising the corresponding questions.

The notion of *habitus* encompasses the notion of ethos, and that's why I use the latter word less and less. The practical principles of classification which constitute the *habitus* are *inseparably* logical and axiological, theoretical and practical. Because practical logic is turned towards practice, it inevitably implements values. That's why I have abandoned the distinction, to which I resorted once or twice, between *eidos* as a system of logical schemes and *ethos* as a system of practical, axiological schemes. (All the more so since by compartmentalizing different dimensions of the *habitus*, one tends to reinforce the realist view which thinks in terms of separate faculties.) Moreover, all the principles of choice are 'embodied', turned into postures, dispositions of the body. Values are postures, gestures, ways of standing, walking, speaking. The strength of the ethos is that it is a morality made flesh.

So you can see how I have come to use almost exclusively the concept of *habitus*. The idea of *habitus* has a long tradition behind it. The Scholastics used it to translate Aristotle's *hexis*. You find it in Durkheim, who, in *L'Évolution pédagogique en France*, notes that Christian education had to solve the problems raised by the need to mould a Christian *habitus* with a pagan culture. It's also in Marcel Mauss, in his famous text on the techniques of the body. But neither of those authors gives it a decisive role to play.

Why did I revive that old word? Because with the notion of *habitus* you can refer to something that is close to what is suggested by the idea of habit, while differing from it in one important respect. The *habitus*, as the word implies, is that which one has acquired, but which has become durably incorporated in the body in the form of permanent dispositions. So the term constantly reminds us that it refers to something historical, linked to individual history, and that it belongs to a genetic mode of thought, as opposed to essentialist modes of thought (like the notion of competence which is part of the Chomskian lexis). Moreover, by *habitus* the Scholastics also meant something like a property, a *capital*. And indeed, the *habitus* is a capital, but one which, because it is embodied, appears as innate.

But then why not say 'habit'? Habit is spontaneously regarded as repetitive, mechanical, automatic, reproductive rather than productive. I wanted to insist on the idea that the *habitus* is something powerfully generative. To put it briefly, the *habitus* is a product of conditionings which tends to reproduce the objective logic of those conditionings while transforming it. It's a kind of transforming machine that leads us to 'reproduce' the social conditions of our own production, but in a relatively unpredictable way, in such a way that one cannot move simply and mechanically from knowledge of the conditions of production to knowledge of the products. Although this capacity for generating practices or utterances or works is in no way innate and is historically constituted, it is not completely reducible to its conditions of production not least because it functions in a *systematic* way. One can only speak of a linguistic *habitus*, for example, so long as it is not forgotten that it is only one dimension of the *habitus* understood as a system of schemes for generating and perceiving practices, and so long as one does not autonomize the production of speech *vis-à-vis* production of aesthetic choices, or gestures, or any other possible practice. The *habitus* is a principle of invention produced by history but relatively detached from history: its dispositions are *durable*, which leads to all sorts of effects of hysteresis (of time-lag, of which the example *par excellence* is Don Quixote). It can be understood by analogy with a computer program (though it's a mechanistic and therefore dangerous analogy) – but a self-correcting program. It is constituted from a systematic set of simple and partially interchangeable principles, from which an infinity of solutions can be invented, solutions which cannot be directly deduced from its conditions of production.

So the *habitus* is the principle of a real autonomy with respect to the immediate determinations of the 'situation'. But that does not mean that it is some kind of a-historical essence, of which the existence is merely the development, in short, a destiny defined once and for all. The adjustments that are constantly required by the necessities of adaptation to new and unforeseen situations may bring about durable transformations of the *habitus*, but these will remain within certain limits, not least because the *habitus* defines the perception of the situation that determines it.

The 'situation' is, in a sense, the permissive condition of the fulfilment of the *habitus*. When the objective conditions of fulfilment are not present, the *habitus*, continuously thwarted by the situation, may be the site of explosive forces (resentment) which may await (and even look for) the opportunity to break out and which express themselves as soon as the objective conditions for this (e.g. the power of an authoritarian foreman) are offered. (The social world is an immense reservoir of accumulated violence, which is revealed when it encounters the conditions for its expression.) In short, in reaction against instantaneist mechanism, one is led to insist on the 'assimilatory' capacities of the *habitus*; but the *habitus* is also a power of adaptation, it constantly performs an adaptation to the external world which only exceptionally takes the form of a radical conversion.

Q. *What distinction do you make between a field and an apparatus?*
A. A fundamental one, I think. The idea of the 'apparatus' reintroduces pessimistic functionalism: it's an 'infernal engine', programmed to bring about certain ends. The educational system, the State, the Church, the parties, are not apparatuses, but fields. However, in certain conditions, they may start functioning as apparatuses. Those conditions need to examined.

In a field, agents and institutions are engaged in struggle, with unequal strengths, and in accordance with the rules constituting that field of play, to appropriate the specific profits at stake in that game. Those who dominate the field have the means to make it function to their advantage; but they have to reckon with the resistance of the dominated agents. A field becomes an apparatus when the dominant agents have the means to nullify the resistance and the reactions of the dominated – in other words, when the lower clergy, or the grass-roots activists, or the working classes, etc., can only *suffer* domination; when all movement runs downwards and the effects of domination are such that the struggle and dialectic that are constitutive of the field come to an end. There is history so long as there are people who revolt, who make trouble. The 'total' or totalitarian institution, the asylum, prison or concentration camp as described by Goffman, or the totalitarian state, attempts to institute the end of history.

The difference between fields and apparatuses is seen clearly in revolutions. Revolutionaries behave as if it were sufficient to seize control of the 'state apparatus' and to reprogramme the machine, in order to have a radically different social order. In fact, the political will has to reckon with the logic of the social fields, extremely complex universes in which political intentions may be hijacked, turned upside down (this is as true of the action of the dominant groups as of subversive action, as is shown by everything that is described in the inadequate language of 'recuperation', which is still naïvely teleological). All political action can only be sure of achieving the desired effects so long as it is dealing with apparatuses, that is, organizations in which the dominated agents are reduced to execution, to carrying out orders 'to the death' (activists, soldiers, etc.). Thus apparatuses are just one state, one which can be regarded as pathological, of fields.

Notes

1 A holder of the prestigious teaching qualification, the *agrégation* [translator].

Further reading

For further discussion, see Bourdieu, P. (1975) 'Le fétichisme de la langue', *Actes de la recherche en science sociales*, 4: 2–32; (1977) 'The economics of linguistic exchanges', *Social*

Science Information, 16(6): 645–68; (1975) 'Le langage autorisé: note sur les conditions sociales de l'efficacité du discours rituel', *Actes de la recherche en science sociales*, 5–6: 183–90; (1988) *L'Ontologie politique de Martin Heidegger*, Paris: Éditions de Minuit.

11

CENSORSHIP

I should like to talk briefly about the notion of censorship. The censorship of which every work bears traces is also operating in this gathering. Speaking-time is a scarce resource, and I shall try not to monopolize it by 'taking the floor' for too long.

What I want to say can be summed up in a generative formula: every expression is an accommodation between an *expressive interest* and a *censorship* constituted by the field in which that expression is offered; and this accommodation is the product of a process of euphemization which may even result in silence, the extreme case of censored discourse. This euphemization leads the potential 'author' to produce something which is a compromise formation, a combination of what there was to be said, which 'needed' to be said, and what *could* be said, given the structure of a particular field. In other words, what is sayable in a given field is the result of what might be called a form-giving process [*une mise en forme*]: speaking means observing the forms. By that, I mean that discourse owes its most specific properties, its properties of form, and not only its content, to the social conditions of its production, that is, the conditions that determine what is to be said and the conditions that determine the field of reception in which that thing to be said will be heard. That is how one can move beyond the relatively naïve opposition between internal analysis and external analysis of works or utterances.

From the point of view of the sociologist, who has his own principle of pertinence, that is, his own principle for constituting his object of study, expressive interest will be what can be called a political interest in the broad sense, it being understood that in every group there are political interests. Thus, within a restricted field (the one constituted by this group, for example), *politeness* is the result of the transaction between what there is to be said and the external constraints that constitute a field. Let me borrow an example from Lakoff: observing his hosts' new carpet, a visitor will not say, 'Oh, what a beautiful carpet, how much did it cost?' but rather, '*May I ask* how much you paid for it?' The 'may I?' corresponds to the work of euphemization, which consists in applying the appropriate forms. Having to express a certain intention, one may or may not apply the forms, the forms by which one recognizes, for example, a philosophical discourse,

Contribution to colloquium on 'la science des œuvres', Lille, May 1974, published in *Social Science Information*, 16(3–4), 1977: 385–8 which itself, by the same token, announces itself as requiring to be received within the appropriate forms, that is, as form and not as content. One of the properties of a 'well-formed' discourse is that it imposes the norms of its own perception; it says, 'Treat me with due form', that is, in accordance with the forms I give myself, and above all *don't reduce me* to what I *deny* by taking on these forms. In other words, I am arguing here for the right to perform 'reduction': euphemized discourse exercises a symbolic violence which has the specific effect of forbidding the only violence that it deserves, which consists in reducing it to what it says but in a form such that it claims not to be saying it. Literary discourse is a discourse that says 'Treat me as I ask to be treated, that is, semiologically, as a structure.' If the history of art and the sociology of art are so *backward*, it's because artistic discourse has succeeded only too well in imposing its own norm of perception. It's a discourse that says 'Treat me as purposiveness without purpose,' 'Treat me as form and not as substance.'

When I say that the field functions as a censorship, I mean that the field is a certain structure of the distribution of a certain kind of capital. This capital may be academic capital, intellectual prestige, political power, physical strength, etc., depending on the particular field. The authorized spokesman is the holder, either in person (charisma) or by delegation (if he's a priest or a teacher), of an institutional capital of authority, which means that he is given credit, credence, he is given the power to speak. Émile Benveniste, analysing the Greek word *skeptron*, says it was a token passed to the orator who was about to speak, to mark the fact that his speech was authorized speech, a speech that people obey, if only by listening to it.

So, if a field functions as a censorship, that's because someone who enters the field is immediately situated in a certain structure, the structure of the distribution of capital. The group does, or does not, grant him the right to speak; it does, or does not, *credit* him. In this way the field exercises a censorship on what he might like to say, on the deviant discourse, *idios logos*, to which he might wish to give vent, and forces him to utter only what is appropriate, what is sayable. It excludes two things: what cannot be said, given the structure of the distribution of the means of expression – the unsayable – and what *could* be said, almost too easily, but which is censored – the unnameable.

The work of euphemization would seem to be a simple process of giving form, of working on the form, but in the end what is produced is inseparable from the form in which it is manifested. The question of what would have been said in another field, that is, in another form, is strictly meaningless: Heidegger's discourse only makes sense as philosophical discourse. The substitution of 'authentic' and 'inauthentic' for 'distinguished' (or 'unique') and 'common' (or 'vulgar') brings about a sea change. Firstly, what functions as euphemism is the whole system. I used the word 'euphemism' with some hesitation, because euphemism substitutes one word for another (the taboo word). In fact the euphemization that I am describing here is performed by the whole discourse. For example, Heidegger's famous text on *Das Man* is 'about', on the one hand, public transport, and, on the other hand, what some people call the 'mass media'. Those are two perfectly real referents that are the possible subject of an ordinary discourse, but they are masked by the system of relations that constitutes philosophical discourse. It's not just one word being used for another, it's the discourse as such, and through it the whole field, that functions as an instrument of censorship.

That's not all: if we want, for example, to determine the structure of what is said in the place where we are, it's not sufficient to make an analysis of the discourse; we have to grasp the discourse as the product of a whole process of work on the group (invitation and non-invitation, etc.). In short, one needs an analysis of the social conditions of the constitution of the group in which the discourse is produced, because that is where one finds the true principle of what could and what could not be said there. More profoundly, one of the most effective ways a group has of reducing people to silence is by excluding them from the positions from which one can speak. Conversely, one of the ways for a group to control discourse consists in filling the positions from which one *can* speak with people who will only say what the field authorizes and calls for. To understand what can be said in an educational system, one has to understand the mechanisms of recruitment of the teaching staff, and it would be naïve to suppose that what can be said there, and why, is something that can be grasped at the level of the teachers' discourse.

Every expression is a kind of symbolic violence which cannot be exerted by the person who exerts it, and cannot be undergone by the person who undergoes it, except in so far as it is misrecognized as such. And if it is misrecognized as such, that is partly because it is exerted through the mediation of a process of euphemization. Yesterday, someone was referring to the problem of reception (in connection with the efficacy of an ideology); what I am saying encompasses both production and reception. When, for example, in *L'Éducation sentimentale*, Flaubert projects his whole 'representation' of the structure of the dominant class, or, more precisely, his relationship to his position in the dominant class, in the form of the impossibility of seeing that class differently, he projects something that he is himself unaware of, or rather, that he denies and misrecognizes because the work of euphemization that he applies to that structure helps to conceal it from him, and something that is also denied and misrecognized by the commentators (because they are the product of the very same structures that governed the production of the work). In other words, in order for Flaubert to be read hermeneutically, one needs the whole system of which his own discourse is itself a product among others. So when one speaks of a science of works of art, it is important to know that, simply by treating works autonomously, one grants them what they want, that is to say, everything.

Further reading

For further discussion see Bourdieu, P. (1988) *L'Ontologie politique de Martin Heidegger*, Paris: Éditions de Minuit.

12

'YOUTH' IS JUST A WORD

Q. *How does a sociologist approach the problem of young people?*
A. The professional reflex is to point out that the divisions between the
ages are arbitrary. It's the paradox identified by Pareto, who said that we
don't know when old age begins, just as we don't know where wealth
begins. Indeed, the frontier between youth and age is something that is
fought over in all societies. For example, a few years ago I was reading an
article on relations between young men and their elders in sixteenth-century
Florence; it showed how the elders of the city offered its young men the
ideology of virility – *virtù* – and violence, which was a way of keeping
wisdom – and therefore power – for themselves. In the same way, Georges
Duby shows how in the Middle Ages the limits of youth were manipulated
by the holders of the patrimony, so as to keep the young nobles, who might
otherwise aspire to the succession, in a state of youth, that is,
irresponsibility.

Entirely equivalent things would be found in sayings and proverbs, or
simply in stereotypes of youth, or again in philosophy, from Plato to Alain,
which assigns its specific passion to each age of man – love to adolescence,
ambition to maturity. The ideological representation of the division
between young and old grants certain things to the youngest, which means
that in return they have to leave many things to their elders. This is seen very
clearly in the case of sport, in rugby, for example, with the glorification of
'tough young players', docile, good-natured brutes assigned to the rough
and tumble of the forward game exalted by managers and commentators
('Just use your strength and keep your mouth shut, don't think'). This
structure, which is also found elsewhere (e.g. in relations between the sexes)
reminds us that the logical division between young and old is also a
question of power, of the division (in the sense of sharing-out) of powers.
Classification by age (but also by sex and, of course, class . . .) always means
imposing limits and producing an *order* to which each person must keep,
keeping himself in his place.

Q. *What do you mean by 'old'? Adults? Those involved in
production? Pensioners?*

Interview with Anne-Marie Métailié in *Les Jeunes et le premier emploi*, Paris:
Association des Âges, 1978: 520–30

A. When I say young/old, I am taking the relationship in its most general form. One is always somebody's senior or junior. That is why the divisions, whether into age-groups or into generations, are entirely variable and subject to manipulation. For example, the anthropologist Nancy Munn shows that in some societies in Australia, the rejuvenating magic that old women use to restore their youth is regarded as thoroughly diabolical, because it overturns the boundaries between the ages, so that no one knows any longer who's young and who's old. My point is simply that youth and age are not self-evident data but are socially constructed, in the struggle between the young and the old.

The relationship between social age and biological age is very complex. If one were to compare young people from the different fractions of the dominant class, for example all the students entering the École Normale, the École Nationale d'Administration, Polytechnique, etc., in the same year, one would see that the closer they are to the pole of power, the more these 'young men' take on the attributes of the adult, the old man, the noble, the notable, etc. As one moves from the intellectuals to the managing director, so everything that gives a 'young' look – long hair, jeans, etc. – disappears.

As I have shown in relation to fashion or artistic and literary production, each field has its specific laws of ageing. To understand how the generations are divided, you have to know the specific laws of functioning of the field, the specific prizes that are fought for and the divisions that emerge in the struggle (*nouvelle vague, nouveau roman, nouveaux philosophes*, 'the new judges', etc.). All that is fairly banal, but it demonstrates that age is a biological datum, socially manipulated and manipulable; and that merely talking about 'the young' as a social unit, a constituted group, with common interests, relating these interests to a biologically defined age, is in itself an obvious manipulation. At the very least one ought to analyse the differences between different categories of 'youth', or, to be brief, at least *two* types of 'youth'. For example, one could systematically compare the conditions of existence, the labour market, the time management, etc., of 'young people' who are already in work, and of adolescents of the same (biological) age who are students. On one side there are the constraints of the real economic universe, barely mitigated by family solidarity; on the other, the artificial universe of dependency, based on subsidies, with low-cost meals and accommodation, reduced prices in theatres and cinemas, and so on. You'd find similar differences in all areas of existence: for example, the scruffy, long-haired kids who take their girlfriends for a ride on a clapped-out scooter are the very same ones who get picked up by the police.

In other words, it's an enormous abuse of language to use the same concept to subsume under the same term social universes that have practically nothing in common. In one case, you have a universe of adolescence, in the true sense, in other words, one of provisional irresponsibility: these 'young people' are in a kind of social no man's land, they are adults for some things and children for others, they have it both ways. That's why many bourgeois adolescents dream of prolonging their adolescence indefinitely: it's the complex of Frédéric in Flaubert's *Éducation sentimentale*, who eternally extends his adolescence. Having said that, the 'two youths' are simply two opposing poles, the two extremes of a space of possibilities offered to 'young people'. One of the interesting things that emerge from Laurent Thévenot's work is that it shows that between these extreme positions – the bourgeois student at one end and, at the other, the young worker who does not even have an adolescence – one finds nowadays all the intermediate positions.

Q. *Isn't it the transformation of the educational system that has produced this kind of continuity, where previously there was a more clear-cut difference between the classes?*
A. One of the factors in this blurring of the oppositions between young people in the different classes is the fact that in all classes a higher proportion pass through secondary education, so that a proportion of (biologically) young people whose parents did not experience adolescence have discovered this temporary status, the half-way house between childhood and adulthood. I think that's a very important social fact. Even in the milieux apparently most remote from the student condition of the nineteenth century, that's to say in small villages, where the children of peasants and craftsmen now go to the local secondary school even in that case, adolescents are placed, for a relatively long period, at an age when previously they would have been working, in those positions almost outside the social universe which define the adolescent condition. It seems that one of the most powerful effects of the situation of adolescents derives from this kind of separate existence, which puts them *socially out of play*. The 'schools of power', and especially the *grandes écoles*, place young people in enclosures separated from the world, quasi-monastic spaces where they live a life apart, a retreat, withdrawn from the world and entirely taken up with preparing for the most 'senior positions'. They do perfectly gratuitous things there, the sorts of things one does at school, exercises with blank ammunition. For some years now, all young people have had access to a version of this experience, more or less fully developed and, above all, more or less long. However brief and superficial it may have been, this experience is decisive, because it is sufficient to produce to some degree a break with self-evidences. There's the classic case of the miner's son who wants to go down the mine as soon as possible, because that's his route into the world of adults.

Even today, one reason why working-class adolescents want to leave school and start work very early is the desire to attain adult status, and the associated economic capacities, as soon as possible. It's very important for a boy to earn money so he can keep up with his peers, go out with his mates and with girls, be seen, and see himself, as a 'man'. That's one of the factors behind working-class children's resistance to the raising of the school leaving age.

All the same, the fact of being placed in the 'student' situation induces all sorts of things which are constitutive of the scholastic situation. They have their bundle of books tied up with a string, they sit on scooters and chat up girls, they associate with others of their own age, of both sexes, outside of work, and at home they are absolved from material tasks on the grounds that they are studying (and it's an important factor that the working classes go along with this tacit contract which leads students to be set 'out of play').

I think that this symbolic setting-aside has a certain importance, especially since it is accompanied by one of the fundamental effects of the educational system, which is the manipulation of aspirations. People always forget that school is not just a place where you learn things, where you acquire knowledge and skills: it's also an institution which awards qualifications – and therefore entitlements – and so confers aspirations. The old school system produced less confusion than the present system with its complicated tracks which lead people to have aspirations that are ill-adjusted to their real chances. The tracks used to be fairly clear: if you went beyond the primary school certificate, you went to a *cours complémentaire*, or a 'higher primary school', or a *collège*, or a *lycée*; there was a clear hierarchy among these routes, and no one was in any doubt. Now, there is a host of routes through the system that are difficult to tell apart and you have to be very alert in order to avoid running into a siding or a dead-end, and also to avoid devalued courses and qualifications. That helps to encourage a degree of disconnection of people's aspirations from their real chances. The previous state of the system meant that limits were very strongly internalized; it led people to accept failure or limits as just or inevitable . . ..
For example, primary school teachers were people who were selected and trained, consciously or unconsciously, so that they would be cut off from peasants and workers, while at the same time being completely separate from secondary teachers. Now that the system gives the status of *lycéen*, albeit devalued, to children from social classes for whom secondary education was formerly quite inaccessible, it encourages these children and their families to expect what the system provided for *lycée* pupils at a time when those schools were closed to them. To enter secondary education is to enter into the aspirations that were inscribed in entering secondary education in a earlier stage of the system; going to *lycée* means putting on, like a pair of boots, the aspiration to become a *lycée* teacher, or a doctor, a lawyer or a notary, all positions that were opened up by the *lycée* in the inter-war period. Now, at the time when working-class children were not in the system, the system was not the same. Consequently, there's been devaluation as a simple effect of inflation, and also as a result of the change in the 'social quality' of the qualification holders. The effects of educational inflation are more complicated than people generally imply: because a

qualification is always worth what its holders are worth, a qualification that becomes more widespread is *ipso facto* devalued, but it loses still more of its value because it becomes accessible to people 'without social value'.

Q. *What are the consequences of this inflation?*

A. The phenomena that I've just described mean that the aspirations objectively inscribed in the system as it was in its earlier state are disappointed. The mismatch between the aspirations that the school system encourages through the set of effects that I have alluded to is the principle of the collective disappointment and collective refusal that contrast with the collective adherence of the former period (I mentioned the example of the miner's son) and the submission in advance to the objective chances which was one of the tacit conditions of the functioning of the economy. It is a kind of breaking of the vicious circle whereby the miner's son wanted to go down the pit, without even wondering whether he had any choice. Of course, what I have described is not valid for all young people: there are still masses of adolescents, especially bourgeois adolescents, who are still in the circle, as before – who see things as they used to be seen, who want to get into a *grande école*, MIT, or Harvard Business School, who want to sit for every exam you could imagine, just as before.

Q. *And working-class kids end up as misfits in the world of work?*

A. One can be sufficiently at home in the school system to be cut off from the world of work, but not enough to succeed in finding work with the aid of qualifications. (That was already a theme in the conservative literature of the 1880s, which was already talking about unemployed *bacheliers* and worrying about the effects of breaking the circle of opportunities and aspirations and the associated self-evidences.) One can be very unhappy in the educational system, feel completely out of place there, but still participate in the student subculture, the gang of *lycéens* who hang around dance halls, who cultivate a student style and are sufficiently integrated into that lifestyle to be alienated from their families (whom they no longer understand and who no longer understand their children – 'With all the advantages they've had!') – and at the same time have a feeling of disarray, despair, towards work. In fact, as well as this effect of the breaking of a circle, there is also, despite everything, the confused realization of what the educational system offers some people – the confused realization, even through failure, that the system helps to reproduce privileges.

I think – and I wrote it ten years ago – that in order for the working class to be able to discover that the educational system functions as an instrument of social reproduction, they had to pass through the system. So long as they had nothing to do with the system, except at primary school, they might well accept the old Republican ideology of 'schooling as a liberatory force', or indeed, whatever the spokesmen say, have no opinion about it all. Now, in the working class, both among adults and among adolescents, the discovery is taking place, even if it has not yet found a language to express itself, that the educational system is a vehicle for privileges.

Q. *But then how do you explain the apparently much greater depoliticization that we've seen over the last three or four years?*

A. The confused revolt – the questioning of work, school, and so on – is a comprehensive one; it challenges the educational system as a whole and is absolutely different from the experience of failure in the earlier state of the system (though that hasn't entirely disappeared, of course – you only have to listen to interviews: 'I was no good at French, I didn't get on at school, etc.'). What is going on through the more or less anomic and anarchic forms of revolt is not what is normally understood as politicization, that is, something that the political apparatuses are prepared to register and reinforce. It's a broader, vaguer questioning, a kind of unease at work, something that is not political in the established sense, but which could be; something that strongly resembles certain forms of political consciousness that are obscure to themselves, because they have not found their own voice, and yet of an extraordinary revolutionary force, capable of overwhelming the political apparatuses, that one also finds in sub-proletarians or in first-generation industrial workers of peasant origin. To explain their own failure, to make it bearable, these people have to question the whole system, the educational system, and also the family, with which it is bound up, and all institutions, identifying the school with the barracks and the barracks with the factory. There's a kind of spontaneous ultra-leftism which reminds one of the language of sub-proletarians in more ways than one.

Q. *And does that have an influence on the conflicts between the generations?*

A. One very simple thing, which people don't think of, is that the aspirations of successive generations, parents and children, are formed in relation to different states of the distribution of goods and of the chances of obtaining the different goods. What for the parents was an extraordinary privilege (for example, when they were twenty, only one person in a thousand of their age and their milieu owned a car) has become statistically banal. And many clashes between generations are clashes between systems of aspirations formed in different periods. Something that for generation one was the conquest of a lifetime is given at birth to generation two. The discrepancy is particularly great in the case of classes in decline, who don't even have what they had at the age of twenty – at a time when all the privileges of those days (skiing, seaside holidays, etc.) have become *common*. It's no accident that anti-youth racism (which is very visible in the statistics, although unfortunately we don't have analyses by class fraction) is characteristic of declining classes (such as craftsmen or small shopkeepers), or individuals in decline and the old in general. Not all old people are anti-youth, of course, but old age is also a social decline, a loss of social power, and in that way the old share in the relation to the young that is also characteristic of the declining classes. Naturally, the old people of the declining classes, that's to say old craftsmen, old shopkeepers and so on, combine all these symptoms in an extreme form: they are against young people but also against artists, against intellectuals, against protest, against everything that changes and stirs things up, precisely because their future lies behind them, because they have no future, whereas young people are defined as having a future, as those who will define the future.

Q. *But isn't the educational system the source of conflicts between the generations in so far as it can bring together, in the same social positions, people who have been trained in different states of the school system?*

A. We can start from a concrete case: at present, in many middle-ranking positions in the civil service that one can reach by learning on the job, you find, side by side, in the same office, young holders of the baccalaureate, or even a *licence* [university degree], taken on straight from the educational system, and people in their fifties who started out thirty years earlier with the primary *certificat d'études*, at a stage in the development of the educational system when that certificate was still a relatively rare qualification, and who, through self-teaching and seniority, have reached managerial positions that are now only open to *bacheliers*. The opposition here is not between young and old, but virtually between two states of the educational system, two states of the differential rarity of qualifications; and this opposition takes the form of conflicts over classifications. Because the old cannot say that they are in charge because they are old, they will invoke the experience associated with seniority, whereas the young will invoke the competence guaranteed by qualifications. The same opposition can also be found in the field of trade unionism (for example, within the union Force Ouvrière in the Post Office), in the form of tension between young bearded Trotskyists and old activists whose sympathies lie with the old-style Socialist Party, the SFIO. You also find, side by side, in the same office, in the same jobs, engineers some of whom come from Arts et Métiers[1] and others from Polytechnique. The apparent identity of status conceals the fact that one group has, as the phrase goes, a future before it and is only passing through a position which for the others is a point of arrival. In this case, the conflicts may well take other forms, because the 'old-young' ('old' because *finished*) are likely to have internalized a respect for academic qualifications as markers of differences in nature.

That's why, in many cases, conflicts that are experienced as conflicts of generations are in fact acted out through persons or age-groups based on different relations to the educational system. One of the unifying principles of a generation is (nowadays) to be found in a common relationship to a particular state of the school system, and in the specific interests, which are different from those of the generation defined by its relationship to a different state of the system. What is common to all young people, or at least all those who benefited to any extent from the school system, who have derived at least some basic qualification from it, is that, overall, that generation is more qualified in a given job than the previous generation. (Incidentally, it may be noted that women, who, through a kind of discrimination, arrive in jobs through a kind of hyper-selection, are constantly in this situation, i.e. they are almost always more qualified than men in equivalent positions.)

It is certain that, beyond all class differences, young people have collective, generational interests, because, quite apart from the effect of 'anti-young' discrimination, the mere fact that they have encountered different states of the educational system means that they will always get less out of their qualifications than the previous generation would have got. There's a structural deskilling of the generation. That's probably important in trying to understand the kind of disenchantment that is relatively common to the whole generation. Even in the bourgeoisie some of the current conflicts are probably explained by this, by the fact that the time-lag for succession is lengthening, the fact that, as Le Bras has clearly shown in an article in *Population*, the age at which inheritances or positions are handed on is getting later and later and the juniors of the dominant class are champing at the bit. That is probably not unrelated to the contestation to be seen in the professions (among the architects, the lawyers, the doctors, and so on) and in the universities. Just as the old have an interest in pushing young people back down into youth, so the young have an interest in pushing the old into old age.

There are periods when the pursuit of the 'new', through which the 'newcomers' (who are usually also biologically youngest) push the incumbents into the social death of 'has-beens', intensifies and when, by the same token, the struggles between the generations take on greater intensity. They are times when the trajectories of the youngest and the oldest overlap and the young aspire to the succession 'too soon'. These conflicts are avoided so long as the old are able to adjust the tempo of the rise of the young, to channel their careers and apply the brake to those who cannot hold themselves back, the 'high-flyers' who jostle and hustle for advancement. In fact, most of the time, the old do not need to apply the brakes because the 'young' – who may be fifty-something – have internalized the limits, the modal ages, that is, the age at which one can 'reasonably aspire' to a position, and would not even think of claiming it earlier, before 'their time has come'. When the 'sense of the limits' is lost, then conflicts arise about age limits and limits between the ages, in which what is at stake is the transmission of power and privileges between the generations.

Note

1   The Conservatoire National des Arts et Métiers, providing vocational training for 'mature' students (in contrast to the École Polytechnique) [translator].

13

MUSIC LOVERS: ORIGIN AND EVOLUTION OF THE SPECIES

Q. *You seem to have a kind of reluctance to talk about music. Why is that?*

A. First, discourse about music is one of the most sought-after occasions for intellectual window-dressing. Talking about music is the opportunity *par excellence* for flaunting the range and universality of one's culture. I'm thinking for example of the radio programme *Le Concert égoïste*. The list of works chosen, the remarks made to justify the choice, the tone of intimate and inspired confidence, are so many strategies for self-presentation, intended to give the most flattering image of oneself, the one closest to the legitimate definition of the 'cultivated man', that is, a person who is 'original' within the limits of conformity. Nothing gives more opportunities than music for exhibiting one's 'class', and there's nothing by which one is more inevitably classified.

But the display of musical culture is not a cultural display like others. Music is the most spiritualistic of the arts and the love of music is a guarantee of 'spirituality'. You only have to think of the extraordinary value that is nowadays placed on the vocabulary of 'listening' by the secularized versions of religious language (psychoanalysis, for example); or to consider the concentrated, meditative poses and postures that listeners feel called upon to adopt at public performances of music. Music is hand-in-glove with the soul: there are innumerable variations on the soul of music and the music of the soul ('inner music'). Every concert is a sacred concert ... To be 'indifferent to music' is a particularly shameful form of barbarism: the 'élite' and the 'mass', the soul and the body ...

But that's not all. Music is the 'pure art' *par excellence*. Placing itself beyond words, music says nothing and has *nothing to say*; having no expressive function, it is diametrically opposed to theatre, which, even in its most rarefied forms, remains the bearer of a social message and can only be 'put over' on the basis of an immediate, deep agreement with the values and expectations of the audience. The theatre divides and is divided: the opposition between (in Paris) right-bank theatre and left-bank theatre,[1] between bourgeois 'boulevard' theatre and avant-garde theatre, is inseparably aesthetic and political. There is nothing quite like that in music

Interview with Cyril Huvé in *Le Monde de la musique*, 6, 1978: 30–1 (leaving aside a few recent exceptions). Music represents the most radical, the most absolute form of denial of the world, and especially of the social world, that is achieved by any art form.

It only has to be borne in mind that there is no activity more classifying, more distinctive, that is, more closely linked to social class and educational capital, than concert-going or the playing of a 'noble' instrument (rarer activities, other things being equal, than visiting museums or even contemporary-art galleries) to understand why the concert was predisposed to become one of the great bourgeois celebrations.

Q. *But how do you explain why musical tastes are so deeply revealing?*
A. Musical experiences are rooted in the most primitive bodily experience. There are probably no tastes – except perhaps in food – more deeply rooted in the body than musical tastes. That's why, as La Rochefoucauld put it, 'Our pride suffers more impatiently the condemnation of our tastes than of our opinions.' Our tastes do indeed express us or betray us more than our judgements, in politics for example. And perhaps nothing is harder to bear than other people's 'bad' taste. Aesthetic intolerance can be terribly violent. Tastes are inseparable from *distastes*: aversion to different lifestyles is perhaps one of the strongest barriers between the classes. That's why *de gustibus non est disputandum*. Think of the uproar provoked by the slightest change in the routine of so-called cultural radio stations.

What is intolerable for those who have a certain taste, that's to say, a certain acquired disposition to 'differentiate and appreciate' as Kant puts it, is above all the *mixing* of genres, the confusion of domains. Radio or television producers who juxtapose a classical violinist and a fiddler (or, worse, a tzigane violinist), an interview with Janos Starker and a chat with an Argentinian tango director, and so on, are – sometimes knowingly, sometimes unconsciously – performing ritual barbarisms, sacrilegious transgressions, by mixing what ought to be separated, the sacred and the profane, and combining that which the embodied classifications, tastes, require to be separated.

Q. *And these deep-seated tastes are linked to particular social experiences?*
A. Absolutely. For example, when in a very fine article Roland Barthes describes aesthetic enjoyment as a kind of direct communication between the 'inner' body of the interpreter – present in the 'grain of the singer's voice' or the 'pads of the pianist's fingers' – and the body of the listener, he's referring to a particular experience of music, that given by an early, domestic knowledge, acquired by practice.[2] Incidentally, Barthes is quite right to reduce the 'communication of souls', as Proust called it, to a communication of bodies. It's useful to remember that St Teresa of Avila

and St John of the Cross speak of divine love in the language of human love. Music is a 'bodily thing'. It ravishes, moves, stirs, carries away; it is not so much beyond words as below them, in movements of the limbs and body, rhythms, excitements and slowings, tensions and releases. The most 'mystical', the most 'spiritual' of the arts is perhaps simply the most corporeal. That's probably what makes it so difficult to speak of music except in adjectives or exclamations. Cassirer used to say that the key words of religious experience, *mana*, *wakanda*, *orenda*, and so on, are exclamations, that's to say, expressions of ravishment.

But to return to variations in taste according to social conditions, I will not surprise anyone by saying that a person's social class, or 'class' (as in 'he's got class'), can be identified as infallibly from his preferred music (or simply the radio station he listens to) as from the aperitif – Pernod, Martini or whisky – that he drinks. But surveys show that one can go further in describing and explaining differences in tastes than the simple distinction of a 'cultured' taste, a 'popular' taste and a 'mainstream' taste that combines the most 'noble' of popular productions, such as, among singers, Brel and Brassens, with the most popularized classical works, Strauss waltzes or Ravel's *Boléro*. (In every epoch, 'distinguished' works fall into 'vulgarity' through 'popularization': a perfect example is Albinoni's *Adagio*, which passed in a few years from the status of a musicologist's discovery to that of typically 'mainstream' jingle; the same could be said of a number of works by Vivaldi.)

The most subtle differences that separate aesthetes from amateurs as regards the works or interpreters of the most recognized repertoire derive, not (or not only) from ultimate and ineffable preferences, but from differences in the mode of acquisition of musical culture, in the form of the earliest experiences of music. For example, the opposition that Barthes establishes, in the same article, between Fischer-Dieskau, the professional of the record industry, and Panzera, who brings to perfection the qualities of the amateur, is typical of a particular relation to music, which refers back to particular conditions of acquisition and makes one particularly sensitive and lucid (again the taste/distaste link) towards the 'shortcomings' of the new mainstream culture, characteristic of the age of high-fidelity recording. On the one hand, there is an expressive, dramatic and emotionally clear art with a 'grainless' voice; on the other, the art of diction that is realized in French *mélodie*, Duparc, late Fauré, Debussy, with the death of Mélisande, the antithesis of the (too eloquent, too dramatic) death of Boris.

Having identified the generative scheme that underlies this opposition, one can endlessly enumerate the tastes and distastes: on the one hand, the expressive sound and fury of the orchestra, on the other the intimism of the piano, the maternal instrument *par excellence*, and the intimacy of the bourgeois living-room.

At the basis of this classification, this taste, there are the two ways of acquiring musical culture: on the one hand, intimate, early familiarity, on the other the passive, scholastic taste of the LP collector. Two relations to music that spontaneously develop in relation to each other: tastes are always distinctive, and the exaltation of certain artists of the past (Panzera or Cortot), who are loved even for their imperfections which evoke the freedom of the amateur, implies disparagement of the modern performers and their impeccable recordings for mass production.

The radio programme *Tribune des critiques de disques* almost always follows this triangular pattern: a famous artiste of the old school, Schnabel for example; some modern performers, soulless professionals discredited by the imperfect perfection of their technique; and a newcomer who combines the old virtues of the inspired amateur with the impeccable technique of the professional, such as Pollini or Abbado.

It's because tastes are distinctive that they change: the exaltation of artists of the past – as confirmed by the countless reissues of 78s or of radio recordings – is undoubtedly related to the appearance of a musical culture based on records rather than on playing an instrument or concert-going, and on the increasing familiarity of the instrumental perfection that is demanded by the record industry and the economic and cultural competition among artists and producers.

Q. *In other words, the evolution of musical production is indirectly one of the causes of the changing of tastes?*
A. Undoubtedly. Here too, production helps to produce consumption. But the economics of musical production still remains to be studied. If it is not to mean simply moving from mystical celebration into the most crudely reductive economism, then it would require one to describe the whole set of mediations through which the record industry manages to impose a repertoire, sometimes even an interpretation and a style, on artists, even the greatest of them (Karajan must by now have recorded the complete Beethoven symphonies at least three times), thereby helping to impose a particular definition of legitimate tastes.

What makes that undertaking so difficult is that, in the field of cultural goods, production implies the production of consumers, that is to say, more precisely, the production of the taste for music, the need for music, belief in music. To give an adequate account of that, which is what is most essential, would mean analysing the whole network of relationships of competition and complementarity, complicity in competition, which hold together the whole set of agents concerned, famous and unknown composers and performers, record producers, critics, radio producers, teachers, etc., in short, all those who have an interest in music and interests that depend on music, musical investments – in both the economic and psychological senses – who are caught up in the game and taken in by the game.

Notes

1   Or perhaps, in London, West End theatre and the South Bank or the Royal Court [translator].

2   Barthes, R. (1977) 'The grain of the voice', in R. Barthes, *Image, Music, Text*, London: Fontana, 179–89.

14

THE METAMORPHOSIS OF TASTES

How do tastes change? Can the logic of the transformation of tastes be scientifically described?

Before I try to answer these questions, I must indicate how *tastes* are defined. They emerge as choices made among practices (sports, pastimes, etc.) and properties (furniture, hats, ties, books, pictures, spouses, etc.) through which *taste*, in the sense of the principle underlying these choices, manifests itself.

In order for there to be tastes, there have to be goods that are classified, as being in 'good' or 'bad' taste, 'distinguished' or 'vulgar' – classified and thereby classifying, hierarchized and hierarchizing – and people endowed with principles of classification, tastes, that enable them to identify, among those goods, those that suit them, that are 'to their taste'. In fact there can be taste without goods (taste in the sense of a principle of classification, a principle of division, a capacity for distinction), and goods without a taste. One might say for example, 'I went to every shop in Neuchâtel and found nothing to my taste.' That raises the question of what this taste is that exists prior to the goods capable of satisfying it (contradicting the maxim *ignoti nulla cupido*, of the unknown there is no desire).

But there will also be cases where goods do not find the 'consumers' who would find them to their taste. The example *par excellence* of these goods which precede the taste of the consumers is that of avant-garde painting or music, which, since the nineteenth century, have not found the tastes that they 'call for' until long after the time they are produced, sometimes long after the death of the producer. That raises the question of whether the goods that precede tastes (apart from the producers' taste, of course) help to make tastes; the question of the symbolic efficacy of the supply of goods or, more precisely, of the effect of the embodiment of a particular taste, that of the artist, in the form of goods.

Thus we arrive at a provisional definition: tastes, understood as the set of practices or properties of a person or group, are the product of an encounter (a pre-established harmony) between goods and a taste (when I say 'My house is to my taste,' I mean I have the house that suits my taste, in which my taste feels at home). Among these goods one must, at the risk of shocking some people, include all the objects of election, of elective affinity, such as the objects of sympathy, friendship or love.

Talk given at the University of Neuchâtel, May 1980

A moment ago I raised the question in an elliptical way: to what extent does the good that realizes my taste, which is its realized potentiality, create the taste that feels at home in it? The love of art often speaks the same language as romantic love: 'love at first sight' is the miraculous encounter between an expectation and its realization. It's also the relationship between a people and its prophet or its spokesman: 'you would not seek me if you had not found me' (Pascal). The person who is spoken-for is someone who had something to say latent within in him and who does not know it until he is told it. In a sense, the prophet brings nothing; he only preaches to the converted. But preaching to the converted still means doing something. It means performing the typically social, and quasi-magical, operation of the encounter between an already objectified discourse and an implicit expectation, between a language and certain dispositions that only exist in the practical state. Tastes are the product of this encounter between two histories, one existing in the objectified state, the other in the incorporated state, which are objectively attuned to one another. Hence, no doubt, one dimension of the miracle of the encounter with a work of art: to discover something to one's taste is to discover oneself, to discover what one wants ('Just what I wanted'), what one had to say and didn't know how to say and, consequently, didn't know.

In the encounter between a work of art and the consumer, there is an absent third party, the person who produced the work, who has made something to his taste through his capacity to transform his taste into an object, to transform it from a state of mind, or rather, a state of the body, into something visible corresponding to his taste. The artist is this professional practitioner of the transformation of the implicit into the explicit, the objectification that transforms taste into an object, who realizes the potential, in other words a practical sense of beauty that can know itself only by realizing itself. Indeed, this practical sense of beauty is purely negative and made up almost exclusively of *refusals*. The objectifier of taste stands in the same relation to the product of his objectification as the consumer: he may or may not find it to his taste. He is acknowledged to have the competence necessary to objectify a taste. More precisely, the artist is someone whose audience recognizes him as such by recognizing itself in what he has made, recognizing in what he has made what they would have made if they had known how to. He is a 'creator', a magical word that can be used once one has defined the artistic operation as a magical, that is, typically social, operation. (When one speaks of a 'producer' of art, as one often must, in order to break with the ordinary representation of the artist as a creator – which means denying oneself all the immediate complicities that this terminology is bound to elicit both from the 'creators' and the consumers, who like to think of themselves as 'creators', with the theme of reading as re-creation – one is liable to forget that the artistic act is an act of production of a quite particular kind, since it has to bring to full existence something that was already there, in the very expectation of its appearance, and to make it exist quite differently, as a sacred thing, an object of belief.)

So tastes, defined as the sets of choices made by particular persons, are the product of an encounter between the objectified taste of the artist and the taste of the consumer. We now have to clarify how it is that, at a given moment, there are goods for all tastes (even if there are perhaps not tastes for all goods), with the most varied clients all finding goods to their taste. (In my whole analysis, one could mentally replace 'work of art' with 'religious good or service'. Thus the analogy with the Catholic Church shows that the rather hasty *aggiornamento* has replaced a fairly uniform product with a very diversified supply, so that there is now something for all tastes, with the Mass in French, in Latin, in robes, in trousers, and so on.) To account for this quasi-miraculous adjustment between supply and demand (apart from a degree of excess supply over demand), one could, with Max Weber, invoke the conscious pursuit of adjustment, a calculated transaction by the clerics with the expectations of the laity. That would be to assume that the avant-garde priest who offers the inhabitants of a working-class suburb a 'liberated' Mass, or the traditionalist who says Mass in Latin, has a cynical or at least calculated relationship with his clientele, that he enters with it into a quite conscious supply-and-demand relationship, that he is informed as to the demand – it's not clear how, since it cannot formulate itself and can only become conscious by recognizing itself in its objectification – and that he strives to satisfy it (there is always this suspicion against a successful author: their books have succeeded because they have gone out to meet the demands of the market, i.e., by implication, the lowest, most facile demands, those least deserving to be satisfied). So it is assumed that, thanks to some kind of more or less cynical or sincere 'acumen' or 'business sense', the producers adjust to the demand: the one who succeeds is the one who has found a 'niche' in the market.

The hypothesis I shall put forward in order to account for the universe of tastes at a given moment is quite different, even if conscious intentions and transactions are, of course, never excluded from cultural production. (Some sectors of the space of production – it's one of their distinctive properties – quite cynically obey the calculated pursuit of profit, and therefore the 'market niche': you give a subject, you give six months and a million francs, and the 'writer' has to produce a novel that will be a best-seller.) So the model I am putting forward represents a break with the model that is spontaneously accepted, which sees the cultural producer – writer, artist, priest, prophet, sorcerer, or journalist – as a rational economic calculator who, through some kind of market survey, manages to sense and satisfy needs that are scarcely formulated or not even known, so as to draw the maximum possible profit from his capacity to steal a march on his competitors. In fact, there are spaces of production in which the producers work with their eyes fixed much less on their clients, that is, what is called the target audience, than on their competitors. (But that's another teleological formulation which relies too much on conscious strategy.) More exactly, they work in a space in which what they produce depends very closely on their position in the space of production (I must apologize to those who are not accustomed to sociology; I'm obliged to put forward an analysis without being able to justify it in simple terms). In the case of journalism, the critic of *Le Figaro* writes not with his eyes on his public but by reference to the critic of *Le Nouvel Observateur* (and vice versa). In order to do so, he does not need to consult what the other has written; he simply has to follow his taste, his own inclinations, in order to define himself against what the critic on the opposite side – who does just the same thing – thinks or says. He thinks against the *Nouvel Observateur* critic without this even becoming conscious. That can be seen in his rhetoric, which is that of anticipated contradiction – you are going to call me a reactionary philistine because I criticize Arrabal, but I understand Arrabal well enough to assure you that there is nothing to understand. In reassuring himself, he reassures his public, who are worried by works that worry them because they are unintelligible – although this public always understands them well enough to sense that they mean things that it understands only too well. To put it in somewhat objectivist and determinist terms, the producer is governed in his production by the position he occupies in the space of production. Producers produce diversified products by the logic of things and without pursuing distinction. (It is clear that what I have tried to show is diametrically opposed to all the theses on conspicuous consumption which make the conscious pursuit of difference the sole principle of change in cultural production and consumption.)

So there is a logic of the space of production that leads producers to produce different goods, whether they aim to or not. The objective differences may, of course, be subjectively reinforced, and for a long time now, artists, who are objectively distinguished, have also sought to distinguish themselves – in particular, in the *manner*, the form, which is specifically theirs, as opposed to the subject, the function. To say, as I sometimes have, that intellectuals, like phonemes, only exist through difference does not imply that all difference arises from the pursuit of difference: it is, fortunately, not sufficient to seek difference in order to find it, and sometimes, in a universe in which most people seek difference, it is sufficient not to seek it in order to be very different . . .

And on the consumers' side, how are people going to choose? On the basis of their taste, which most often means negatively (one can always say what one doesn't like, which often means other people's tastes). This taste is constituted through confrontation with already realized tastes; it teaches itself what it is by recognizing itself in objects that are themselves already objectified tastes.

So, to understand tastes, to analyse sociologically what people have, their properties and practices, first means understanding, on the one hand, the conditions in which the products on offer are produced, and on the other hand, the conditions in which the consumers 'produce themselves'. For example, to understand the sports that people do, one has to know not only their dispositions, but also the supply, which is the product of historical inventions. This means that the same taste might, in another state of the supply, have been expressed in practices that are phenomenally quite different, but structurally equivalent. (It's our practical intuition of these structural equivalences between phenomenally different but practically interchangeable objects that leads us to say, for example, that Robbe-Grillet is to the twentieth century what Flaubert was to the nineteenth; which means that the person who chose Flaubert from the supply of the time would nowadays be in a position homologous to that of the reader who chooses Robbe-Grillet.)

Now that I have outlined how tastes are generated in the encounter between a supply and a demand, or, more precisely, between classified objects and systems of classification, we can examine how these tastes change. First on the side of production, the supply: the artistic field is the site of permanent change, so much so that, as we have seen, to disqualify an artist, as an artist, it is sufficient to relegate him to the past, by showing that his style merely reproduces a style attested in the past, that he is a fossil or a counterfeiter, a mere imitator who is totally devoid of value because he is totally devoid of originality.

The artistic field is the site of partial revolutions which shake up the structure of the field without calling into question the field as such and the game that is played there. In the religious field, there's the dialectic of orthodoxy and heresy – or 'reform', the model of specific subversion. Artistic innovators, like reformers, are people who say to those dominant in the field, 'You've betrayed, we must go back to the source, the message.' For example, the oppositions around which literary struggles have been organized, right through the nineteenth century and up to the present day, can be traced back in the last analysis to the opposition between the young, that is, the newcomers, the latest arrivals, and the old, the established, the establishment. Obscure/clear, difficult/facile, profound/superficial, and so on – ultimately these oppositions are between artistic ages and generations, that is, different positions in the artistic field that the native language contrasts as advanced/outmoded, avant-garde/rearguard, etc. (It can be seen, incidentally, that the description of the structure of a field, of the specific power relations that constitute it as such, contains a description of the history of the field.)

To enter the game of production, to exist intellectually, is to 'make an epoch' [faire date] and, by the same token, to relegate into the past those who, at another date, also 'made an epoch'. (To 'make an epoch' is to make history, which is the product of the struggle and even the struggle itself; when there is no more struggle, there is no more history. So long as there is struggle there is history, and therefore hope. As soon as there is no more struggle, no more resistance from the dominated, the dominant have a monopoly and history stops. The dominant, in all fields, see their domination as the end of history – the 'end' in the sense both of conclusion and goal – which has no 'beyond' and therefore becomes eternal.)

To make an epoch, then, means relegating those who were once dominant into the past, making them *passé*, 'has-beens'. Those who are thrust in this way into the past may become merely outmoded, but they may also become 'classic', eternal (the conditions of this 'eternization', and the role of the educational system in creating 'classics', would merit analysis).

Haute couture is the field in which the model I have described is seen most clearly, so clearly that it's almost too easy and one is liable to understand too quickly, easily, but only partially (which often happens in the social sciences – fashion is one of those mechanisms that one never stops trying to understand because they are understood too easily). For example, Bohan, the successor of Dior, talks about his dresses in the language of good taste, discretion, moderation, sobriety, implicitly condemning all the eye-catching provocations of those who are to his 'left' in the field; he speaks of his left as the *Figaro* journalist speaks of *Libération*. As for the avant-garde couturiers, they speak of fashion in the language of politics (our survey was done just after the events of 1968), saying that fashion has to be 'brought on to the streets', and that '*Haute couture* should be within reach of everyone.' It can be seen that there are equivalences between these autonomous fields such that language can pass from one to the other with apparently identical but really different meanings. This raises the question whether, when people talk about politics in certain relatively autonomous spaces, they are not doing the same as Ungaro talking about Dior.

That gives us a first factor of change. Will things follow on the other side? One can imagine a field of production which takes off and 'grows' its consumers. That has been true of the field of cultural production, or some sectors of it at least, since the nineteenth century. But it also happened, quite recently, in the religious field. Supply preceded demand; the consumers were not asking for it . . . That is a case where the logic of the field is operating 'in neutral', confirming the central idea that I am putting forward, namely that change does not result from adjustment of the product to the demand. Without forgetting these cases of mismatch, we can say that, in general, the two spaces, the space of production of goods and the space of production of tastes, change at broadly the same rate.

One of the factors which determine change in demand is undoubtedly the quantitative and qualitative rise in the level of demand that accompanies the raising of the level of education (or the length of schooling). This means that an ever greater number of people will enter the race for the appropriate cultural goods. The effect of a rising level of education makes itself felt, among other things, through what I call the effect of assignment by status (*noblesse oblige*). This leads the holders of a given educational qualification, which functions like a title of nobility, to behave in ways – visiting museums and galleries, buying a record player, reading *Le Monde* – that are inscribed in their social definition, one might almost say in their 'social essence'. In this way, the general lengthening of education and especially the intensified use made of the educational system by classes that are already intensive users explain the growth in all cultural practices (a development which, in the case of museums, was predicted by the model that we put forward in 1966).[1] And it is not surprising, in terms of this logic, that the proportion of people who say they can read a musical score or play an instrument rises strongly as one moves towards the youngest generations. The contribution of change in demand to change in tastes is seen clearly in a case like that of music, where the rise in the level of demand coincides with a lowering of the level of supply, with the *record* (the same thing is seen in the area of reading, with the paperback). The rise in the level of demand induces a translation of the structure of tastes, a hierarchical structure, which runs from the rarest, Berg or Ravel nowadays, to the least rare, Mozart or Beethoven. To put it more simply, all the goods offered tend to lose some of their relative scarcity and their distinctive value as the number of consumers both inclined and able to appropriate them grows. Popularization devalues. *Déclassé* goods no longer give class; goods that belonged to the 'happy few' become commonplace. Those who once marked their membership of the cultural élite by reading *L'Éducation sentimentale* or Proust must now turn to Robbe-Grillet, or further, to Claude Simon, Tony Duvert, etc. The rarity of the product and the rarity of the consumer decline in parallel. That is why records and record collectors 'threaten' the rarity value of the music lover. If the latter then set Panzera against Fischer-Dieskau, the impeccable product of the LP industry, as others contrast Mengelberg with Karajan, they manage to reintroduce the lost rarity. The cult of 'vintage' records and live recordings can be understood in the same terms. In all these cases, it is a question of bringing back scarcity: nothing is more commonplace than the Strauss waltzes, but what charm they have when conducted by Fürtwängler; and as for Mengelberg's Tchaikovsky! Another example: Chopin, long discredited as a composer of piano pieces for the finishing school, has gone full circle and has passionate supporters among the young musicologists. (If, for the sake of brevity, I sometimes use the language of intentionality and strategy to describe these processes, it has to be remembered that these rehabilitation operations are perfectly sincere and 'disinterested' and largely stem from the fact that those who rehabilitate in opposition to those who disqualify did not experience the conditions encountered by those who disqualified Chopin.)

So rarity can come from the world of listening (records, concerts, or performance in person), from the interpreter, and from the work itself. When it is threatened on one side, it can be brought back from another angle. And the supreme elegance may be found by playing with fire, either by combining the rarest tastes for the most difficult music with the most acceptable forms of popular music, preferably exotic, or by relishing strictly and highly controlled performances of the most 'accessible' and potentially most vulgarized works. It hardly needs to be said that the games of the consumers retrace the games of some composers who, like Mahler or Stravinsky, enjoy playing with fire, by using, at the second degree, elements of popular or even 'vulgar' music, borrowed from the music hall or dance hall.

These are only some of the strategies – usually unconscious – through which the consumers defend their rarity by defending the rarity of the products they consume or the way in which they consume them. In fact, the most elementary, the simplest strategy, consists in shunning works that have become popularized, devalued and disqualified. A 1979 survey by the Institut Français de Démographie showed that there are composers, Albinoni or Chopin for example, the 'consumption' of which rises steadily as one moves towards both the oldest and also the least educated respondents. The music they offer is both 'outmoded' and *déclassé*, in other words vulgarized and commonplace.

The abandonment of outmoded and 'common' music is accompanied by an endless search for the music that is rarest at the moment in question, which means, of course, the most modern music. And it can also be seen that the rarity of music, as measured by the mean rating it is given by a representative sample of listeners, increases as one moves towards more modern works, as if the objective difficulty of the works increased with the quantity of *accumulated history* they contain – the extent of their references to the history of music – and with the time it takes to acquire the competence they demand, in other words the rarity of that competence. The scores range from 3.0 out of 5 for Monteverdi, Bach and Mozart, to 2.8 for Brahms, 2.4 for Puccini, and (a slight inversion) 2.3 for Berg (but the work was *Lulu*) and 1.9 for Ravel (*Concerto for the Left Hand*). In short, one might predict that the most 'informed' public would continuously move (and concert programmes confirm this) towards modern, and increasingly modern, music. But there are also reversions – we have seen the case of Chopin – and renovations – baroque music played by Harnoncourt or Malgoire. This leads to cycles exactly comparable to those of fashion in dress, except that the period is longer. This would be the key to understanding the successive styles in Bach interpretation, from Busch to Leonhardt, through Münchinger, each one reacting against the preceding style.

It can be seen that the distinction 'strategies' of the producer and the distinction 'strategies' of the best informed, that is, the most distinguished, consumers meet up with each other without needing to seek each other out. That is why the encounter with a work of art is so often experienced in terms of a miracle and 'love at first sight'; and why the love of art is expressed and experienced in the language of love.

Note

1   Cf. P. Bourdieu, A. Darbel and D. Schnapper (1966), *L'Amour de l'Art: les musées d'art européens et leur public*, Paris: Éditions de Minuit [translator].

Further reading

For further discussion, see Bourdieu, P. (1980) 'The production of belief: contribution to an economy of symbolic goods', *Media, Culture and Society* 2(3): 261–93. Reprinted as pp. 131–63 in (1986) *Media, Culture and Society: A Critical Reader*, London: Sage.

15

HOW CAN ONE BE A SPORTSMAN?

I speak neither as a historian nor as a historian of sport, and so I appear as an amateur among professionals and can only ask you, as the phrase goes, to be 'good sports'.... But I think that the innocence which comes from not being a specialist can sometimes lead one to ask questions that specialists tend to forget, because they think they have answered them and because they have taken for granted a certain number of presuppositions that are perhaps fundamental to their discipline. The questions I shall raise come from outside; they are the questions of a sociologist who, among the objects he studies, encounters sporting activities and entertainments, in the form, for example, of the statistical distribution of sports activities by educational level, age, sex, and occupation, and who is led to ask himself questions not only about the relationship between the practices and the variables, but also about the meaning which the practices take on in those relationships.

I think that, without doing too much violence to reality, it is possible to consider the whole range of sporting activities and entertainments offered to social agents – rugby, football, swimming, athletics, tennis, golf, etc. – as a supply intended to meet a *social demand*. If such a model is adopted, two sets of questions arise. First, is there a field of production, endowed with its own logic and its own history, in which 'sports products' are generated, that is, the universe of the sporting activities and entertainments available and socially acceptable at a given moment in time? Secondly, what are the social conditions of possibility of the appropriation of the various 'sports products' that are thus produced – playing golf or cross-country skiing, reading *L'Équipe* or watching the World Cup on TV? In other words, how is the demand for 'sports products' produced, how do people acquire the 'taste' for sport, and for one sport rather than another, whether as an activity or as an entertainment? More precisely, according to what principles do agents choose between the different sports activities or entertainments which, at a given moment in time, are offered to them as being possible?

It seems to me that we should first consider the historical and social conditions of possibility of a social phenomenon which we too easily take for granted: 'modern sport'. In other words, what social conditions made

Keynote address given at the International Congress of the History of Sport and Physical Education Association, held in March 1978 at the Institut National des Sports et de l'Éducation physique

possible the constitution of the system of institutions and agents directly or
indirectly linked to the existence of sporting activities and entertainments?
The system includes public or private 'sports associations', whose function
is to represent and defend the interests of the practitioners of a given sport
and to draw up and impose the standards governing that activity, the
producers and vendors of goods (equipment, instruments, special clothing,
etc.) and services required in order to pursue the sport (teachers,
instructors, trainers, sports doctors, sports journalists, etc.) and the
producers and vendors of sporting entertainments and associated goods
(T-shirts, photos of stars, the *tiercé*, etc.). How was this body of specialists,
living directly or indirectly off sport, progressively constituted (a body to
which sports sociologists and historians also belong – which probably does
not help the question to emerge)? And, more exactly, when did this system
of agents and institutions begin to function as a *field of competition*, the site
of confrontations between agents with specific interests linked to their
positions within the field? If it is the case, as my questions tend to suggest,
that the system of the institutions and agents whose interests are bound up
with sport tends to function as a field, it follows that one cannot directly
understand what sporting phenomena are at a given moment in a given
social environment by relating them directly to the economic and social
conditions of the corresponding societies: the history of sport is a relatively
autonomous history which, even when marked by the major events of
economic and social history, has its own tempo, its own evolutionary laws,
its own crises, in short, its specific chronology.

Thus one of the most important tasks for the social history of sport could
well be to establish its own foundations by constructing the historical
genealogy of the emergence of its object as a *specific reality* irreducible to
any other. It alone can answer the question – which has nothing to do with
an academic question of *definition* – as to the moment (it is not a matter of a
precise date) from which it is possible to talk of sport, that is, the moment
from which there began to be constituted a field of competition within
which sport was defined as a specific practice, irreducible to a mere ritual
game or festive amusement. This amounts to asking if the appearance of
sport in the modern sense of the word is not correlative with a break (which
may have taken place in several stages) with activities which may appear to
be the 'ancestors' of modern sports, a break which is itself linked to the
constitution of a field of specific practices, endowed with its own specific
rewards and its own rules, where a whole specific competence or culture is
generated and invested (whether it be the inseparably cultural and physical
competence of the top-level athlete or the cultural competence of the sports
manager or journalist) – a culture which is in a sense esoteric, since it
separates the professional from the layman. This leads me to cast doubt on
the validity of all those studies which, by an essential anachronism, pursue
analogies between the *games* of European or non-European pre-capitalist
societies, erroneously treated as pre-sporting practices, and *sports* in the

strict sense, whose historical appearance is contemporary with the constitution of a field of production of 'sports products'. Such a comparison is only justified when, taking a path diametrically opposed to the search for 'origins', it aims, as in Norbert Elias's work, to grasp the specificity of sporting practice or, more precisely, to determine how certain pre-existing physical exercises, or others which may have received a radically new meaning and function – as radically new as in the case of simple invention, for example volleyball or basketball – become sports, defined with respect to their rewards, their rules, and also the social identity of their participants – players or spectators – by the specific logic of the 'sporting field'.

So one of the tasks of the social history of sport might be to lay the real foundations of the legitimacy of a social science of sport as a *distinct scientific object* (which is not at all self-evident), by establishing from what moment, or rather, from what set of social conditions, it is really possible to speak of sport (as opposed to the simple playing of games – a meaning that is still present in the English word 'sport' but not in the use made of the word in countries outside the Anglo-Saxon world where it was introduced *at the same time* as the radically new social practices which it designated). How was this terrain constituted, with its specific logic, as the site of quite specific social practices, which have defined themselves in the course of a specific history and can only be understood in terms of that history (e.g. the history of sports laws or the history of *records*, an interesting word that recalls the contribution which historians, with their task of *recording* and celebrating noteworthy exploits, make to the constitution of a field and its esoteric culture)?

Not possessing the historical culture needed to answer these questions, I have tried to mobilize what I knew of the history, particularly of football and rugby, so as at least to try to formulate them better. (There is of course no reason to suppose that the process of constitution of a field took the same form in all cases, and it is even likely that, as with Gerschenkron's model of economic development, the sports which came into existence later than others consequently underwent a different history, largely based on borrowings from older and therefore more 'advanced' sports.) It seems to be indisputable that the shift from games to sports in the strict sense took place in the educational establishments reserved for the 'élites' of bourgeois society, the English public schools, where the sons of aristocratic or grand-bourgeois families took over a number of *popular* – that is, *vulgar* – games, while changing their meaning and function in exactly the same way as the field of learned music transformed the folk dances – bourrées, sarabands, gavottes, etc. – which it introduced into high-art forms such as the suite.

To characterize this transformation briefly, that is, as regards its principle, we can say that the bodily exercises of the 'élite' are disconnected from the ordinary social occasions with which folk games remained associated (agrarian feasts, for example) and divested of the social (and, *a fortiori*, religious) functions still attached to a number of traditional games (such as the ritual games played in a number of pre-capitalist societies at certain turning points in the farming year). The school, the site of *schole*, leisure, is the place where practices endowed with social functions and integrated into the collective calendar are converted into *physical exercises*, activities which are an end in themselves, a sort of physical art for art's sake, governed by specific rules, increasingly irreducible to any functional necessity, and inserted into a specific calendar. The school is the site, *par excellence*, of what are called gratuitous exercises, where one acquires a distant, neutralizing disposition towards language and the social world, the very same one which is implied in the bourgeois relation to art, language and the body: gymnastics makes a use of the body which, like the scholastic use of language, is an end in itself. What is acquired in and through experience of school, a sort of retreat from the world and from real practice, of which the great boarding schools of the 'élite' represent the fully developed form, is the propensity towards activity for no purpose, a fundamental aspect of the ethos of bourgeois 'élites', who always pride themselves on disinterestedness and define themselves by an elective distance – manifested in art and sport – from material interests. 'Fair play' is the way of playing the game characteristic of those who do not get so carried away by the game as to forget that it *is* a game, those who maintain the 'role distance', as Goffman puts it, that is implied in all the roles designated for the future leaders.

The autonomization of the field of sport is also accompanied by a process of *rationalization* intended, as Weber expresses it, to ensure predictability and calculability, beyond local differences and particularisms: the constitution of a corpus of specific rules and of specialized governing bodies recruited, initially at least, from the 'old boys' of the public schools come hand in hand. The need for a body of fixed, universally applicable rules makes itself felt as soon as sporting 'exchanges' are established between different educational institutions, then between regions, etc. The relative autonomy of the field of sport is most clearly affirmed in the powers of self-administration and rule-making, based on a historical tradition or guaranteed by the State, which sports associations are recognized as having: these bodies are invested with the right to lay down the standards governing participation in the events which they organize, and they are entitled to exercise a disciplinary power (banning, fines, etc.) in order to ensure observance of the specific rules which they decree. In addition, they award specific titles, such as championship titles and also, as in England, the status of trainer.

The constitution of a field of sports practices is linked to the development of a philosophy of sport which is necessarily a *political* philosophy of sport. The theory of amateurism is in fact one dimension of an aristocratic philosophy of sport as a disinterested practice, finality without an end, analogous to artistic practice, but even more suitable than art for affirming the manly virtues of future leaders: sport is conceived as a training in courage and manliness, 'forming the character' and inculcating the 'will to win' which is the mark of the true leader, but a will to win within the rules. This is 'fair play', conceived as an aristocratic disposition utterly opposed to the plebeian pursuit of victory at all costs. (And then one would have to explore the link between the sporting virtues and the military virtues: remember the glorification of the deeds of old Etonians or Oxfordians on the field of battle or in aerial combat.) This aristocratic ethic, devised by aristocrats (the first Olympic committee included innumerable dukes, counts and lords, and all of ancient stock) and guaranteed by aristocrats, all those who constitute the self-perpetuating oligarchy of international and national organizations, was clearly adapted to the requirements of the times, and, as one sees in the works of Baron Pierre de Coubertin, incorporates the most essential assumptions of the bourgeois ethic of private enterprise, baptized *self-help* (English often serves as a euphemism). This glorification of sport as an essential component in a new type of apprenticeship requiring an entirely new educational institution, which is expressed in Coubertin's writings, particularly *L'Éducation en Angleterre* and *L'Éducation anglaise en France*, reappears in the work of Demolins, another of Frédéric Le Play's disciples. Demolins founded the École des Roches and was the author of *À quoi tient la supériorité des Anglo-Saxons* and *L'Éducation nouvelle*, in which he criticizes the Napoleonic barracks-style *lycée* (a theme which has subsequently become one of the common-places of the 'sociology of France' produced at the Paris Institut des Sciences Politiques and at Harvard). What is at stake, it seems to me, in this debate (which goes far beyond sport), is a definition of bourgeois education which contrasts with the petty-bourgeois and academic definition: it is 'energy', 'courage', 'willpower', the virtues of 'leaders' (military or industrial), and perhaps above all personal initiative, (private) 'enterprise', as opposed to knowledge, erudition, 'scholastic' submissiveness, symbolized in the great *lycée*-barracks and its disciplines, etc. In short, it would be a mistake to forget that the modern definition of sport that is often associated with the name of Coubertin is an integral part of a 'moral ideal', that is, an ethos which is that of the dominant fractions of the dominant class and is brought to fruition in the major private schools intended primarily for the sons of the heads of private industry, such as the École des Roches, the paradigmatic realization of this ideal. To value *education* over *instruction*, *character* or *willpower* over *intelligence*, *sport* over *culture*, is to affirm, within the educational universe itself, the existence of a hierarchy irreducible to the strictly scholastic hierarchy which favours the second term in those oppositions. It means, as it were, disqualifying or discrediting the values recognized by other fractions of the dominant class or by other classes (especially the intellectual fractions of the petite-bourgeoisie and the 'sons of schoolteachers', who are serious challengers to the sons of the bourgeoisie on the terrain of purely scholastic competence);

it means putting forward other criteria of 'achievement' and other principles for legitimizing achievement as alternatives to 'academic achievement'. (In a recent survey of French industrialists, I was able to demonstrate that the opposition between the two conceptions of education corresponds to two routes into managerial positions in large firms, one from the École des Roches or the major Jesuit schools via the Law Faculty or, more recently, the Institut des Sciences Politiques, the Inspection des Finances or the École des Hautes Études Commerciales, the other from a provincial *lycée* via the École Polytechnique.) The glorification of sport as the training-ground of character, etc., implies a certain anti-intellectualism. When one remembers that the dominant fractions of the dominant class always tend to conceive their relation to the dominated fraction – 'intellectuals', 'artists', 'professors' – in terms of the opposition between the male and the female, the virile and the effeminate, which is given different contents depending on the period (e.g. nowadays short hair vs. long hair; 'economic and political' culture vs. 'artistic and literary' culture, etc.), one understands one of the most important implications of the exaltation of sport and especially of 'manly' sports like rugby, and it can be seen that sport, like any other practice, is an object of struggles among the fractions of the dominant class and also among the social classes.

The field of sporting practices is the site of struggles in which what is at stake, *inter alia*, is the monopolistic capacity to impose the legitimate definition of sporting practice and of the legitimate function of sporting activity – amateurism vs. professionalism, participant sport vs. spectator sport, distinctive (élite) sport vs. popular (mass) sport; and this field is itself part of the larger field of struggles over the definition of the *legitimate body* and the *legitimate use of the body*, struggles which, in addition to trainers, managers, gymnastics masters and all the other purveyors of sporting goods and services, involve moralists and especially the clergy, doctors (in particular, health specialists), educators in the broadest sense (marriage guidance counsellors, dietitians, etc.), the arbiters of fashion and taste (couturiers, etc.). The struggles for the monopolistic power to impose the legitimate definition of this particular class of body uses, sporting uses, no doubt present some invariant features. I am thinking, for example, of the opposition, from the point of view of the definition of legitimate exercise, between the professionals in physical education (gymnasiarchs, gymnastics teachers, etc.) and doctors, that is, between two forms of specific *authority* ('pedagogic' vs. 'scientific'), linked to two sorts of *specific capital*; or the recurrent opposition between two antagonistic philosophies of the use of the body, a more ascetic one which, in the paradoxical expression *culture physique* ('physical culture'), emphasizes culture, the *antiphysis*, the counter-natural, straightening, rectitude, effort, and another, more hedonistic one which privileges nature, *physis*, reducing the culture of the body, physical culture, to a sort of *laisser-faire* or a return to *laisser-faire* – as *expression corporelle* ('physical expression' – 'anti-gymnastics') does nowadays, teaching its devotees to unlearn the superfluous disciplines and restraints imposed, among other things, by ordinary gymnastics. Since the relative autonomy of the field of bodily practices entails, by definition, a relative dependence, the development, within the field, of practices oriented towards one or the other pole, asceticism or hedonism, depends to a large extent on the state of the power relations among the fractions of the dominant class and among the social classes within the field of struggles for monopolistic definition of the legitimate body and the legitimate uses of the body. Thus the progress made by everything that is referred to as 'physical expression' can only be understood in relation to the progress, seen for example in parent–child relations and more generally in all that pertains to pedagogy, of a new variant of bourgeois morality, preached by certain rising fractions of the bourgeoisie (and petite-bourgeoisie) and favouring liberalism in child-rearing and also in hierarchical relations and in sexuality, in place of ascetic severity (denounced as 'repressive').

It was necessary to sketch in this first phase, which seems to me a decisive one, because in states of the field that are none the less quite different, sport still bears the marks of its origins. Not only does the aristocratic ideology of sport as disinterested, gratuitous activity, which lives on in the ritual themes of celebratory discourse, help to mask the true nature of an increasing proportion of sporting practices, but the practice of sports such as tennis, riding, sailing or golf doubtless owes part of its 'interest', as much nowadays as it did at the beginning, to its distinguishing function and, more precisely, to the *gains in distinction* which it brings (it is no accident that the majority of the most select, i.e. selective, clubs are organized around sporting activities which serve as a focus or pretext for elective gatherings). The distinctive gains are all the greater when the distinction between noble – distinguished and distinctive – practices, such as the 'smart' sports, and the 'vulgar' practices which popularization has made of a number of sports originally reserved for the 'élite', such as football (and to a lesser extent rugby, which will perhaps retain for some time to come a dual status and a dual social recruitment), is combined with the even sharper opposition between participation in sport and the mere consumption of sporting entertainments. We know that the probability of practising a sport beyond adolescence (and *a fortiori* beyond early manhood or into old age) declines markedly as one moves down the social hierarchy (as does the probability of belonging to a sports club), whereas the probability of watching one of the reputedly most popular sporting spectacles, such as football or rugby, on television (stadium attendance as a spectator obeys more complex laws) declines markedly as one rises in the social hierarchy.

Thus, whatever the importance of taking part in sport – particularly team sports like football – for working-class and lower-middle-class adolescents, it cannot be ignored that the so-called popular sports, cycling, football or rugby, *also* and mainly function as spectacles (which may owe part of their interest to imaginary participation based on past experience of real practice). They are 'popular' but in the sense this adjective takes on whenever it is applied to the material or cultural products of mass production, whether cars, furniture or songs. In brief, sport, which sprang from 'popular' games, that is, games produced by the people, returns to the people, like 'folk music', in the form of spectacles produced for the populace. Sport as a spectacle would appear more clearly as a mass commodity, and the organization of sporting entertainments as one branch among others of show business, if the value collectively bestowed on practising sports (especially now that sports contests have become a measure of relative national strength and hence a political stake) did not help to mask the divorce between practice and consumption and consequently the functions of simple passive consumption.

It might be wondered, in passing, whether some recent developments in sporting practices – such as doping, or the increased violence both on the pitch and on the terraces – are not in part an effect of the evolution which I have too rapidly sketched. One only has to think, for example, of all that is implied in the fact that a sport like rugby (in France – but the same is true of American football) has become, through television, a mass spectacle, transmitted far beyond the circle of present or past 'practitioners', that is, to a public very imperfectly equipped with the specific competence needed to decipher it adequately. The 'connoisseur' has schemes of perception and appreciation which enable him to see what the layman cannot see, to perceive a necessity where the outsider sees only violence and confusion, and so to find in the promptness of a movement, in the unforeseeable inevitability of a successful combination or the near-miraculous orchestration of a team strategy, a pleasure no less intense and learned than the pleasure a music-lover derives from a particularly successful rendering of a favourite work. The more superficial the perception, the less it finds its pleasure in the spectacle contemplated in itself and for itself, and the more it is drawn to the search for the 'sensational', the cult of obvious feats and visible virtuosity and, above all, the more exclusively it is concerned with that other dimension of the sporting spectacle, suspense and anxiety as to the result, thereby encouraging players and especially organizers to aim for victory at all costs. In other words, everything seems to suggest that, in sport as in music, extension of the public beyond the circle of amateurs helps to reinforce the reign of the pure professionals. When Roland Barthes, in an article entitled 'Le grain de la voix', contrasts Panzera, a French singer of the inter-war period, with Fischer-Dieskau, whom he sees as the archetypal product of middle-brow culture, he makes one think of those who contrast the inspired rugby of a Dauger or a Boniface with the 'well-oiled machinery' of the Béziers team or France captained by Fouroux. This is the viewpoint of the 'practitioner', past or present, who, as opposed to the mere consumer, the armchair musician or sportsman, recognizes a form of excellence which, as even its imperfections testify, is simply the limiting case of the competence of the ordinary amateur. In short, there is every reason to suppose that, in music as in sport, the purely passive competence, acquired without any personal performance, of publics newly won by records or television is at least a negative, that is, permissive, factor in the evolution of production (one sees, incidentally, the ambiguity of a certain style of 'ultra-left' critique: denunciation of the vices of mass production – in sport as in music – is often combined with aristocratic nostalgia for the days of amateurism).

More than by the encouragement it gives to chauvinism and sexism, it is undoubtedly through the division it makes between professionals, the virtuosi of an esoteric technique, and laymen, reduced to the role of mere consumers, a division that tends to become a deep structure of the collective consciousness, that sport produces its most decisive political effects. Sport is not the only area in which ordinary people are reduced to the role of 'fans', the extreme caricatural form of the activist, condemned to an imaginary participation which is only an illusory compensation for the dispossession they suffer at the hands of experts.

In fact, before taking further the analysis of the effects, we must try to analyse more closely the determinants of the shift whereby sport as an élite practice reserved for amateurs became sport as a spectacle produced by professionals for consumption by the masses. It is not sufficient to invoke the relatively autonomous logic of the field of production of sporting goods and services or, more precisely, the development, within this field, of a sporting entertainments industry which, subject to the laws of profitability, aims to maximize its efficiency while minimizing its risks. (This leads, in particular, to the need for specialized executive personnel and scientific management techniques that can rationally organize the training and upkeep of the physical capital of the professional players: one thinks, for example, of American football, in which the squad of trainers, doctors and public relations men is more numerous than the team of players, and which almost always serves as a publicity vehicle for the sports equipment and accessories industry.)

In reality, the development of sporting activity itself, even among working-class youngsters, doubtless results partly from the fact that sport was predisposed to fulfil, on a much larger scale, the very same functions which underlay its *invention* in the late-nineteenth-century English public schools. Even before they saw sport as a means of 'improving character' in accordance with Victorian belief, the public schools, 'total institutions' in Goffman's sense, which have to carry out their supervisory task twenty-four hours a day, seven days a week, saw sport as 'a means of filling in time', an economical way of occupying the adolescents who were their full-time responsibility. When the pupils are on the sports field, they are easy to supervise, they are engaged in 'healthy' activity and they are venting their violence on each other rather than destroying the buildings or shouting down their teachers. This is surely one factor in the spreading of sport and the growth of sports associations, which, originally organized on a *voluntary* basis, progressively received recognition and aid from the public authorities. This *extremely economical* means of mobilizing, occupying and controlling adolescents was predisposed to become an instrument and a stake in struggles between all the institutions totally or partly organized with a view to the mobilization and symbolic conquest of the masses and therefore competing for the symbolic conquest of youth. These include political parties, unions, and churches, of course, but also paternalistic bosses, who, with the aim of ensuring *complete and continuous containment* of the working population, provided their employees not only with hospitals and schools but also with stadiums and other sports facilities (a number of sports clubs were founded with the help and under the control of private employers, as is still attested today by the number of stadiums named after employers). We are familiar with the competition which has never ceased to be fought out in the various political arenas over questions of sport from the level of the village (with the rivalry between secular or religious clubs, or, more recently, the debates over the priority to be given to sports facilities) to national level (with, for example, the opposition between the Fédération du Sport de France, controlled by the Catholic Church, and the Fédération Sportive et Gymnique du Travail controlled by the left-wing parties). And indeed, in an increasingly disguised way as State recognition and subsidies increase, and with them the apparent neutrality of sports organizations and their officials, sport is an object of political struggle. This competition is one of the most important factors in the development of a social, that is, socially constituted, need for sporting practices and for all the accompanying equipment, instruments, personnel and services. Thus the imposition of sporting needs is most evident in rural areas where the appearance of facilities and teams, as with youth clubs and senior citizens' clubs nowadays, is almost always the result of the work of the village petite-bourgeoisie or bourgeoisie, which finds here an oppor-tunity to impose its political services of organization and leadership and to accumulate or maintain a political capital of renown and honourability which is always potentially convertible into political power.

It goes without saying that the popularization of sport, down from the élite schools to the mass sporting associations, is necessarily accompanied by a change in the functions which the sportsmen and their organizers assign to this practice, and also by a transformation of the very logic of sporting practices which runs parallel to the transformation of the expectations and demands of the audience which now extends far beyond the former practitioners. The exaltation of 'manliness' and the cult of 'team spirit' that are associated with playing rugby – not to mention the aristocratic ideal of 'fair play' – have a very different meaning and function for bourgeois or aristocratic adolescents in English public schools and for the sons of peasants or shopkeepers in south-west France. This is simply because, for example, a sporting career, which is practically excluded from the field of acceptable trajectories for a child of the bourgeoisie – setting aside tennis or golf – represents one of the few paths of upward mobility open to the children of the dominated classes; the sports market is to the boys' physical capital what the system of beauty prizes and the occupations to which they lead – hostess, etc. – is to the girls' physical capital; and the working-class cult of sportsmen of working-class origin is doubtless explained in part by the fact that these 'success stories' symbolize the only recognized route to wealth and fame. Everything suggests that the interests and values which practitioners from the working and lower-middle classes bring into the conduct of sports are in harmony with the corresponding requirements of professionalization (which can, of course, coexist with the appearances of amateurism) and of the rationalization of preparation for and performance of the sporting exercise that are imposed by the pursuit of maximum specific efficiency (measured in 'wins', 'titles', or 'records') combined with the minimization of risks (which we have seen is itself linked to the development of a private or State sports entertainments industry).

We have here a case of a supply, that is, the particular definition of sporting practice and entertainment that is put forward at a given moment in time, meeting a demand, that is, the expectations, interests and values that agents bring into the field, with the actual practices and entertainments evolving as a result of the permanent confrontation and adjustment between the two. Of course, at every moment each new entrant must take account of a determinate state of the division of sporting activities and entertainments and their distribution among the social classes, a state which he cannot alter and which is the result of the whole previous history of the struggles and competition among the agents and institutions engaged in the 'sporting field'. But while it is true that, here as elsewhere, the field of production helps to produce the need for its own products, none the less the logic whereby agents incline towards this or that sporting practice cannot be understood unless their dispositions towards sport, which are themselves one dimension of a particular relation to the body, are reinserted into the unity of the system of dispositions, the *habitus*, which is the basis from which lifestyles are generated (for example, it would be easy to demonstrate the homologies between the relation to the body and the relation to language that are characteristic of a class or class fraction).

In other words, faced with the statistical table representing the distribution of the various sporting practices by social class which I mentioned at the beginning, one must first consider the variations in the social significance and function that the different social classes give to the different sports. It would not be difficult to show that the different social classes do not agree as to the effects expected from bodily exercise, whether on the outside of the body (bodily *hexis*), such as the visible strength of prominent muscles which some prefer or the elegance, ease and beauty favoured by others, or inside the body, health, mental equilibrium, etc. In other words, the class variations in these practices derive not only from the variations in the factors which make it possible or impossible to meet their economic or cultural costs but also from the variations in the perception and appreciation of the immediate or deferred profits that are supposed to accrue from the different sporting practices. Thus, the different classes are very unequally attentive to the 'intrinsic' profits (real or imaginary, it does not matter much, since they are real inasmuch as they are really expected) for the body itself: Jacques Defrance shows for example that gymnastics may be asked to produce either a strong body, bearing the outward signs of strength – this is the working-class demand, which is satisfied by body-building – or a healthy body – this is the bourgeois demand, which is satisfied by a gymnastics or other sports whose function is essentially hygienic. It is no accident that the 'strong-man' was for a long time one of the most typically popular entertainments – remember the famous Dédé la Boulange who performed in the Square d'Anvers, alternating feats of strength with a mountebank's patter – or that weight-lifting, which is supposed to develop the muscles, was for many years, especially in France, the favourite working-class sport; nor is it an accident that the Olympic authorities took so long to grant official recognition to weight-lifting, which, in the eyes of the aristocratic founders of modern sport, symbolized mere strength, brutality and intellectual indigence, in short the working classes.

Similarly, the different classes are very unequally concerned about the social profits to be derived from pursuing certain sports. It can be seen, for example, that in addition to its strictly health-giving functions, golf has a *distributional significance* which, unanimously recognized and acknowledged (everyone has a practical grasp of the probability of the various classes practising the various sports), is entirely opposed to that of *pétanque*, whose purely health-giving function is perhaps not very different but which has a distributional significance very close to that of Pernod and all types of food that are not only economical but strong (in the sense of spicy) and supposed to give strength because they are heavy, fatty and spicy. There is in fact every reason to think that the logic of distinction plays a decisive part, along with spare time, in the distribution among the classes of a practice which, like *pétanque*, requires practically no economic or cultural capital, or even physical capital. Increasing steadily until it reaches its greatest frequency in the lower-middle classes, and especially among primary teachers and clerical workers in the medical services, it then declines, increasingly so as the concern to distinguish oneself from the commonplace becomes stronger, as it does among artists and members of the professions.

The same is true of those sports which, requiring only 'physical' qualities and bodily competences, the conditions for acquiring which seem to be more or less equally distributed, are equally accessible within the limits of the available time and, secondarily, the available physical energy. The probability of practising them would undoubtedly grow as one moves up the social hierarchy if it were not the case that, in accordance with a logic that is observed in other areas (photography, for example), the concern for distinction and a lack of taste for them turned away the members of the dominant class. In fact, most of the collective sports – basketball, handball, rugby, soccer – which surveys show to be strongest among clerical workers, technicians and shopkeepers, and also, no doubt, the most typically popular sports such as boxing and wrestling, combine all the reasons for repelling the members of the dominant class: the social composition of their audience, which underlines the vulgarity implied in their popularization, the values involved, such as competitiveness, and the virtues required – strength, endurance, a disposition towards violence, a spirit of 'sacrifice', docility and submission to collective discipline, the perfect antithesis of the 'role distance' implied in bourgeois roles, etc.

So everything suggests that the probability of practising the different sports depends, to a different degree for each sport, primarily on economic capital and secondarily on cultural capital and spare time; it does so through the affinity between the ethical and aesthetic dispositions associated with a particular position in the social space and the profits which, on the basis of these dispositions, appear to be offered by the various sports. The relationship between the different sports and age is more complex, since it is only defined – through the intensity of the physical effort required and the disposition towards that effort which is an aspect of class ethos – within the relationship between a sport and a class. The most important property of the 'popular' sports is the fact that they are tacitly associated with youth, which is spontaneously and implicitly credited with a sort of provisional licence expressed, among other ways, in the squandering of an overflow of physical (and sexual) energy, and that they are abandoned very early (usually at the moment of entry into adult life, marked by marriage). By contrast, the 'bourgeois' sports, mainly practised for their functions of physical maintenance and for the social profit they bring, have in common the fact that their age-limit lies far beyond youth and perhaps comes all the later the more prestigious and exclusive they are (e.g. golf).

In reality, even apart from any search for distinction, it is the relation to one's own body, a fundamental aspect of the *habitus*, which distinguishes the working classes from the privileged classes, just as, within the latter, it distinguishes fractions that are separated by the whole universe of a lifestyle. On one side, there is the instrumental relation to the body which the working classes express in all the practices centred on the body, whether in dieting or beauty care, relation to illness or medication, and which is also manifested in the choice of sports requiring a considerable investment of effort, sometimes of pain and suffering (e.g. boxing) and sometimes a gambling with the body itself (as in motor-cycling, parachute-jumping, all forms of acrobatics, and, to some extent, all sports involving fighting, among which we may include rugby). On the other side, the inclination of the privileged classes towards the 'stylization of life' is confirmed in their tendency to treat the body as an end in itself, with variants according to whether the emphasis is placed on the intrinsic functioning of the body as an organism, which leads to the macrobiotic cult of health, or on the appearance of the body as a perceptible configuration, the 'physique', that is, the body-for-others.

Everything seems to suggest that the concern to cultivate the body appears, in its most elementary form, that is, as the cult of health, often implying an ascetic exaltation of sobriety and dietetic rigour, among the lower-middle classes, who indulge particularly intensively in gymnastics – the ascetic sport *par excellence* since it amounts to a sort of training for training's sake. Gymnastics or strictly health-oriented sports like walking or jogging, which, unlike ball games, do not offer any competitive satisfaction, are highly rational and rationalized activities. This is firstly because they presuppose a resolute faith in reason and in the deferred and often intangible benefits which reason promises (such as protection against ageing, an abstract and negative advantage which only exists by reference to a thoroughly theoretical referent); secondly, because they generally only have meaning by reference to a thoroughly theoretical, abstract knowledge of the effects of an exercise which is itself often reduced, as in gymnastics, to a series of abstract movements, decomposed and reorganized by reference to a specific and technically defined end (e.g. 'the abdominals') and is opposed to the total movements of everyday situations, oriented towards practical goals just as marching, broken down into elementary movements in the sergeant-major's handbook, is opposed to ordinary walking.

Thus it is understandable that these activities encounter and fulfil the ascetic dispositions of upwardly mobile individuals who are prepared to find their satisfaction in effort itself and to accept – such is the whole meaning of their existence – the deferred gratifications that will reward their present sacrifice. The health-giving functions tend increasingly to be associated with and even subordinated to what might be called aesthetic functions, at higher levels of the social hierarchy (especially, other things being equal, among women, who are more imperatively required to submit to the norms defining what the body ought to be, not only in its perceptible configuration but also in its motion, its gait, etc.). It is no doubt among the professions and the well-established business bourgeoisie that the health-giving and aesthetic functions are most clearly combined with social functions; there, sports take their place, along with parlour games and social exchanges (receptions, dinners, etc.), among the 'gratuitous' and 'disinterested' activities which enable the accumulation of social capital. This is seen in the fact that, in the extreme form it assumes in golf, shooting, and polo in smart clubs, sporting activity tends to become a mere pretext for select encounters or, to put it another way, a technique of sociability, like bridge or dancing.

In conclusion, I will simply indicate that the principle of the transformations of sporting practices and consumption has to be sought in the relationship between changes in the supply and changes in demand.

Changes in supply (with the invention or importing of new sports or new equipment, the reinterpreting of old sports and games, etc.) arise through the competitive struggles to impose legitimate sporting practice and to win the loyalty of the ordinary practitioners (sports proselytism), struggles between the different sports and, within each sport, between the different schools or traditions (e.g. in skiing, on-piste, off-piste and cross-country), struggles between the different categories of agents involved in this competition (top-level sportsmen and women, trainers, PE teachers, equipment manufacturers, etc.). Changes in demand are one aspect of the transformation of lifestyles and therefore obey the general laws of that transformation. The correspondence that is observed between these two series of changes is no doubt to be ascribed, here as elsewhere, to the fact that the space of the producers (i.e. the field of the agents and institutions that are in a position to contribute to changes in supply) tends to reproduce, in its divisions, the divisions of the space of the consumers. In other words, the taste-makers who are able to produce or impose (or even sell) new practices or new forms of old practices (such as the 'Californian' sports or the various kinds of 'physical expression'), as well as those who defend the old practices or the old ways of practising, put into operation the dispositions and convictions that constitute a *habitus* though which a particular position in the field of specialists, and also in the social space, is expressed. They are therefore predisposed to give voice to the more or less conscious expectations of the corresponding fractions of the lay public and, by objectifying those expectations, to realize them.

16

HAUTE COUTURE AND HAUTE CULTURE

My title is not intended as a joke. I do indeed intend to talk about the relationship between *haute couture* and culture. Fashion is a very prestigious subject in the sociological tradition, at the same time as being apparently rather frivolous. The hierarchy of research areas is regarded as one of the most important areas in the sociology of knowledge, and one of the ways in which social censorships are exerted is precisely this hierarchy of objects regarded as worthy or unworthy of being studied. This is one of the very ancient themes of the philosophical tradition; and yet the old lesson of the *Parmenides*, that there are Ideas of everything, including dirt and body hair, has not been taken very far by the philosophers, who are generally the first victims of this social definition of the hierarchy of objects. I think that this preamble is not superfluous, because, if there is one thing that I want to communicate this evening, it is that there are scientific profits to be drawn from scientifically studying 'unworthy' objects.

My argument is based on the structural homology between the field of production of one particular category of luxury goods, namely fashion garments, and the field of production of that other category of luxury goods, the goods of legitimate culture such as music, poetry, philosophy and so on. It follows that when I speak of *haute couture* I shall never cease to be speaking also of *haute culture*. I shall be talking about the production of commentaries on Marx or Heidegger, the production of paintings or discourse about paintings. You may say, 'Why not talk about them directly?' Because these legitimate products are protected by their legitimacy against the scientific gaze and against the desacralization that is presupposed by the scientific study of sacred objects (I think that the sociology of culture is the sociology of religion of our day). In talking about a less well guarded subject I hope that I shall also convey more effectively what might be rejected if I were to say it about more sacred things.

My intention is to make a contribution to the sociology of intellectual production, that's to say the sociology of the intellectuals, as well as to analysis of fetishism and magic. There too, you may say, 'But why not go and study magic in "primitive" societies, rather than in the Paris fashion

Talk given to *Noroit* (Arras) in November 1974 and published in *Noroit*, 192, 1974: 1–2, 7–17, and 193–4, 1975: 2–11 scene?' I think that one of the functions of ethnological discourse is to say things that are bearable so long as they apply to remote populations, with the respect we owe them, but much less so when they are related to Western societies. At the end of his essay on magic, Marcel Mauss asks himself, 'Where is the equivalent in our society?' I would like to show that the equivalent is to be looked for in *Elle* or *Le Monde* (especially the literary page). The third topic for consideration would be: What is the function of sociology? Aren't sociologists trouble-makers who come in and destroy magical communions? Those are questions that you will be able to decide when you have heard me.

I'll start by describing very rapidly the structure of the field of production of *haute couture*. By 'field' I mean an area, a playing field, a field of objective relations among individuals or institutions competing for the same stakes. The players who are dominant in the particular field of *haute couture* are the designers who possess in the highest degree the power to define objects as rare by means of their signature, their label, those whose label has the highest price. In a field (and this is the general law of fields), the occupiers of the dominant position, those who have the most specific capital, are opposed in a whole host of ways to the newcomers, the new entrants to the field, *parvenus* who do not possess much specific capital.

The established figures have *conservation strategies*, aimed at deriving profit from progressively accumulated capital. The newcomers have *subversion strategies*, oriented towards an accumulation of specific capital which presupposes a more or less radical reversal of the table of values, a more or less revolutionary subversion of the principles of production and appreciation of the products and, by the same token, a devaluation of the capital of the established figures. Watching a TV debate between the designers Balmain and Scherrer, you would have understood, just from their diction, which one was on the 'right' and which on the 'left' (in the relatively autonomous space of the field).

(Here I must open a parenthesis: when I say 'right' and 'left', I know as I say it that the practical equivalent that each of us has – with a particular reference to the political field – of the theoretical construction that I am putting forward will compensate for the inevitable inadequacy of oral presentation. But, at the same time, I know that this practical equivalent is liable to act as a screen – because if I had only had the notions of right and left in my head to understand this, I would never have understood anything. The particular difficulty of sociology comes from the fact that it teaches things that everybody knows in a way, but which they don't want to know or cannot know because the law of the system is to hide those things from them.)

To return to the debate between Balmain and Scherrer: Balmain in very long, rather pompous sentences, defended 'French quality', creation, and so on; Scherrer spoke like a student leader in May '68, with unfinished sentences, dramatic pauses, and so on. Similarly, I've identified in the women's magazines the adjectives most often associated with the different designers. On the one hand, 'luxurious, exclusive, elegant, traditional, classic, refined, select, balanced, made to last'; on the other, 'super-chic, kitsch, funny, appealing, witty, cheeky, radiant, free, enthusiastic, structured, functional'. On the basis of the positions that the various agents or institutions occupy in the structure of the field, which correspond fairly well in this case to their seniority, it's possible to predict, or at least to understand, the aesthetic positions they will adopt, as expressed in the adjectives used to describe their products or in any other indicator. The further you move from the dominant pole towards the dominated pole, the more trousers there are in the collections; the fewer fittings; the more the grey carpeting and the monograms give way to aluminium and to sales-girls in miniskirts; the more one moves from the right bank to the left bank.

To counter the subversion strategies of the newcomers, the possessors of legitimacy, that's to say those who are in the dominant position, will always utter the vague and pompous discourse of the ineffable, of what 'goes without saying'. Like the dominant groups in the field of relations between the classes, they have conservative, defensive strategies, which can remain silent, tacit, because these people only have to be what they are in order to be *comme il faut*. By contrast, the left-bank couturiers have strategies that aim to overthrow the very principles of the game – but always in the name of the game, the spirit of the game. Their strategies of returning to the sources consist in turning against the dominant figures the very principles in the name of which they justify their domination. These struggles between the establishment and the young pretenders, the challengers, who, as in boxing, have to 'make all the running', take all the risks, are the basis of the changes which occur in the field of *haute couture*.

But the precondition for entry to the field is recognition of the values at stake and therefore recognition of the limits not to be exceeded on pain of being excluded from the game. It follows that the internal struggle can only lead to partial revolutions that can destroy the hierarchy but not the game itself. Someone who wants to achieve a revolution in the cinema or in painting says, 'That is not *real* cinema' or 'That is not *real* painting'. He pronounces anathemas, but in the name of a purer, more authentic definition of the principles in whose name the dominant dominate.

Thus each field has its own forms of revolution, and therefore its own periodization; and the breaks occurring in the different fields are not necessarily synchronized. All the same, the specific revolutions have a certain relationship with external changes. Why did Courrèges effect a revolution, and in what ways is the change brought in by Courrèges different from the change that came in every year in the form 'a bit longer, a bit shorter'? Courrèges made statements that went far beyond fashion: he was no longer talking about fashion, but about the modern woman, who had to be free, uninhibited, sporty, relaxed. In fact, I think that a specific revolution, something that marks a 'turning-point' in a given field, is the synchronization of an internal revolution and of something outside, in the wider world. What does Courrèges do? He does not talk about fashion; he talks about lifestyle and says: 'I want to dress the modern woman, who must be both active and practical.' Courrèges has a 'spontaneous' taste, that is, one produced in certain social conditions, which means that he only has to 'follow his taste' in order to respond to the taste of a new bourgeoisie that is abandoning one kind of etiquette, abandoning the style of Balmain, which is described as fashion for old ladies. It abandons that fashion for a fashion that allows the body to be seen, shows it off, and therefore presupposes that the body is tanned and athletic. Courrèges carried out a specific revolution in a specific field because the logic of the internal distinctions led him to meet up with something that already existed outside.

The permanent struggle within the field is the motor of the field. It can be seen, incidentally, that there is no contradiction between structure and history and that what defines the structure of the field as I have defined it is also the principle of its dynamics. Those who struggle for dominance cause the field to be transformed, perpetually restructured. The opposition between right and left, rearguard and avant-garde, the consecrated and the heretical, orthodoxy and heterodoxy, constantly changes in content but remains structurally identical. The new entrants are able to unseat the 'establishment' only because the implicit law of the field is distinction in all senses of the word. Fashion is the latest fashion, the latest difference. An emblem of class (in all senses) withers once it loses its distinctive power. When the miniskirt reaches the mining villages of northern France, it's time to start all over again.

The dialectic of pretension and distinction that is the basis of the transformations of the field of production reappears in the field of consumption. It characterizes what I call the competitive struggle: an unbroken, unending struggle among the classes. One class possesses a particular property, another class catches up with it, and so on. This dialectic of competition implies a race towards the same goal and implicit recognition of that goal. Pretension is always bound to lose, because, by definition, it allows the goal of the race to be imposed on it, thereby accepting the handicap that it strives to make up. What are the favourable conditions (since this cannot be done without a conversion of consciousness) in order for some of the competitors to stop running and drop out of the race – and in particular, the middle classes, those who are in the middle of the bunch? What is the moment when the probability of having one's interests satisfied by remaining in the race ceases to be greater than the probability of having them satisfied by leaving the race? I think that that is how the historical question of revolution arises.

Here, a parenthesis to deal with the traditional pairs of alternatives, such as conflict/consensus, or static/dynamic, which are perhaps the main obstacle to scientific knowledge of the social world. In fact, there is a form of struggle which implies consensus on what is at stake in the struggle and which is seen particularly clearly in the area of culture. This struggle, which takes the form of a chase (I'll have what you have, etc.), is *integrative*; it's a change that tends to ensure permanence. I'll take the example of education since it was in that area that the model became clear to me. You calculate the probabilities of access to higher education at time t, you find a distribution giving so much for working-class children, so much for the lower-middle classes, and so on; you calculate the probabilities at time $t + 1$; you find a homologous structure. The absolute values have increased but the overall form of the distribution has not changed. In fact, the translation of structure that is observed is not a mechanical phenomenon but the aggregate product of a host of small individual races ('now we can send the kid to high school', etc.), the resultant of a particular form of competition which implies recognition of the prizes at stake. Countless strategies, developed in relation to very complex systems of references, underlie the process described by the mechanical metaphor of translation. People too often think in simple dichotomies: 'Either it changes, or it doesn't change.' 'Static or dynamic.' Auguste Comte thought that way, but that is no excuse. What I try to show is that there are invariants that are the product of variation.

Like the field of the social classes and of lifestyles, the field of production has a structure that is the product of its earlier history and the principle of its subsequent history. The principle of change within it is the struggle for the monopoly of distinction, that is, the monopolistic power to impose the latest legitimate difference, the latest fashion, and this struggle ends with the progressive fall of the defeated into the past. This brings us to another problem, that of *succession*. I found a wonderful article in *Marie-Claire* entitled 'Can anyone replace Chanel?' For a long time we wondered what would happen for de Gaulle's succession; it was a problem worthy of *Le Monde*. Replacing Chanel is a problem to preoccupy *Marie-Claire*; in fact, it's exactly the same problem. It's what Max Weber called the 'routinization of charisma': how can the unique irruption which brings discontinuity into a universe be turned into a durable institution? How can the continuous be made out of the discontinuous? 'Three months ago Gaston Berthelot, who had overnight been appointed . . . ' ('appointed' is rather a bureaucratic term, the very opposite of the vocabulary of creation) . . . overnight been appointed "artistic director" . . .' (here the language of bureaucracy is yoked to the language of art) '. . ."artistic director" of the House of Chanel in January 1971, on the death of Mademoiselle, has been no less rapidly "thanked for his services". His "contract" has not been renewed. Rumour has it that he was not able to "impose his authority". It has to be said that Gaston Berthelot's natural discretion was strongly encouraged by the trustees.' Here too it becomes very interesting: he failed because he was put in conditions in which he was bound to fail: 'No interviews, no self-promotion, no fuss.' (That may seem a casual remark by a journalist, but it's crucial.) There were also the comments by his team on each of his proposals: 'Was the model faithful and respectful? No need of a designer for that; just bring out the old suits and carry on. But give them a new skirt and a different pocket – Mademoiselle would never have stood for that.' Such are the paradoxes of charismatic succession.

The field of fashion is very interesting because it occupies an intermediate position (in an abstract theoretical space, of course) between a field that is designed to organize succession, like the field of bureaucratic administration, where the agents must by definition be interchangeable, and a field in which people are radically irreplaceable, such as the field of artistic and literary creation or prophetic creation. One doesn't ask 'How is Jesus to be replaced?' or 'Who can take the place of Picasso?' It's inconceivable. Here, we have a field where there is both affirmation of the charismatic power of the creator and affirmation of the possibility of replacing the irreplaceable. Gaston Berthelot did not succeed, because he was caught between two contradictory types of demands. The first condition his successor laid down was to be allowed to talk. If you think of avant-garde painting, conceptual art, you'll realize that it is crucial for the creator to be able to create himself as a creator by producing the utterances that accredit his creative power.

The problem of succession shows that what is in question is the possibility of transmitting a creative power. Anthropologists would say a kind of mana. The couturier performs an operation of *transubstantiation*. Take a supermarket perfume at 3 francs; the label makes it a Chanel perfume worth 30 francs. The mystery is the same with Duchamp's urinal, which is constituted as an *objet d'art*, both because it is marked by a painter who has signed it and because it is exhibited in a consecrated place which, in receiving it, makes it a work of art, now transmuted economically and symbolically. The creator's signature is a mark that changes not the material nature but the social nature of the object. But this mark is a proper name – and at once the problem of succession arises, because you can only inherit common names or common functions, but not proper names.

But then, how is this power of the proper name produced? People have wondered, for example, how it is that the painter, for example, is endowed with the power to create value. The easiest, most obvious argument has been given in reply: the uniqueness of the work. In fact, however, what is involved is not the rarity of the product, but *the rarity of the producer*. But how is that produced?

We need to go back to Mauss's essay on magic. Mauss starts by asking, 'What are the particular properties of magical operations?' He sees that that won't work. Then he asks, 'What are the specific properties of magical representations?' He eventually finds that the motor is belief, which refers him back to the group. In my language, what makes the power of the producer is the field, that is, the system of relations as a whole. The energy is the field. What Dior mobilizes is something that is not definable outside of the field; what they all mobilize is what the field produces, that is, a power based on faith in *haute couture*. And the higher they are placed in the hierarchy which structures the field, the more of that power they can mobilize.

If what I'm saying is true, then Courrèges's criticisms of Dior, or Hechter's attacks on Courrèges and Scherrer, all help to build up the power of Courrèges, Scherrer, Hechter and Dior. The two extremes of the field agree at least in saying that Retro and girls who dress any old how are all very nice, very pretty, but only up to a point. For what are girls who buy their clothes at jumble sales doing? They are challenging the monopoly of the legitimate manipulation of the sacred in matters of fashion, just as heretics challenge the priestly monopoly of legitimate reading of Scripture. If people start challenging the monopoly of legitimate reading, if any Tom, Dick or Harriet can read the Gospel or make dresses, then the specialist field is destroyed. That is why revolt within the field always has its limits. Writers' quarrels always have as their boundary respect for literature.

What makes the system work is what Mauss called collective belief. I would rather call it collective misrecognition. Mauss said of magic, 'A society always pays itself in the counterfeit coin of its own dream.' That means that in this game one has to play the game: those who mislead are misled, and the greatest misleaders are the most misled, the greatest mystifiers are the most mystified. To play the game, one has to believe in the ideology of creation and, if you're a fashion journalist, it is not advisable to have a sociological view of the world.

What makes the value, the magic, of the label, is the collusion of all the agents of the system of production of sacred goods. This collusion is, of course, perfectly unconscious. The circuits of consecration are all the more powerful when they are long, complex and hidden even from the eyes of those who take part in and benefit from them. Everyone knows the example of Napoleon taking the crown from the hands of the Pope and placing it on his own head. That was a very short cycle of consecration, with very limited power to induce misrecognition. An effective cycle of consecration is one in which A consecrates B, who consecrates C, who consecrates D . . . who consecrates A. The more complicated the cycle is, the more invisible it is, the more its structure can be misrecognized, and the greater the effect of belief. (One ought to analyse in this light the circular circulation of flattering reviews or the ritual exchange of citations.) For a 'native', whether producer or consumer, the system acts as a screen. Between Chanel and her label, there is a whole system, which Chanel understands better than anyone, and at the same time less well than anyone.

Further reading

For further discussion, see Bourdieu, P. (1975) 'Le couturier et sa griffe, contribution à une théorie de la magie', *Actes de la recherche en sciences sociales*, 1: 7–36.

17

BUT WHO CREATED THE 'CREATORS'?

Sociology and art do not make good bedfellows. That's the fault of art and artists, who are allergic to everything that offends the idea they have of themselves: the universe of art is a universe of belief, belief in gifts, in the uniqueness of the uncreated creator, and the intrusion of the sociologist, who seeks to understand, explain, account for what he finds, is a source of scandal. It means disenchantment, reductionism, in a word, vulgarity or (it amounts to the same thing) sacrilege: the sociologist is someone who, just as Voltaire expelled kings from history, wants to expel artists from the history of art. But it's also the fault of the sociologists, who have done their best to confirm received ideas about sociology, and especially the sociology of art and literature.

The first received idea is that sociology can give an account of cultural consumption but not of cultural production. Most general accounts of the sociology of cultural products accept this distinction, which is a purely social one. It tends in fact to reserve a separate, sacred space and a privileged treatment for the work of art and its uncreated 'creator', while abandoning to sociology the consumers, that's to say the inferior, even repressed aspect (especially as regards its economic dimension) of intellectual and artistic life. And research aimed at determining the social factors of cultural practice (visits to museums, theatres or concerts, etc.) gives apparent confirmation to this distinction, which is based on no theoretical foundation. In fact, as I shall try to show, the most specific feature of production, that is to say the production of value, cannot be understood unless one takes into account simultaneously the space of producers and the space of consumers.

Second received idea: that sociology – and its favoured instrument, statistics – belittles and crushes, flattens and trivializes artistic creation; that it sets the great and the small on the same footing, at all events fails to grasp what makes the genius of the greatest artists. Here too, and probably more clearly, the sociologists have largely proved their critics right. I shall not dwell on literary statistics, which, both in the inadequacy of its methods and

Talk given at the École Nationale Supérieure des Arts Décoratifs, Paris, April 1980, published in *Art: sur 10 ans, aujourd'hui, 1981*, Paris: Ministère de la Culture, 1981: 71–84 the poverty of its results, dramatically confirms the most pessimistic views of the guardians of the literary temple. I shall hardly discuss the tradition of Lukács and Goldmann, which tries to relate the content of the literary work to the social characteristics of the class that is assumed to be its privileged audience. This approach, which, in its most caricatural forms, subordinates the writer or artist to the constraints of a milieu or the direct demands of a clientele, succumbs to a naïve teleology or functionalism, directly deducing the work from the function that is alleged to be socially assigned to it. Through a kind of *short circuit*, it abolishes the specific logic of the space of artistic production.

In fact, on this point too, the 'believers' are entirely right in opposition to reductive sociology when they insist on the autonomy of the artist and, in particular, on the autonomy that results from the specific history of art. It is true that, as Malraux put it, 'art imitates art' and that works of art cannot be explained purely in terms of demand, that is, in terms of the aesthetic and ethical expectations of the various fractions of the audience. But that does not mean that one is confined to the *internal history of art*, the sole authorized complement of the *internal reading of the work of art*.

The sociology of art and literature in its ordinary form in fact forgets what is essential, namely the universe of artistic production, a social universe having its own traditions, its own laws of functioning and recruitment, and therefore its own history. The autonomy of art and the artist, which the hagiographic tradition accepts as self-evident in the name of the ideology of the work of art as 'creation' and the artist as uncreated creator, is nothing other than the (relative) autonomy of what I call a *field*, an autonomy that is established step by step, and under certain conditions, in the course of history. The specific object of the sociology of cultural works is neither the individual artist (or any purely statistical set of individual artists), nor the relationship between the artist (or, which amounts to the same thing, the artistic school) and any particular social group conceived either as the efficient cause or determining principle of the contents and forms of expression or as the final cause of artistic production, that is, as a demand, with the history of contents and forms being *directly* attached to the history of the dominant groups and their struggles for domination. In my view, the sociology of cultural products must take as its object the whole set of relationships (objective ones and also those effected in the form of interactions) *between the artist and other artists*, and beyond them, the whole set of agents engaged in the production of the work, or, at least, of the *social value* of the work (critics, gallery directors, patrons, etc.). It is opposed both to a positivist description of the social characteristics of the producers (early upbringing, education, etc.) and to a sociology of reception which (as Antal does for the Italian art of the fourteenth and fifteenth centuries) directly relates works to the conception of life of the different fractions of the audience of patrons, that is, to 'society considered in its capacity for reception with respect to art'. In fact, most of the time, these two perspectives merge, as if it were assumed that artists are predisposed by their social origin to sense and satisfy a certain social demand (it is remarkable that, in terms of this logic, the analysis of the *content* of works of art takes precedence – it is even true of Antal – over analysis of the *form*, that is, of what *specifically* belongs to the producer).

It can moreover be pointed out that the short-circuit effect is not found only among the standard whipping-boys of the champions of pure aesthetics, like poor Hauser, or even in a Marxist as concerned for distinction as Adorno (when he writes about Heidegger), but also in one of those who have been most eager to denounce 'vulgar sociologism' and 'deterministic materialism', Umberto Eco. In *The Open Work*, apparently on the basis of the idea that there is a unity among all the cultural works of an epoch, and with the aid of quite arbitrary analogies, he directly relates the properties that he ascribes to the 'open work', such as overt plurivocality, deliberate unpredictability, etc., to the properties of the world as presented by science.

The sociology of works of art, as I conceive it, rejects these different ways of ignoring *production* itself. It takes as its object the field of cultural production and, inseparably from this, the relationship between the field of production and the field of consumers. The social determinisms of which the work of art bears the traces are exerted partly through the producer's *habitus*, referring back to the social conditions of his production as a social subject (family, etc.) and as a producer (schooling, professional contacts, etc.), and partly through the social demands and constraints inscribed in the *position* he occupies in a particular, more or less autonomous, field of production.

What is called 'creation' is the encounter between a socially constituted *habitus* and a particular position that is already instituted or *possible* in the division of the labour of cultural production. The labour through which the artist makes his work and, inseparably from this, makes himself as an artist (and, when it is part of the demands of the field, as an original, individual artist) can be described as the dialectical relationship between his 'post', which often exists prior to him and outlives him (entailing obligations, such as 'the artist's life', attributes, traditions, modes of expression, etc.), and his *habitus*, which more or less totally predisposes him to occupy that post or – and this may be one of the prerequisites inscribed in the post – more or less completely to transform it.

In short, the producer's *habitus* is never entirely the product of his post – except perhaps in some craft traditions where family training (and therefore the conditionings of the class of origin) and professional training are completely merged with one another. Conversely, one can never move directly from the social characteristics of the producer – his social origin – to the characteristics of his product: the dispositions linked to a particular social origin – plebeian or bourgeois – may express themselves in very different forms, while conserving a family resemblance, in different fields.

One only has to compare, for examples, the two parallel couples of the plebeian and the patrician, Rousseau and Voltaire or Dostoevsky and Tolstoy. If the post makes the *habitus* (more or less completely), a *habitus* that is made in advance (more or less completely) for the post (through the mechanisms determining vocation and co-option) helps to make the post. And this is probably increasingly true, the greater the distance between its social conditions of production and the social demands inscribed in the post and also the greater the degree of liberty and space for innovation explicitly inscribed in the post. There are those who are made for taking up ready-made positions and those who are made for making new positions. Explaining this would require a long analysis, and I simply want to indicate here that it's especially when trying to understand intellectual or artistic revolutions that one needs to remember that the autonomy of the field of production is a partial autonomy which does not exclude dependence. Specific revolutions, which overthrow the power relations within a field, are only possible in so far as those who import new dispositions and want to impose new positions find, for example, support outside the field, in the new audiences whose demands they both express and produce.

Thus, the originating subject of a work of art is neither an individual artist – the apparent cause – nor a social group (such as the banking and commercial bourgeoisie that rose to power in Quattrocento Florence, according to Antal, or the *noblesse de robe*, in Goldmann's theory). Rather, it is the *field of artistic production as a whole* (which stands in a relation of relative autonomy, greater or lesser depending on the period and the society, with respect to the groups from which the consumers of its products are recruited, i.e. the various fractions of the ruling class). Sociology or social history cannot understand anything about a work of art, least of all what makes its *singularity*, when it takes as its object an author or a work in isolation. In fact, all single-author studies that try to get beyond hagiography and anecdote are led to consider the field of production as a whole, but because they generally fail to take on that work of constructing the field as an explicit project, they most often do so in an imperfect and partial way. And, contrary to what might be thought, statistical analysis does no better, since, in grouping authors in broad pre-constructed categories (schools, generations, genres, etc.), it destroys all the pertinent differences whereas a preliminary analysis of the structure of the field would show that certain positions (especially the *dominant* ones, such as the position Sartre occupied in the French intellectual field between 1945 and 1960) may only have *place for one*, and that the corresponding classes may contain just one person, which is a challenge for statistics.

So the subject of the work is a *habitus* in relationship with a 'post', a position, that is, with a field. To show this and, I hope, demonstrate it, I'd need to reproduce here the analyses I've devoted to Flaubert, in which I tried to show how the real key to the Flaubertian project, which Sartre tries desperately, and interminably, to understand, lies outside the individual,

Flaubert, in the objective relationship between, on the one hand, a *habitus* shaped in certain social conditions (defined by the 'neutral' position of the professions, the 'capacities' as they were called, within the dominant class and by Gustave's position, as a child, within his family, in terms of his birth rank and his relation to the educational system) and, on the other hand, a particular position in the field of literary production, this itself being situated in a particular position in the field of the dominant class.

To be a little more specific: Flaubert, as an advocate of art for art's sake, occupies a *neutral* position in the literary field, defined by a twofold negative relationship (which he experienced as a twofold refusal), to 'social art' on the one hand and 'bourgeois art' on the other. This field, itself located in a *dominated* position in the field of the dominant class (hence the denunciation of the 'bourgeois' and the recurrent dream of a clerisy on which the artists of the time generally agreed), is thus organized in accordance with a structure homologous with that of the dominant class as a whole (this homology being, as we shall see, the principle of an automatic, and not cynically pursued, adjustment of the products to the various categories of consumers).

This would need to be developed. But it is immediately clear that, on the basis of such an analysis, one *understands* the logic of some of the most fundamental properties of Flaubert's *style*. I'm thinking, for example, of *discours indirect libre*, which Bakhtin interprets as the mark of an ambivalent relationship to the groups whose thoughts he relates, a kind of hesitation between the temptation to identify with them and the concern to keep his distance. I'm also thinking of the chiastic structure that reappears obsessively in his novels, and even more clearly in his drafts, in which Flaubert expresses, in a transformed and 'negated' form, the dual relationship of twofold negation which sets him, as an artist, against both the 'bourgeois' and the 'populace', and, as a 'pure' artist, against 'bourgeois art' and 'social art'.

Having thus established Flaubert's 'post', his position in the division of literary labour (and therefore in the division of the work of domination), we can turn back again to the social conditions of production of the *habitus* and ask what Flaubert had to be in order to occupy and (simultaneously) produce the 'post' of 'art for art's sake' and *create* the Flaubert position. We can try to establish what are the pertinent features of the social conditions of the production of Gustave (e.g. the role of 'idiot of the family' so well analysed by Sartre) which will enable us to understand how he was able to fulfil and make the post of Flaubert.

Contrary to what the functionalist approach would suggest, the adjustment of production to consumption results mainly from the structural homology between the space of production (the artistic field) and the field of consumers (i.e. the field of the dominant class). The internal divisions of the field of production are reproduced in an automatically (and also to some extent consciously) differentiated supply which meets the automatically (and also consciously) differentiated demands of the various categories of consumers. Thus, quite apart from any pursuit of adjustment or any direct subordination to a demand expressly formulated (through commissions or patronage), each class of clients can find products to its taste and each class of producers has some chance of finding consumers for its products, at least in the long run (which may sometimes mean posthumously).

In fact, most acts of production function in accordance with a logic in which two birds are killed with one stone. When a producer, for example the theatre critic of *Le Figaro*, produces products adjusted to the taste of his audience (which is almost always the case – he says so himself), it's not that he has tried to flatter the taste of his readers (we can believe him when he says this), or obeyed aesthetic or political directives, or responded to warnings from his editor, his readers or the government (all of which are presupposed by formulae such as 'capitalist lackey' or 'spokesman of the bourgeoisie', of which the standard theories are more or less subtly euphemized versions). In fact, having chosen *Le Figaro*, because it felt right for him, and having been chosen by its editors because he felt right for them, he only has to give free rein to his taste (which, in the theatre, has clear political implications), or rather to his distastes (taste almost always being a distaste for other people's tastes), to the loathing he feels for the plays (as he well knows) his colleague and rival at *Le Nouvel Observateur* will infallibly enjoy, in order to satisfy, as if by a miracle, the taste of his readers (who are to the readers of *Le Nouvel Observateur* as he is to its theatre critic). And he will bring them in addition something that is expected of a professional, namely an intellectual's riposte to another intellectual, a critique, which will reassure the 'bourgeois', of the highly sophisticated arguments with which the intellectuals justify their taste for the avant-garde.

The correspondence that is established *objectively* between the producer (artist, critic, journalist, philosopher, etc.) and his audience is clearly not the product of a conscious pursuit of adjustment, conscious and self-interested transactions and calculated concessions to the demands of the audience. Nothing can be understood about a work of art, not even its informative content, its themes and theses or what is loosely called its 'ideology', by relating it directly to a group. This relationship functions only as an additional and almost accidental extra, through the relationship that a producer has – on the basis of his position in the space of positions constituting the field of production – with the space of the aesthetic and ethical postures that are effectively possible at a given moment, in view of the relatively autonomous history of the artistic field. This space of aesthetic and ethical positions, which is the product of a historical accumulation, is the common system of references in relation to which all those who enter the field are objectively defined. What makes the unity of an epoch is not so much a common culture as the common set of problems, which is nothing other than the set of aesthetic/ethical 'positions' attached to the set of positions marked out in the field. There is no other criterion of the existence of an intellectual, an artist or a school than his or its capacity to win recognition as holding a position in the field, a position in relation to which the others have to situate and define themselves; and the 'problem area' of the time is nothing other than the set of these *relations* between positions, which are also, necessarily, relations between aesthetic and ethical 'positions'. Concretely, that means that the emergence of an artist, a school, a party or a movement as a position within a field (an artistic, political or any other field) is marked by the fact that its existence 'poses problems' for the occupiers of the other positions, that the theses it puts forward become an object of struggles, that these theses provide one of the terms of the major oppositions around which the struggle is organized (for example, left/right, clear/obscure, scientism/anti-scientism, etc.).

Thus the proper object of a science of art, literature or philosophy can be nothing other than this structure of two inseparable spaces, the space of the products and the space of the producers (artists or writers, and also critics, publishers, etc.), which are like two translations of the same sentence. The autonomizing of works is unjustifiable both theoretically and practically. For example, any attempt at a socio-logical analysis of a discourse which is restricted to the work itself is denied the necessary movement which swings back and forth between the thematic or stylistic features of the work which reveal the social position of the producer (his/her interests, view of society, etc.) and the characteristics of the social position of the producer which cast light on his/her stylistic 'choices', and vice versa. In short, for a full understanding of even the most strictly 'internal' features of the work, one has to abandon the opposition between internal analysis (linguistic or any other) and external analysis.

Furthermore, the scholastic opposition between structure and history also has to be superseded. The set of 'problems' that is constituted in the field in the form of authors and 'key works', the beacons by which others situate themselves, is history through and through. The reaction against the past, which makes history, is also what makes the historicity of the present, negatively defined by what it rejects. In other words, the refusal which is the principle of change supposes and proposes and thereby recalls to the present, by opposing it, what it is opposed to. For example, the reaction against anti-scientific and individualistic Romanticism, which led the Parnassians to valorize science and integrate its achievements into their work, led them to find in Quinet's *Le Génie des religions* (or in the work of Burnouf, the restorer of the mythic epics of India) the antithesis and antidote to Chateaubriand's *Génie du Christianisme*, just as it inclined them to the cult of ancient Greece, the antithesis of the Middle Ages and the symbol of the perfect form through which, in their eyes, poetry is akin to science.

I'm tempted to digress here. To remind historians of ideas who believe that what circulates in the intellectual field, and especially between intellectuals and artists, is *ideas*, I shall simply point out that the Parnassians associated Greece not only with the idea of perfect form, exalted by Gautier, but also the idea of *harmony*, which was part of the spirit of the age – it's also found in the theories of social reformers like Fourier. What circulates in a field, and especially between specialists of different arts, is stereotypes, which are more or less polemical and reductive (and which the producers have to reckon with); titles of works that everybody talks about (e.g. *Romances sans paroles*, a title of Verlaine's taken from Mendelssohn); vogue words and the ill-defined ideas they convey (e.g. '*saturnien*', or the theme of *Les Fêtes galantes*, launched by the Goncourts). In short, one might wonder if what is common to all the producers of cultural goods in a given period is not this kind of cultural vulgate, a mass of smart commonplaces that the tribe of essayists, critics and semi-intellectual journalists produces and peddles and which is inseparable from a style and a mood. This vulgate, which is clearly the most 'fashionable', dated and perishable aspect of the production of an epoch, is also no doubt what is most common to its whole set of cultural producers.

I'll return to the example of Quinet, which shows one of the most important properties of all fields of production, namely the permanent presence of the past of the field, which is endlessly recalled even in the very breaks which dispatch it to the past. These reminders, like direct evocations, references, allusions, etc., are so many nudges and winks addressed to other producers and to those consumers who define themselves as legitimate consumers by showing themselves capable of picking them up. *Le Génie des religions* defines itself in opposition to *Génie du Christianisme*. Distinction, which pushes the past into the past, presupposes it and perpetuates it in the very gap it creates with respect to it. One of the most fundamental properties of fields of cultural production lies in the fact that the acts performed there and the products produced there contain practical (and sometimes explicit) reference to the history of the field. For example, what separates the writings of Jünger or Spengler on technology, time and history from what Heidegger writes on the same subjects is the fact that, by situating himself in the problematics of philosophy, and therefore in the philosophical field, Heidegger reintroduces the whole history of philosophy of which those problematics are the outcome. Similarly, Luc Boltanski has shown that the construction of a field of the strip cartoon was accompanied by the development of a body of cartoon historians and, simultaneously, the appearance of works making 'scholarly' reference to the history of the genre. The same could be shown for the history of the cinema.

It is true that 'art imitates art', or, more precisely, that art is born of art, and usually the art with which it contrasts. And the autonomy of the artist finds its basis not in the miracle of his creative genius but in the social product of the social history of a relatively autonomous field – methods, techniques, styles, etc. By defining the means and the limits of the thinkable, the history of the field causes what happens in the field to be never the direct *reflection* of external constraints or demands, but rather a symbolic expression, *refracted* by the whole specific logic of the field. The history that is deposited in the very structure of the field and also in the *habitus* of the agents is the prism which intervenes between the world external to the field and the work of art, causing all external events – economic crisis, political reaction, scientific revolution – to undergo refraction.

To conclude, I would like to complete the circle and return to the starting-point, the antinomy between art and sociology, and take seriously, not the denunciation of scientific sacrilege, but what is implied in that denunciation, that is, the sacred character of art and the artist. I think that the sociology of art has to take as its object not only the social conditions of production of the producers (i.e. the social determinants of the training or selection of artists) but also the social conditions of production of the field of production as the site of work tending (and not *aiming*) to produce the artist as a producer of sacred objects, fetishes; or, which amounts to the same thing, producing the work of art as an object of belief, love and aesthetic pleasure.

To make things clearer, I'll take the example of *haute couture*, which provides an enlarged image of what happens in the world of painting. We know that the magic of the designer's label, stuck on any object, perfume, shoes or even, it's a real example, a bidet, can multiply its value in an extraordinary way. This is indeed a magical, alchemical act, since the social nature and value of the object are changed without any change in its physical or (thinking of perfume) its chemical nature. Painting, since Duchamp, has provided countless examples, of which you are all aware, of magical acts which, like those of the couturier, so clearly owe their value to the social value of the person who produces them that the question to ask is not what the artist creates, but who creates the artist, that is, the transmuting power that the artist exercises. It's the question that Marcel Mauss came round to when, in despair, after seeking all the possible foundations of the magician's power, he finally asks who makes the magician. You may raise the objection that Duchamp's urinal and bicycle (and we've seen better still, since then) are exceptional limiting cases. But one only has to analyse the relationship between the 'authentic' original and the fake, the replica or the copy, or again the effects of *attribution* (the main, if not exclusive aim of traditional art history, which perpetuates the tradition of the connoisseur and the expert) on the social and economic value of the work, to see that what makes the value of the work is not the rarity (the uniqueness) of the product but the rarity of the producer, manifested by the *signature*, the equivalent of the designer label, that is, the collective belief in the value of the producer and his product. I'm thinking of Warhol, who, moving on from the example of Jasper Jones and his Ballantine's beer bottle in bronze, signs fifteen-cent cans of Campbell's soup and sells them at six dollars.

The analysis would need to be spelled out in more detail. Here I shall simply point out that one of the main tasks of art history would be to describe the genesis of a field of artistic production capable of producing the artist as such (as opposed to the craftsman). This would not mean raising yet again, as has been done, obsessively, in the social history of art, the question of when and how the artist emerged from the status of craftsman. It means describing the economic and social conditions of the constitution of an artistic field capable of underpinning belief in the quasi-godlike powers attributed to the modern artist. In other words, it's not just a matter of destroying what Walter Benjamin called 'the fetish of the name of the master'. (That's one of the easy acts of sacrilege by which sociology has too often been tempted. Like black magic, sacrilegious inversion contains a form of recognition of the sacred. The joys of desacralizing prevent one from taking seriously, and therefore explaining, the fact of sacralization and the sacred.) The point is to take note of the fact that the name of the master is indeed a fetish and to describe the social conditions of possibility of the figure of the artist as master, that is, as the producer of the fetish of the work of art. In a word, the aim would be to describe the historical constitution of the field of artistic production, which as such, produces belief in the value of art and in the value-creating power of the artist. And that would give a basis for what I posited at the beginning, namely that the 'subject' of artistic production and its product is not the artist but the whole set of agents who are involved in art, are interested in art, have an interest in art and the existence of art, who live on and for art, the producers of works regarded as artistic (great and small, famous – i.e. 'celebrated' – or unknown), critics, collectors, go-betweens, curators, art historians, and so on.

So we've come full circle. And we are caught inside.

Further reading

For further discussion, see Bourdieu, P. (1975) 'La critique du discours lettré', *Actes de la recherche en science sociales*, 5–6: 4–8; (1980) 'The production of belief: contribution to an economy of symbolic goods', *Media, Culture and Society*, 2(3): 261–93 (reprinted in (1986), *Media, Culture and Society: A Critical Reader*, London: Sage, 131–63); (1980) 'Lettre à Paolo Fossati à propos de la *Storia dell'arte italiana*', *Actes de la recherche en science sociales*, 31: 90–2; (1971) 'Champ du pouvoir, champ intellectuel et habitus de classe', *Scolies*, Cahiers de recherches de l'École Normale Supérieure, 1: 7–26; (1987) 'The invention of the artist's life', *Yale French Studies*, 73: 75–103; (1988) *L'Ontologie politique de Martin Heidegger*, Paris: Éditions de Minuit.

18

PUBLIC OPINION DOES NOT EXIST

I would first like to make it clear that it is not my intention to denounce opinion polls in a mechanical and casual way, but to make a rigorous analysis of their functioning and their functions. That presupposes calling into question the three postulates that they implicitly depend on.

Every opinion survey assumes that everyone can have an opinion; in other words, that producing an opinion is something available to all. At the risk of offending a naïvely democratic sentiment, I would contest this first premise. Secondly: it is assumed that all opinions are of equal value. I think it can be shown that this is untrue and that the cumulation of opinions that do not all have the same strength leads to the production of meaningless artefacts. The third implicit postulate is this: putting the same question to everyone assumes that there is a consensus on what the problems are, in other words that there is agreement on the questions that are worth asking. These three postulates, it seems to me, entail a whole series of distortions that are found even when all the conditions of methodological rigour are fulfilled in collecting and analysing the data.

Various technical objections are often made against opinion polls. For example, the representativeness of the samples is questioned. I think that in the present state of the tools available to the polling organizations, this objection is unfounded. It is complained that they ask biased questions or bias the answers by the way they are formulated; there is rather more truth in this, and it is often the case that the answer is induced by the way the question is asked. For example, an elementary principle of questionnaire design that requires one to 'give scope' for every possible answer is often violated by omitting a possible option from the questions or the suggested answers, or the same option may be offered several times in different guises. There are all kinds of biases of this type, and it would be interesting to enquire into the social conditions of the appearance of these biases. Most of the time they result from the conditions in which the people who design the questionnaires have to work; but they are often due to the fact that the problems defined by the opinion poll institutes are subordinated to a particular type of demand. For example, when we undertook to analyse a major national survey on what the French thought of their education system, we examined all the questions asked about education in the

Talk given to *Noroit* (Arras) in January 1971, reprinted in *Les Temps modernes*, 318, 1973: 1292–1309 archives of a number of polling agencies. We found that more than two hundred questions had been asked about education since May 1968, as against only twenty or so between 1960 and 1968. This means that the problem areas that present themselves to a polling organization are closely linked to the political climate of the day and dominated by a particular type of social demand. The question of education, for example, cannot be raised by a polling institute until it becomes a political problem. One immediately sees the differences between these institutions and academic research centres, which generate their problematics, perhaps not in an unclouded sky, but at least with much greater distance from social demand in its direct and immediate form.

A rapid statistical analysis of the questions asked showed that the great majority of them were directly linked to the political preoccupations of professional politicians. If we were to play a parlour game this evening and I were to ask you to write down the five questions that you thought most urgent as regards education, we would certainly arrive at a list very different from the one we derived from noting the questions actually asked by the pollsters. The question (or variants of it) 'Should politics be brought into schools?' was very often asked, whereas the question 'Should curricula be changed?' or 'Should teaching methods be changed?' was asked only rarely. The same with 'Do teachers need retraining?' All of these are important questions, from another point of view at least.

The problematics offered by the polling agencies are subordinated to political interests, and this very strongly governs both the meaning of the answers and the meaning given to them on publication of the findings. At present, the opinion poll is an instrument of political action: perhaps its most important function is to impose the illusion that there is something called public opinion in the sense of the purely arithmetical total of individual opinions; to impose the illusion that it is meaningful to speak of the average of opinions or the average opinion. The 'public opinion' that is manifested on the front pages of newspapers ('60 per cent of French people are in favour of . . .') is a pure and simple *artefact* whose function is to disguise the fact that the state of opinion at a given time is a system of forces, tensions, and that nothing more inadequately expresses the state of opinion than a percentage.

We know that every exercise of power is accompanied by a discourse aimed at legitimizing the power of the group that exercises it; we can even say that it is characteristic of every power relation that it takes on its full force only in so far as it disguises the fact that it is a power relation. In a word, the politician is someone who says 'God is on our side'. The modern equivalent of 'God is on our side' is 'Public opinion is on our side'. That is the fundamental effect of the opinion poll: it creates the idea that there is such a thing as a unanimous public opinion, and so legitimizes a policy and strengthens the power relations that underlie it or make it possible.

Having said at the beginning what I wanted to say at the end, I shall try to indicate very rapidly what are the operations through which this *consensus effect* is produced. The first operation, which starts from the premise that everyone must have an opinion, consists in ignoring the non-responses and 'don't knows', labelled in France 'no answer'. For example, you ask people 'Are you in favour of the Pompidou government?' You record 30 per cent 'no answer', 20 per cent 'yes' and 50 per cent 'no'. You can say there are more against than for, and then there are 30 per cent left over. Or you can recalculate the percentages of 'yes' and 'no', leaving out the 'no answers'. This simple choice is a theoretical operation with enormous implications, which I would like to examine with you.

Eliminate the 'no answers'. That's what is done in an election where there are blank or void voting slips. It means imposing the implicit philosophy of an election on an opinion survey. Looking closer, it can be seen that there are generally more 'no answers' among women than men and that the gap between women and men rises as the questions become more directly political. A further observation: the more the question deals with problems of knowledge and information, the greater is the gap between the 'no answers' of the better educated and the less educated. By contrast, when the questions deal with ethical problems, the 'no answers' vary little in relation to education (for example: 'Should parents be severe with their children?'). Again, the more a question raises conflictual problems, touches on a site of contradictions, generates tensions for a particular category (e.g. the situation in Czechoslovakia after 1968 for people who vote Communist), the greater the number of 'no answers' in that category. As a result, simple statistical analysis of failure to answer provides information both on what the question means and on the category in question, the latter being defined as much by its *probability of having an opinion* as by its conditional probability of having an opinion for or against.

Scientific analysis of opinion polls shows that there exists practically no catch-all problem: no question which is not reinterpreted in relation to the interests of the people to whom the question is posed. Thus the first imperative in evaluating a poll is to ask what question the different categories of people thought they were answering. One of the most pernicious effects of opinion surveys is to put people in a position where they must answer a question they have never thought about. Questions having to do with moral issues, for example, the punishment of children, relations between teachers and pupils, and so on, are problems which are increasingly perceived as ethical problems as one moves down the social hierarchy, but which can be political problems for the upper classes. One of the distorting effects of surveys is the transformation of ethical responses into political responses by the simple imposition of a particular problematic.

In fact, there are several principles which can be used to generate a response. First of all, there is what could be called 'political competence', a notion that corresponds to a definition of politics which is both arbitrary and legitimate, both dominant and concealed as such. This political competence is not universally distributed. It varies, roughly speaking, with level of education. In other words, the probability of having an opinion on all the questions which presuppose a certain political knowledge can be compared to the probability of going to a museum. Some astonishing variations can be found: whereas a student involved in a far-left movement perceives forty-five different divisions to the left of the Parti Socialiste Unifié, a middle-level executive sees none at all. In the political scale (far left, left, centre left, centre, centre right, right, far right, etc.) which 'political science' polls use as if it were self-evident, certain social categories make intensive use of a very small sector of the extreme left; others use only the centre, while still others use the whole range. An election is in the end the aggregation of totally different spaces; people who measure in centimetres are added together with those who measure in kilometres, or to use an image familiar to teachers, those who mark on a scale of 0 to 20 with those who use only 9 to 11. Competence is measured, among other things, by the degree of refinement of one's perception (the same is true of aesthetics, where some people can distinguish the five or six stages in the development of a single painter).

This comparison can be pushed even further. In aesthetic perception, there is a prerequisite: people must first think of the work of art as a work of art, and once they have done so, they need to have perceptual categories in order to construct and structure it, etc. Now, take a question formulated in the following way: 'Are you for directive or non-directive child-rearing?' For some people, this can be constituted as a political question, the representation of the parent–child relationship being integrated into a systematic vision of society; for others it is purely a moral question. In the questionnaire I mentioned earlier, in which we asked people 'For you, is it political or not to go on strike, wear long hair, participate in a rock festival, etc?', very great variations by social class emerged. The first condition for responding adequately to a political question is therefore to be capable of seeing it as political; the second, once the question has been constituted as political, is to be capable of applying political categories to it, categories which may be more or less adequate, more or less refined, etc. These are the specific conditions for the production of opinions, conditions which opinion surveys assume to be universally and uniformly fulfilled when they first postulate that everyone can produce an opinion.

The second principle according to which people may produce an opinion is what I call 'class ethos' (rather than 'class ethic'), by which I mean a system of implicit values which people have internalized from childhood and from which they generate answers to very different types of questions. An example: I think the opinions which people exchange at the end of a football match between Roubaix and Valenciennes owe a great deal of their coherence and logic to a class ethos. Many answers which are treated as political answers are in reality produced by a class ethos and may take on a totally different meaning when they are interpreted in political terms.

Here I must refer to a specific sociological tradition, prevalent especially among political sociologists in the United States, who commonly speak of the conservatism and authoritarianism of the working classes. These ideas are based on international comparison of surveys or elections which tend to show that each time the working classes are asked, in any country, about problems concerning relations of authority, individual liberty, freedom of the press, etc., they give answers which are more 'authoritarian' than those of the other classes. So the general conclusion is drawn that there is a conflict between democratic values (the author I am thinking of, Lipset, means American democratic values) and the authoritarian and repressive values that have been internalized by the working classes. This then leads to a kind of eschatological vision: let's raise the standard of living and the level of education and, since the propensity to repression and authoritarianism, etc., is linked to low income and low levels of education, etc., in that way we will produce good citizens of American democracy.

It appears to me that the crux of the problem is the meaning of the answers to certain questions. Imagine a group of questions like the following: 'Are you in favour of sexual equality?', 'Are you in favour of the sexual independence of married couples?', 'Are you in favour of non-repressive education?', 'Do you believe in the new society?'[1] Now imagine another type of question, like: 'Should teachers go on strike when their jobs are threatened?', 'Should teachers act in solidarity with other civil service employees during periods of social conflict?' These two groups of questions receive replies structured inversely in relation to social class. The first group of questions, which deal with a certain kind of change in social relations, in the symbolic form of social relations, provokes responses which are increasingly favourable as one ascends the social hierarchy and the hierarchy by level of education; inversely, the questions which deal with real transformation of the power relations between classes provoke increasingly unfavourable answers as one ascends the social hierarchy.

Thus the statement 'The working classes are repressive' is neither true nor false. It is true to the extent that the working classes tend to have a much more rigid and authoritarian idea about moral problems concerning relations between parents and children or between the sexes. Concerning problems of political structure, which bring into play the maintenance or transformation of the social order, and not just the conservation or transformation of the modes of relationship between individuals, the working classes are much more favourable towards a transformation of the social structure. You can see how some of the problems posed in May 1968, and often poorly posed, in the conflict between the Communist party and the far left, are closely linked to the central problem that I have just tried to present, concerning the nature of the answers people give in reply to the questions asked, that is, the principle upon which they produce their answers. The opposition I made between these two groups of questions actually amounts to the opposition between the two principles in the production of opinions, an authentically political principle and an ethical one, and the problem of the conservatism of the working classes is produced because this difference is ignored.

The effect of the imposition of a problematic, an effect produced by all opinion polls and all political questioning (not least by elections), results from the fact that the questions asked in an opinion survey are not questions which arise spontaneously for the people questioned, and that the responses are not interpreted in terms of the problematic actually referred to in their answers by the different categories of respondents. Thus the *dominant problematic*, a picture of which is provided by the list of questions posed in the last two years by the polling institutes, is the problematic which essentially interests the people who hold power and who want to be informed about the means of organizing their political action. This problematic is very unequally possessed by the different social classes, who, it is important to remember, also vary greatly in their capacity to produce a counter-problematic. Following up the theme of a televised debate between Jean-Jacques Servan-Schreiber and Valéry Giscard d'Estaing, a polling institute posed questions like 'Is educational success a function of talent, intelligence, work, or personal merit?' The answers received in fact provided some information (albeit hidden from those who gave the answers) about the extent to which the different social classes are aware of the laws governing the hereditary transmission of cultural capital. Attachment to the myth of talent, of social mobility through the school system, of the impartiality of the system, of equity in the distribution of jobs according to qualifications, etc., is very strong in the working classes. The counter-problematic may exist for a few intellectuals but it has no social force even though it has been taken up by a few parties and groups. Scientific truth is subject to the same laws of diffusion as ideology. A scientific proposition is like a papal encyclical on birth control: it only preaches to the converted.

The idea of objectivity in an opinion survey is associated with asking questions in the most neutral terms so as to give an equal chance to all possible answers. In reality, an opinion poll would no doubt be closer to what happens in reality if it were to break all the rules of 'objectivity' and give people the chance to situate themselves as they really do in real practice, that is, in relation to already formulated opinions. For example, instead of asking 'Some people are in favour of birth control, others against; how about you? . . .', it would provide a series of explicit positions taken by groups mandated to establish and diffuse opinions, so that people could place themselves in relation to responses which have already been constituted. We commonly speak in French of '*taking* a position'; the positions are there already to be taken. But we do not take them haphazardly. We take the positions which we are predisposed to take on the basis of our position in a certain field. A rigorous analysis of ideologies should seek to explain the relation between the structure of positions to be taken and the structure of the field of positions objectively occupied.

It is known that opinion polls are very bad at detecting the latent state of opinion and, more precisely, the movement of opinion. This is because the situation in which they grasp opinions is entirely artificial. In the situations in which opinion is constituted, and especially in crisis situations, people are faced with constituted opinions, opinions supported by groups, so that choosing between opinions clearly means choosing between groups. That is the principle of the *politicizing effect* of a crisis: one has to choose between groups which define themselves politically, and to take more and more positions on the basis of explicitly political principles. In fact, what seems to me to be important is that opinion polls treat public opinion as a simple sum of individual opinions, collected in a situation which is ultimately that of the polling booth, where the individual secretively expresses an isolated opinion in isolation. In real situations, opinions are forces and relations between opinions are power relations between groups.

A further law emerges here: the greater the *interest* one has in a problem, the more opinions one has on it. For example, on the education system, the rate of response is very closely related to the respondents' degree of proximity to the system itself, and the likelihood of their having an opinion varies as a function of the likelihood of having power over what they are answering about. The opinion that asserts itself, as such, spontaneously, is the opinion of people whose opinion 'carries weight', as we say. If a minister of education were to act on the basis of an opinion poll (or at least, a superficial reading of a poll), he would not do what he does when he really acts as a politician, that is, in response to the telephone calls he receives, a visit by a trade union leader, a dean, and so on. In fact, he acts on the basis of those really constituted forces of opinion which enter his perception only in so far as they have force, and in so far as they have some force because they are mobilized.

When trying to forecast what will happen to the university system in the next ten years, I think that the best basis for prediction is mobilized opinion. However, the fact that, as the 'no answers' show, the dispositions of some categories do not reach the status of opinion, in the sense of a constituted discourse aspiring to coherence, seeking to be heard, taken notice of, etc., should not lead us to the conclusion that, in crisis situations, people who had no opinion will choose one at random. If the problem is one that for them is constituted politically (for manual workers, questions of pay or working conditions), they will choose in terms of political competence. If the problem is one that for them is not constituted politically (repressive relationships within the company) or is still in the process of becoming so, they will be guided by the profoundly unconscious system of dispositions that orients their choices in extremely different areas ranging from aesthetics to everyday economic decisions. Traditional opinion surveys ignore both pressure groups and the latent dispositions which may not express themselves in the form of an explicit discourse. That is why the opinion survey is incapable of generating any kind of reasonable prediction about what would happen in a crisis situation.

Consider a problem like that of the education system. You can ask: 'What do you think of the policies of [Education Minister] Edgar Faure?' This type of question is very much like an electoral survey: it's night and all cats are grey. Everybody agrees more or less without knowing what it is they agree about – just like the National Assembly which passed his reforms unanimously. Then you ask: 'Are you in favour of bringing politics into secondary schools?' Here we find a very clear division, and the same thing happens when you ask 'Should teachers be allowed to go on strike?' Among the working classes there is a kind of transfer of specific political competence and people know exactly what to say. You can also ask: 'Should the curriculum be changed?' 'Are you in favour of continuous assessment?' 'Should parents be represented on school boards?' 'Should the *agrégation* be abolished?' – and so on. Behind the question 'What do you think of the policies of Edgar Faure?' there were all these other questions, and people were having to take a position instantly on a set of problems that a good questionnaire could only grasp if it used at least sixty questions, whose variations in every direction could then be observed. In the case of one type of question, the opinions would be related positively to position in the social hierarchy, and in another, they would be related negatively, or perhaps just a bit, or up to a certain point, or even not at all.

As soon as you realize that a national election is the extreme case of a question like 'What do you think of the policies of Edgar Faure?', you understand why specialists in political sociology are able to note that the relationship between social class and practices or opinions, which is usually observed in almost every area of social practice, is very weak when it comes to electoral phenomena, indeed so weak that some of them do not hesitate to conclude that there is no relation whatsoever between social class and the fact of voting for the right or for the left. If we keep in mind that an election poses in a single syncretic question what could only be reasonably understood in two hundred questions; that some people measure in centimetres and others in kilometres; that the candidates' strategy is to pose problems misleadingly and as far as possible to muddy the waters in order to obscure the divisions and win floating votes, together with so many other effects, then we may conclude that we ought perhaps to turn upside-down the traditional question of the relationship between voting behaviour and social class and to ask why we do, in spite of everything, find a relationship at all, albeit a weak one; and to consider the function of the electoral system, a tool which, by its very logic, tends to attenuate conflicts and cleavages.

In short, I did indeed mean to say that public opinion does not exist, at least in the form which some people, whose existence depends on this illusion, would have us believe. I've said that there is, on the one hand, mobilized opinion, formulated opinion, pressure groups mobilized around a system of explicitly formulated *interests*; and, on the other hand, there are dispositions which, by definition, are not opinion if one means by that, as I have throughout this talk, something that can be formulated in discourse with some claim to coherence. That definition of opinion is not my opinion about opinion. It's simply the explicit form of the definition assumed by opinion polls when they ask people to take a position on formulated opinions and when, by simple statistical aggregation of the opinions thus produced, they produce the artefact of public opinion. I'm simply saying that public opinion in the sense implicitly accepted by those who carry out opinion polls or those who use their findings . . . simply does not exist.

Notes

1 *La nouvelle société*, a vision of a less rigid French society put forward by Prime Minister Jacques Chaban-Delmas in 1969 [translator]

19

CULTURE AND POLITICS

I would very much like to escape from the ritual of the lecture, and I consider what I have to say as a kind of offer, a 'supply', hoping that in response to the supply that I have to offer, a demand will emerge and that we shall be able to do business.

One of the difficulties in communication between the sociologist and his readers lies in the fact that the readers are confronted with a product and very often have little idea how it has been produced. Now, strictly speaking, knowledge of the conditions of production of the product is one of the conditions of rational communication of the findings of social science. Readers have to deal with a finished product that is given to them in an order which is not that of discovery (inasmuch as it tends to move towards a deductive order, which often leads the sociologist to be suspected of having produced his theories fully armed out of his head and of having then found some empirical validations to illustrate them). The finished product, the *opus operatum*, conceals the *modus operandi*. What circulates between the science and the non-specialists, or even between a science and the specialists of other sciences (I'm thinking, for example, of linguistics, at the time when it dominated the social sciences), and what is conveyed by the great vehicles of cultural celebration, is, at best, the results, but never the operations. You are never taken into the back-rooms, the kitchens of science. Of course, I cannot give here a real-time film of the research that led me to what I am going to tell you. I shall try to give you a speeded-up and somewhat selective replay, with the aim of giving an idea of how the sociologist works.

After May 1968, I wanted to study the conflicts which take place in and about the educational system, and I started to analyse all the surveys that had been produced by public opinion agencies on the subject of the educational system, as well as the findings of a survey of the changes people wanted to see in the system, which had been conducted through the press. The most interesting information this survey yielded was the structure of the population of respondents, by social class, level of education, sex, age, and so on. For example, the probability of members of the different classes responding to this survey corresponded closely to their chances of access to higher education. The response to this questionnaire was conceived in accordance with the logic of the petition, and the self-selecting sample of the respondents was nothing other than a pressure group composed of the

---

Talk given at the University of Grenoble, 29 April 1980

people who felt they had a legitimate right to respond because they had a legitimate stake in the educational system. This population, which was not representative in the statistical sense of the word, was very representative of the pressure group which was, *de facto*, going to direct the subsequent development of the system. Thus, leaving aside the information that this survey provided on the educational system, or the power relations between the groups who aspired to affect its transformation, etc., it was possible to look into the distinctive characteristics of the respondents, who, because they had decided to respond on the basis of their particular relationship to the object in question, were saying, first and foremost: I am interested in the educational system and I am interesting for the educational system – I have to be listened to.

Following this logic, I looked with new eyes at the 'no answers', which are roughly equivalent in opinion polls to abstentions in elections, a phenomenon so normal in appearance that no one asks what they mean. The phenomenon of abstention is one of those things that everybody knows about, that everybody talks about, and that political scientists, adopting a purely normative point of view, ritually deplore as an obstacle to the proper functioning of democracy, without really taking it seriously. Now, if one bears in mind what is learned from analysis of the structure (by various variables) of a spontaneous sample, it can immediately be seen that, in the case of a representative sample, the 'no answers' (which, for some questions, may be more frequent than answers, raising the question of the statistical representativeness of the latter) contain some very important information which is wiped out by the mere fact of recalculating the percentages after excluding the 'no answers'.

Every group presented with a problem is characterized by a probability of having an opinion and, if it has an opinion, by a *conditional* probability – that's to say a second-degree and therefore quite secondary probability – of having a positive or negative opinion. Bearing in mind what emerges from analysis of the spontaneous sample of the respondents to the survey on education, we may regard the probability of answering that characterizes a group or category (e.g. men as opposed to women, or townspeople as opposed to country people) as a measure of its 'sense' of being both authorized and able to answer, being a legitimate respondent, having 'a say in the matter'. The mechanism through which opinion is expressed, starting with the vote, is based on a hidden property qualification.

But it was first necessary to enquire into the factors which determine the persons questioned to answer or to 'abstain' (rather than to choose between one reply and another). The variations observed in the rate of non-reply might have been due to two things – either the properties of the respondents or the properties of the question. If we choose to take the non-responses, the abstentions, the silences, seriously – which means we take note of their existence and thereby construct an object – then we immediately see that the most important information that a survey provides about a group is not the rate of 'yes's or 'no's, the proportions for or against, but the level of non-response, that is, the probability, for a member of that group, of *having an opinion*. In the case of opinion polls (which obey a logic quite similar to that of elections), we have the necessary information to analyse the factors that determine this probability, in the form of the rate of non-response according to different variables – sex, education, occupation, the problem posed. It can then be observed that women abstain more frequently than men and that (to put it crudely) the gap between men and women increases as the questions become more political in the ordinary sense of the word, that is, the more they appeal to a specific culture such as the history of the political field (with, for example, knowledge of the names of past and present politicians) or to the set of problems specific to professionals (e.g. constitutional questions or foreign policy issues, the extreme case, in which the rate of 'don't knows' becomes enormous, being 'Do you think there is a connection between the Vietnam War and the Arab–Israeli conflict?'). By contrast, there are moral questions (such as 'Should girls under 18 be given the pill?', etc.), where the gaps between men and women disappear. In a second highly significant variation, rates of non-response are also very strongly correlated with level of education: the higher a person's qualifications (other things being equal), the lower the rate of non-response. A third correlation, partially overlapping the second one, is between rate of non-response and social class (or socio-occupational category; it amounts to the same). There is also a strong correlation with the opposition Paris–provinces. In a word, broadly speaking, the rate of non-response varies in direct ratio to the respondents' position in the various hierarchies.

That seems to mean that people's likelihood of abstaining increases as the questions become more political and as they become politically less competent. But that is a simple tautology. In fact, we have to ask what it means to be competent. Why are women less technically competent than men? Spontaneous sociology immediately offers a score of reasons: they have less time to spare for politics, they do the housework, they are less interested. But why are they less interested? Because they have less *competence*, the word now being used not in the technical sense but in the *legal* sense, as one speaks of a competent court. To be competent is to be entitled and required to deal with something. In other words, the real law that is hidden behind these seemingly anodyne correlations is that technical, political competence, like all competences, is a social competence. That does not mean that technical competence does not exist, but it does mean that the propensity to acquire what is called technical competence rises with social competence, that is, as a function of social recognition of being worthy and therefore called upon to acquire that competence.

This circle, which again looks like a pure tautology, is the form *par excellence* of the specifically social action which consists in producing differences where none existed. Social magic can transform people by telling them they are different. That is what competitive examinations do (the 300th candidate is still something, the 301st is nothing). In other words, the social world constitutes differences by the mere fact of designating them. (Religion, which, according to Durkheim, is defined by the setting-up of a frontier between the sacred and the profane, is simply a particular case of all the acts of instituting *frontiers* through which differences of *nature* are set up between realities that in 'reality' are separated by infinitesimal, sometimes imperceptible differences.) Men are more competent politically because politics is part of their competence. The difference between men and women that we accept as self-evident, because it reappears in all practices, is based on a social imposition, the assignment of a competence. The division of labour between the sexes gives politics to the man, just as it gives him the outside, the public arena, paid work outside the home, etc., whereas it assigns woman to the domestic interior, unrecognized work, and also psychology, feeling, the reading of novels, and so on. However, things are not so simple, and the difference between the sexes varies according to class and class fraction, with the properties allotted to each sex becoming specified in each case. For example, in the two- (or rather three-) dimensional space that I constructed in *Distinction*, as one moves from the bottom to the top and from left to right, towards the fractions of the dominant class that are richest in cultural capital and poorest in economic capital, that is, the intellectuals, so the difference between the sexes tends to disappear: for example, among secondary and higher education teachers, reading of *Le Monde* is almost as common among women as among men. Conversely, as you move up but to the right, towards the traditional bourgeoisie, the difference again declines, but much less strongly. And all the evidence tends to confirm that women situated close to the intellectual pole, who are socially recognized as having political competence, have dispositions and competences in matters of politics which differ infinitely less from those of the corresponding men than do those of women in the other class fractions or the other classes.

So it can be accepted that the technically competent are those who are socially designated as competent, and that it is sufficient to designate someone as competent in order to impose on him or her a propensity to acquire the technical competence which in return is the basis of his or her social competence. This hypothesis is also valid in accounting for the effects of educational capital. In all surveys one observes a very strong correlation between educational capital, as measured by educational qualifications, and competences in areas that the educational system does not teach at all, or that it only pretends to teach, such as music, art history, etc. The direct explanation, in terms of inculcation, cannot be used. In fact, among the most hidden, most secret effects of the educational system is what I call the effect of assignment by status, the *noblesse oblige* effect. The system constantly plays on this through the effect of allocation (for example, if you put a *lycéen* in the reputedly 'high-flying' sixth-form class, our '*seconde C*', you call upon him to be a 'high flyer', to be worthy of the 'class' you attribute to him). And qualifications, especially, of course, the most prestigious ones, act according to the same logic: they assign their holders to classes which demand of them they show 'class'. The fact of being designated as academically competent, and therefore socially competent, 'implies', for example, that you read *Le Monde*, that you go to art galleries, own classical records, and so on, and of course, to come to what concerns us here, that you acquire political competence. It's another effect of that magical power whereby it is possible to distinguish people by telling them, *with authority*, that they are different, *distinguished*; or, more precisely, through the very logic of institutions such as aristocracy or academia, which constitute people as different and produce permanent differences in them, either external ones, detachable from the person, like an officer's stripes, or differences inscribed in the very person as a particular way of talking, an accent or what is called *distinction*. In short, whereas one might naïvely say that people are more politically informed, more politically competent, to the extent that they are more educated, in my view one should say that those who are socially designated as competent, as entitled and required to have political competence, are more likely to become what they are, to become what they are told they are, that is politically competent.

A mechanism such as the one I have just described means that a certain number of people eliminate themselves from the game of politics (just as they eliminate themselves from the educational system, saying that it does not interest them); and that those who disenfranchise themselves *spontaneously* are more or less the ones that the dominant fractions would disqualify if they had the power to do so. (We know that the restricted franchise systems of the past legally disqualified the people who had no right to have a say because they lacked property, qualifications or rank.) But the selective franchise works in a hidden way, and that makes all the difference. These people who disqualify themselves do so largely because they do not see themselves as possessing political competence. The social representation of competence that is socially assigned to them (particularly by the educational system, which has become one of the main agencies for the assigning of competence) becomes an unconscious disposition, a taste. Those who disqualify themselves in a sense collaborate in their own disqualification, which is tacitly recognized as legitimate by those who are its victims.

Thus, the probability of replying to an objectively political question (which will be very unequally perceived as political, depending on the same variables that determine the likelihood of replying) is linked to a set of variables entirely similar to those that govern access to culture. In other words, the chances of producing a political opinion are distributed rather like the chances of visiting museums. But we have also seen that the factors differentiating the chances of replying to questions in general come into play that much more strongly when the questions are couched in a more political language, by which I mean a language more in the style of our institutes of 'political science'. In other words, the gap between men and women and between the most educated and the least educated is particularly great when faced with questions typical of Sciences Po or the École National d'Administration (such as 'Do you think that aid to developing countries should rise with GDP?').

What does that mean? To produce an answer to the question 'Are my friends' friends my friends?', I can, as Pierre Greco points out, either think of my real friends (are the X's really friends of the Y's?) or treat the question in terms of logical calculation (that's the kind of response the educational system expects: you answer without thinking much about reality). These two ways of answering are bound up with two different relations to language, words, the world and other people. 'Strictly political' questions are questions that have to be answered in terms of logical calculation. They are questions that require the 'pure' posture, the one demanded by the educational system and by the academic use of language. Plato says somewhere, 'To opine is to speak.' In the definition of opinion, there is a whole implicit content which we forget because we are products of a system in which you have to speak (sometimes for speaking's sake, sometimes to say nothing) if you want to survive. Opinion as I have implicitly defined it so far is verbalized and verbalizable opinion, produced in response to an explicitly verbalizable question, in a form such that the answer presupposes a neutral and neutralizing relation to language. To answer a political science question in the style of the one I quoted a moment ago ('Is there a connection between the Vietnam War . . . ?') requires a posture similar to that required for writing a dissertation, a disposition that is also presupposed by a whole host of other practices, such as looking at a painting in terms of form and composition rather than subject matter. This means that, faced with opinion defined as discourse and as discourse presupposing a neutral and neutralizing relation to the object, there may be inequalities of the same type as those before a work of art, without it being possible to conclude that those who cannot 'opine', in the sense of speaking, do not have something that I cannot call political opinion, since opinion implies utterance, but which I shall call a political sense.

For example, on the problem of social classes, respondents may show themselves quite incapable of answering the question as to the existence of social classes or even as to their own position in the social structure (do you belong to the lower, middle or upper classes?), while having a quite infallible sense of class. While they cannot thematize and objectify their position, their whole attitude towards the interviewer is governed by a sense of social distance which says exactly where they are and where the interviewer is and what is the social relation between them.

An example comes to mind: an American sociologist has pointed out that the likelihood of talking politics to someone rises with the proximity of that person's political opinions to your own. How do people know that those they are going to talk politics to have the same opinions as themselves? It's a fine example of practical sense. There are some superb analyses by Goffman of meetings between strangers and the work people do to diagnose what they can and can't say, how far they can go, and so on. If in doubt, they can always talk about the weather, the least controversial subject of all.

The sociologist is dealing with people who know better than he does, in the practical mode, what he wants to know. Whether the subject is the bosses or the sub-proletariat, he has to bring to an explicit level things that his respondents know perfectly but in another mode, that's to say without really knowing them. Very often he gets no help from what people say about what they do and what they know. The sense of political orientation can govern some practical political choices without rising to the level of discourse, and it will be disconcerted and disarmed by situations in which an answer is required at the level of discourse. (That's why, except in elections, opinion polls have low predictive value, because they cannot grasp things that are not linguistically constituted.) This means that, contrary to what might be thought, those who abstain, who do not answer or who answer randomly – everything suggests that the likelihood of choosing a multiple-choice answer at random rises with the rate of 'no answers' of the category in question – are not empty vessels whose heads can be filled with *any* policy (another illusion entertained by intellectuals). They are reduced to what the medieval theologians called in a wonderful phrase *fides implicita*, implicit faith, a faith that does not rise to the level of discourse but is reduced to a practical sense. How do they choose? The classes most deprived of the capacity for opinion, those who are reduced to implicit faith, make choices at the second degree. If they are asked, 'Do you think there is a connection between this and that?', they do not know, but they delegate to an institution of their choice (a party, a union . . .) the task of making their choices for them. All Churches love *fides implicita*. The idea of *fides implicita* contains the idea of entrusting oneself.

Politics can be described by analogy with a phenomenon of the market: supply and demand. A body of professional politicians, defined as the holders of the *de facto* monopoly of the production of discourses recognized as political, produces a range of discourses that are offered to people endowed with a political taste, that is, a very unequal capacity for discerning between the discourses on offer. These discourses will be received, understood, perceived, selected, chosen and accepted on the basis of a technical competence, and more precisely a system of classification whose acuity and fineness of discrimination will vary as a function of the variables that define social competence. It becomes impossible to understand the specifically symbolic effect of the products offered if they are seen as directly called forth by the demand or inspired by some kind of direct dealing and conscious bargaining with the audience. When a journalist is described as the hack scribbler of the Catholic lobby or the lackey of capitalism, this assumes that he consciously seeks adjustment with the expectations of his readers and aims to satisfy them directly. In fact, analysis of the fields of cultural production shows that, whether among theatre and film critics or political journalists, whether in the intellectual field or the religious field, producers produce not, or not so much as people think, by reference to their audience, but by reference to their competitors. But this is still too teleological a description and might suggest that they write with the conscious intention of distinguishing themselves. In fact, they produce much more as a function of the position they occupy in a certain competitive space. It's easy to show, for example, that in the sphere of politics, the parties, like the newspapers, are constantly driven by two contrary pressures, one which leads them to sharpen their differences, even artificially, in order to distinguish themselves, to be perceptible to people applying a certain system of classification (e.g., on the right, the RPR and the UDF), and the other which leads them to extend their appeal by blurring their differences.

So, on the side of production, there's an arena of competition, which has its autonomous logic, its own history (its Tours Congress, for example),[1] and that's very important, because in politics as in art, you can't understand the latest strategies if you don't know the history of the field, which is relatively autonomous with respect to general history. On the other side, that of consumption, there's a universe of clients, who will perceive and assess the products offered through categories of perception and appreciation that vary according to several variables. The state of the distribution of political opinions at a given moment is thus the encounter between two relatively independent histories. It's the meeting between a supply developed not in response to demand but to the constraints peculiar to a political space that has a history of its own, and a demand which, although it is the product of all the individual histories in which people's political dispositions have been constituted, is organized in accordance with a homologous structure.

There's one point that I'd like to return to rapidly, because I raised it very elliptically, in a way that might lead to confusion. It's the question of the relationship between the parties, especially the Communist Party, and 'implicit faith'. Everything seems to suggest that the greater the proportion of its clientele a party draws from that sector of the consumers who depend on *fides implicita*, the less constrained it will be and the more its history will be relatively autonomous. The more deprived a social category is (we might take the extreme case of production-line workers who are female – as the majority are – and who live in the provinces, and are illiterate and virtually unqualified), the more it relies on its chosen party, to whom it entrusts itself absolutely in matters of politics. It follows that a party, situated in the relatively autonomous space of the parties, will be that much more free to trim its policies to meet the needs of competition with the other parties (recent events give such a clear empirical demonstration of this that I don't need to argue the point) when a large proportion of its clientele consists of people who have given it a blank cheque once and for all. That's what needs to be borne in mind when considering the process of bureaucratization of revolutionary parties, whether in France or in the Soviet Union. (One also needs to bear in mind, of course, the specific logic of *delegation*, which tends to dispossess, in favour of professional officials, those who did not surrender themselves totally.) This means that the iron law of oligarchies, namely the tendency of power, even revolutionary power, to be concentrated in the hands of a few, which the neo-Machiavellians present as the inevitable tendency of political bureaucracies, is enormously strengthened by this relation of implicit faith.

That is why, in conclusion, I'd want to discuss rapidly the question of the conditions in which the practical political sense can move to the level of explicitness. Labov has shown that American blue-collar workers have a strong resistance to acculturation as regards pronunciation, because, he says, they unconsciously identify their class accent with their virility – as if their class sense were lodged in their throats, as if a certain kind of tough-guy guttural speech were a (quite unconscious) refusal of the dominant diction, a defence of working-class identity that can also be located in a certain way of swinging the shoulders, etc. (This also has an important role in the choice of union delegates: CGT delegates have a quite distinctive manner and look, and we know that in the relations between communists and ultra-leftists, bodily indices, short or long hair, and style of dress play an important part.)

So there's this class sense, hidden away deep in the body, a relation to the body which is a relation to class, and then there is consciousness and class consciousness. This is one of the favourite areas for populist fantasy. From the very beginning, in Marx himself, the problem of the awakening of class consciousness has been posed rather as philosophers pose the problem of the theory of knowledge. I think that what I've said this evening helps to pose the problem rather more realistically in the form of the problem of the shift from the deep-seated, corporeal dispositions in which a class lives without articulating itself as such, to modes of expression both verbal and non-verbal (such as demonstrations).

There's a whole analysis to be done of the ways in which a group is able to constitute itself as a group, to constitute its identity, symbolize itself, to move from a population of workers to a labour movement or a working class. This transition, which presupposes *representation* in the sense of delegation, but also in the theatrical sense of *mise-en-scène*, is a very complicated alchemy in which the specific effect of the 'discursive supply', the range of already existing discourses and available models of action (demos, strikes, etc.), plays an important part.

This can be seen in opinion polls. When the most deprived have to choose between several 'pre-formed' answers, they can always point to one of the already formulated opinions (which masks the essential point here, that they would not necessarily have been able to formulate it, especially in the terms that are used). When they have cues enabling them to recognize the 'right' answer or a party line which designates it, they may even single out the one that best corresponds to their declared political affiliations. If not, they are condemned to what I have called *allodoxia*, the mistaking of one opinion for another, just as from a distance one takes one person for another (the equivalent of what, in other areas, leads people to take Golden Delicious for apples, or leatherette for leather, or Strauss waltzes for classical music). They are endlessly likely to make mistakes about the quality of the product, because they choose with a class sense when what is needed is class consciousness. A politician may be chosen for his (appealing) looks when he should be chosen for what he says. The *allodoxia* effect is partly due to the fact that the producers of opinions unconsciously manipulate class *habitus*, through communications that are set up between class bodies without passing through the consciousness of either the sender or the receiver. Thus one 'class throat' speaks to another. What I am presenting here is obviously problematic; it's not at all the last word on the subject, I simply wanted to show that too often these questions are presented in a way that is both too abstract and too simple.

In any case, and on this I shall conclude, it's only when one gives serious attention to these facts which are so self-evident that they pass for insignificant, these banal things which most of those whose task in life is to understand and articulate the social world would consider unworthy of their attention, that one is able to construct theoretical models that are both very general and yet not 'empty'. One of these, I believe, would be the model I have put forward here of the production and consumption of political opinions, which would also be valid for other cultural products.

Note

1   This took place in 1920, when the French Left split between Communists and Socialists [translator].

20

STRIKES AND POLITICAL ACTION

Could 'strikes' be one of those 'preconstructed' objects that researchers allow to be foisted on them? First of all, it is generally agreed that a strike only has meaning if it is resituated in the field of labour struggles, the objective structure of power relations defined by the struggle between, on the one hand, workers (for whom a strike is the principal weapon) and on the other, employers, with a possible third actor (which may not be one), the State.

One then comes up against the problem (directly posed by the notion of a general strike) of the degree of unification of this field. I would like to give it a more general formulation by referring to a article by the American economist O. W. Phelps. Contrary to the classical theory that conceives the market as a unified set of free transactions, Phelps observes that there is no single labour market but rather *several labour markets*, which have their own structures, by which he means the 'set of mechanisms that permanently govern the question of the different employment functions – recruitment, selection, job allocation, pay – and which, being based on law, contract, custom or national policy, have as their main function to determine the rights and privileges of employees and to bring regularity and predictability into labour management and everything that concerns labour'. Isn't the historical tendency towards a gradual shift from local labour markets (in other words, fields of struggle) to a more integrated labour market, in which local conflicts are more likely to trigger off broader conflicts?

What are the factors of unification? We can distinguish economic factors and specifically 'political' factors, namely the existence of an apparatus for mobilization – the trade unions. It has constantly been assumed here that there is a relationship between the unification of the economic mechanisms and the unification of the field of struggle; and also a relationship between the unification of the apparatus of struggle and the unification of the field of struggle. In fact, there is every reason to think that the 'nationalization' of the economy favours the development of national apparatuses that are increasingly autonomous with respect to their local base, a development which favours the generalization of local conflicts. To what extent is there relative autonomy of the political agents of struggle and to what extent is the unification to be ascribed to the unifying action of the unions? Doesn't

---

Concluding remarks made at a symposium on European social history, organized by the Maison des Sciences de l'Homme, Paris, 2–3 May 1975

the fact that every strike that breaks out can become generalized (obviously with varying success depending on the economic sector, which may be more or less strategic – or symbolic) incline us to overestimate the objective unification of this field? It might be that this unification is much more voluntaristic, much more attributable to the organizations than to objective solidarities. One of the major problems of the future could well be the mismatch between the *national* character of union organizations and the *international* character of firms and the economy.

But, with respect to each state of the field, it is possible to ask how closed it is, and to consider, for example, whether the real centre of the existence of the working class is in the field or outside the field. The problem arises, for example, in the case of a working-class world that is still strongly linked to the peasant world, to which it returns or in which it places its income; or, *a fortiori*, in the case of a foreign sub-proletariat, as in Europe today. By contrast, the whole working-class population may be sharply separated from the external world and have *all its interests* in the field of struggle. And again, variations can be found depending on whether that separation has occurred *within that generation* or *over several generations*.

Seniority in entry into the field measures the duration of what might be called the process of 'operativization' or 'factoryization' (if you will accept that barbarous concept, forged along the lines of the notion of 'asylumization' devised by Goffman to refer to the process whereby people in prisons, barracks and all 'total institutions' progressively adapt to the institution and, in a way, come to terms with it). By that, I mean the process through which workers appropriate their firm and are appropriated by it, appropriate their machinery and are appropriated by it, appropriate their working-class traditions and are appropriated by them, appropriate their union and are appropriated by it, and so on. Several aspects can be distinguished within this process. The first, entirely negative, consists in the abandonment of external interests. These interests or stakes may be entirely real: one thinks of emigrant workers who send their money home to their families, buy land or farm equipment or shops back home. Or they may be imaginary but no less potent: this is the case with emigrant workers who, though having lost all real hope of returning home, remain *in transit* and so never become completely 'operativized'.

Next, whatever the state of their external linkages, workers may identify with their position in the field of struggle, totally embrace the interests associated with it, without changing their deep-rooted dispositions. Thus, as Eric Hobsbawm points out, peasants who have only recently entered industrial labour may engage in revolutionary struggles without losing anything of their peasant dispositions.

At another stage in the process, their deep-rooted dispositions may be modified by the objective laws of the industrial milieu; they may learn rules of behaviour that they have to observe in order to be accepted (as regards rate of work, or solidarity, for example); they may espouse collective values (such as respect for the machines with which they work), or again, take on the collective history of the group, its traditions, especially of struggle, and so on.

Finally, they may be integrated into the *world of organized labour*, losing in the realm of what might be called 'primary' revolt – the often violent and unorganized revolt of peasants suddenly cast into the industrial world – and gaining in the realm of 'secondary', organized revolt. Does trade unionism widen or narrow the range of demands? That is a question which this line of thinking leads to.

Tilly has emphasized the need to consider the system of agents involved in struggle – employers, workers, the State – as a whole. The problem of relations with the other classes is a very important element which Haimson alluded to when describing the ambivalence of some fractions of the working class towards the bourgeoisie. This is where the local/national opposition takes on its full meaning. The objective relations that are described in the form of the triad 'employers–workers–State' take very different concrete forms depending on the size of the firm, but also depending on the social environment of the working life: you do or don't see the boss, you do or don't see his daughter going to church, you do or don't see how he lives, and so on. Ways of life are one of the concrete mediations between the objective structure of the labour market and mental structure, and consequently the experience people can have of the struggle, etc. The objective relations that define the field of struggle are apprehended in all the concrete *interactions* and not only in the workplace (and that is one of the bases of paternalism). Those are the terms in which one has to try to understand that, as Haimson suggests, the city seems more favourable to working-class consciousness, whereas, in a small, entirely working-class town, the growth of class consciousness is less rapid but more radical. The class structure as it is perceived at local level seems to be an important mediation in understanding the strategies of the working class.

We now have to ask how, in each case, this field of struggles functions. There are some structural invariants and we can construct a very abstract 'model' of them in order to analyse the variants. A first question, posed by Tilly, is whether there are two or three positions: does the State simply duplicate the employers? Tilly tries to show that in the case of France, the State is a real agent. Is it a real agent or a euphemized, legitimized expression of the relationship between employers and workers (which exists at least in so far as it has the appearance of reality)? This is a question raised by comparison between the workers' struggles in Russia between 1905 and 1917 and in France under the Third Republic (we might also think of the case of Sweden: what is the particular form taken by the struggle when the State is strongly controlled by the trade unions?). We would need a model of all the possible forms of the relationship between the State and the employers (without excluding the Soviet model) in order to see the form that the workers' struggle takes in each case.

There is a fundamental question that has not been fully brought out: when we talk about the relationship between the State, the employers and the workers, it is not entirely legitimate to contrast the objective reality of this relationship (are the State and the employers interdependent or not; are they allies or does the State have an umpiring role?) with the subjective reality from the point of view of the working class (class consciousness or false consciousness). The fact that the State is seen as autonomous ('our State', 'our Republic') is an objective factor. In the case of France – especially at certain times and in certain circumstances – the State is seen by the working class as independent, as a referee. And the State can be or seem to be a referee, in so far as it acts to maintain order (often against the ruling class, which, in blind defence of its short-term interests, would otherwise cut off the branch on which it sits). In other words, when we talk about the State, are we talking about its material force (army, police, etc.) or its symbolic force, which may consist in the recognition of the State implied in misrecognition of the real role of the State? Legitimacy means misrecognition, and what are called legitimate forms of struggle (a strike is legitimate, sabotage is not) represent a dominant definition which is not perceived as such, which is recognized by the dominated groups to the extent that the interest that the dominant groups have in that definition is misrecognized.

We need to bring into a description of the field of conflicts agencies which have not so far been mentioned, such as the educational system, which helps to inculcate, among other things, a *meritocratic vision* of the distribution of hierarchical positions, through the matching of qualifications to jobs; or national service, which plays a key role in preparing for 'operativization'. Perhaps one should add the legal system, which fixes at every moment the established state of power relations, thus helping to maintain them; or the social services, which now play a central role, and all the other institutions responsible for the soft forms of violence. The idea, inculcated by the educational system, that people have the jobs they deserve on the basis of their education and their qualifications plays a decisive role in imposing hierarchies at work and outside work. To regard educational qualifications as the titles of nobility of our society is no wild analogy. They have a crucial role in this process of inculcating a sense of propriety into class relations. Alongside the tendential law of the unification of struggles, there is a shift from forms of rough violence to forms of soft, symbolic violence.

A second question: in this struggle, how are the legitimate stakes and means, that is, what it is legitimate to fight for and the means that it is legitimate to use, defined? There is struggle over the stakes and means of struggle, not only between the dominant and the dominated, but also among the dominated themselves. One of the subtleties of the power relations between the dominant and the dominated is that, in this struggle, the dominant may exploit the struggle among the dominated over the legitimate means and ends (for example, the opposition between quantitative and qualitative demands, or the opposition between economic and political strikes). There's a whole social history to be done of the discussion about legitimate class struggle: what is it legitimate to do to a boss, and so on? This question was re-posed in practice when workers started locking bosses in their offices after May 1968: why are these acts against the person of the boss regarded as scandalous? It might be wondered if every recognition of limits to struggle, every recognition of the illegitimacy of certain means or certain ends, does not weaken the struggle of the dominated, does not weaken the dominated. Economism, for example, is a strategy of the dominant: it consists in saying that the legitimate demand of the dominated is wages and nothing else. On that point, I refer you back to everything that Tilly said about the French employer's extraordinary interest in his authority, about the fact that he may give way on wages but will refuse to treat the dominated as acceptable partners in dialogue and communicates with them through posters on notice boards, etc.

What is the definition of a legitimate demand? It is essential here, as Michèle Perrot pointed out, to consider the structure of the system of demands and, as Tilly said, the structure of the means of struggle. You cannot study a demand such as a wage claim independently of the system of other claims (working conditions and so on). Similarly, you cannot study a means of struggle, such as a strike, independently of the system of the other means of struggle, if only to note, in some cases, that they are not used. The fact of thinking *structurally* brings out the importance of absences.

It seems that at every moment in workers' struggles, three levels can be distinguished: first, there is an 'unthought' aspect of the struggle (what is 'taken for granted', the doxa), and one of the effects of 'operativization' is that there are things that no one thinks of disputing and demanding because they do not come to mind or are not 'reasonable'; secondly, there is what is *unthinkable*, what is explicitly condemned ('what we know the bosses will not give way on' – sacking a foreman, talking with a workers' delegate, etc.); and, at a third level, there is the claimable, the demandable, the legitimate object of demands.

The same analyses are valid for the definition of the legitimate means (strikes, sabotage, confinement of managers, etc.). The unions are responsible for defining the 'right', 'correct' strategy. Does that mean the most effective strategy in absolute terms – with no holds barred – or the one that is most effective because it is the most 'appropriate' in a social context implying a particular definition of the legitimate and the illegitimate? In the collective production of this *definition of legitimate ends and means*, of what, for example, constitutes a 'fair' and 'reasonable' strike or a 'wildcat strike', journalists and all the professional analysts ('political scientists') – often in fact the same people – now play a decisive role; in this context, the distinction between political strikes and non-political (i.e. purely economic) strikes is a politically motivated one that science cannot take over with impunity. There is a political manipulation of the definition of the political. *The question of what is at stake in the struggle is part of what is at stake in the struggle*: at every moment there is a struggle to say if it is 'appropriate' or not to fight on this or that point. That is one of the channels through which symbolic violence is exercised, as soft, disguised violence. We need an analysis of the 'Geneva conventions' of social conflict, that is, the whole set of norms, clearly varying greatly from period to period and society to society, which impose themselves on the dominated at a given point in time and which oblige the workers to set limits to their action out of a sort of concern for respectability, which leads to acceptance of the dominant definition of acceptable struggle (for example, the concern not to inconvenience the public by a strike). It would be interesting to make a systematic collection of all the reminders of these conventions; and also to see all the mechanisms which work in that direction, including linguistic censorship.

Third question: what factors determine the strength of the different sides in a strike? We may posit that their strategies will depend at every moment, in part at least, on the strength they objectively wield in the power relations (the structure), that is, on the strength they have acquired and accumulated through previous struggles (the history). This is to the extent that these power relations are correctly perceived and appreciated on the basis of the instruments of perception (whether theoretical or grounded in the experience of previous struggles) that are available to the agents.

In the case of the workers, the strike is the main instrument of struggle, because one of the few weapons they have is precisely the *withdrawal of labour*, either total (secession or strike) or partial (a go-slow). It would be interesting to determine the costs and benefits of these different forms of withdrawal for the two sides, and so to provide the means of analysing how, on the basis of this system of costs and benefits, the system of strategies that Tilly refers to will be organized. One illustration of the proposition that strategies depend on the state of the power relations can be found in the dialectic described by Montgommery, with reference to the beginnings of Taylorism in the US: unionization, which increases the workers' strength, leads to lower productivity to which the employers respond with Taylorization and a whole set of new management techniques (the origins of American sociology of labour).

Another weapon available to the workers is their physical strength (which, together with weapons, is a component of fighting strength). In terms of that logic one would have to analyse the values of masculinity and combativeness (which are one of the ways in which the Army may ensnare the working classes by exalting the male virtues, machismo, physical strength). But there is also symbolic violence and, in that respect, the strike is a particularly interesting instrument: it is an instrument of real violence that has symbolic effects through the demonstration and affirmation of the cohesion of the group, the collective break with the everyday order that it produces, and so on.

The distinctive feature of the workers' strategies is that they are effective *only if they are collective*, and therefore conscious and methodical, that is, mediated by an *organization* designed to define the objectives and organize the struggle. That would be sufficient to explain why the working-class condition tends to favour *collectivist* (as opposed to individualist) dispositions, if there were not a whole set of factors, constitutive of their conditions of existence, acting in the same direction – the risks of the work and the uncertainties of the whole of existence, which impose solidarity; experience of the interchangeability of the workers (reinforced by the strategies of deskilling) and of submission to the verdict of the labour market, which tends to exclude the idea of the 'fair price' of labour (an idea so strong among craftsmen and members of the independent professions). (Another difference between the worker and the craftsman is that the worker is less likely to mystify himself and to find his symbolic gratifications in the idea that his work is worth more than its price and that he thereby establishes a relationship of non-monetary exchange with his clientele.) The absence of any idea of 'career' (with seniority sometimes playing a negative role) also introduces a fundamental difference between manual workers and white-collar employees, who may invest in individual competition for promotion what the workers – despite the hierarchies within the working class itself – can only invest in collective struggle. The fact that manual workers can assert their strength and value only collectively structures their whole world view and marks a important separation from the petite-bourgeoisie. In this respect, one would need to analyse the 'economic morality' of the working class – as E. P. Thompson has for the pre-industrial period – and determine the principles of evaluation of the price of labour (relationship of labour time to wage; comparison of wages assigned to equivalent work; relationship of needs – family – to wages, etc.).

It follows from this that the strength of the sellers of labour power depends fundamentally on the mobilization and organization of the mobilized group, and consequently, to some extent at least, on the existence of a (trade union) apparatus capable of fulfilling the functions of expression, mobilization, organization and representation.

But that raises a problem which sociologists have never really thought through – that of the nature of groups and the modes of aggregation. There is a first mode of aggregation which is the *additive* or *recurrent* group $(1+1+1 \ldots)$. The dominant strategies always tend to ensure that there is not a group but a series of individuals (in the nineteenth century, the bosses sought to deal with the workers individually, one by one); the opinion poll or secret ballot is always invoked against the show of hands and delegation. Likewise, bonus systems and many other systems of remuneration are so many divisive strategies, in other words depoliticizing strategies (this is one of the bases of the bourgeois horror of the collective and the exaltation of the individual).

The second mode is *collective mobilization*. This is the group assembling physically in the same place and manifesting its strength by its number (hence the importance of the dispute over numbers – the police always say there were 10,000 demonstrators and the unions 20,000).

Finally, there is *delegation*: the words of the union representative speaking for perhaps half a million people (the second and third modes are not mutually exclusive). We need a comparative sociology and history of the modes and procedures of delegation (for example, it is often said that the French tradition favours the mass meeting), the modes of designation of delegates and the characteristics of delegates (for example, the CGT delegate tends to be a solidly built, serious-minded, respectable family man with a moustache, with many years' service in the firm behind him, etc.). Finally, we would need to consider the *nature of the delegation*: what does it mean to delegate to someone a power to express, represent, mobilize and organize? What is the nature of the opinion produced *by proxy*? Just what is this delegation of the power to produce opinions that so offends bourgeois sensibilities, which are so attached to what they call 'personal opinion', an 'authenticity' which we know is simply the misrecognized product of the same mechanisms?

What do delegates *do*? Do they open or close the range of demands? What does the expressive capacity of a spokesman consist in? There's a pain and then there's a language to name it (one thinks of the patient–doctor relationship). The language gives the means of expressing the pain, but at the same time it *closes off* the range of demands that could spring from a generalized discomfort; it makes the sickness exist, makes it possible to appropriate it by constituting it objectively, but at the same time it dispossesses ('I used to feel bad all over, but now I know it's my liver', 'it used to be the whole job, the working conditions, that made me feel sick, but now I know the pain's in my pay'). The notion of the awakening of consciousness may be defined in maximalist or minimalist terms: is it a question of sufficient consciousness to be able to think and express the situation (the problem of the dispossession and reappropriation of the means of expression) and to organize and direct the struggle, or merely of sufficient consciousness to delegate these functions to apparatuses capable of fulfilling them in the best interests of the delegators (*fides implicita*)?

In fact, this way of posing the problem is typically intellectualist: it's the approach that comes most naturally to intellectuals and also the one that most conforms to the interests of intellectuals, since it makes them the indispensable mediation between the proletariat and its revolutionary truth. In fact, as Thompson has often shown, class consciousness and revolt can spring from processes that have nothing to do with the kind of revolutionary *cogito* that intellectuals imagine (it may be, for example, indignation and revolt aroused by bloodshed).

The fact remains that the mobilization of the working class is linked to the existence of a symbolic apparatus for the production of instruments of perception and expression of the social world and labour struggles – all the more so since the dominant class constantly tends to produce and impose demobilizing models of perception and expression (for example, nowadays the adversaries in labour struggles are described as 'social partners'). If one accepts, as some texts by Marx suggest, that language can be identified with consciousness, then raising the question of class consciousness amounts to asking what apparatus of perception and expression the working class has in order to understand and speak of its condition. A comparative history of the vocabularies of struggle would be very important in this respect: what are the words used (words for 'employers' and 'managers', for example), and the euphemisms (e.g. 'social partners'). How are these euphemisms produced and diffused (for example, we know that the French planning commissions have played a major role in producing these euphemisms and a whole collective discourse which the dominated take over virtually lock, stock and barrel)?

As regards the *employers*, one would need to analyse, among other things, their representation of the labour struggle and what is at stake in it (which is not solely economic but may call into question the image that management has of its authority and its role), and their relationship with the State, which may in some cases defend their interests against themselves (or at least the interests of their class as a whole, at the expense of the most reactionary part of the class), etc.

Having established the system of determinant factors of the structure of power relations, one would finally need to establish the factors tending to reinforce or weaken the action of those factors. These might include: the economic situation of the day, and in particular the degree of tension of the labour market; the political situation and the intensity of repression; the experience of previous struggles which, in the dominant class, favours development of methods of manipulation and the art of concessions, and, in the dominated class, mastery of the proletarian methods of struggle (with a corresponding tendency towards the ritualization of strategies); the degree of homogeneity or heterogeneity of the working class; working conditions, etc. In each historical situation, it is the whole set of factors (which are in any case not all independent) which varies, so defining the power relationship and, consequently, the strategies aimed at transforming it.

21

THE RACISM OF 'INTELLIGENCE'

The first point I would make is that there is no single racism, there are *racisms* in the plural. There are as many racisms as there are groups who need to justify themselves in existing as they exist; this is the invariant function of all racisms.

It seems to me very important to bring analysis to bear on the forms of racism that are the most subtle, the most readily misrecognizable, and therefore the least often denounced, perhaps because those who ordinarily denounce racism possess some of the properties conducive to this form of racism. I am thinking of IQ racism, the racism of intelligence. IQ racism is a racism of the dominant class that differs in a host of ways from what is generally called racism, that's to say the petit-bourgeois racism which is the central target of most classic critiques of racism, including the most vigorous of them, such as that by Sartre.

This racism is characteristic of a dominant class whose reproduction depends to a large extent on the transmission of cultural capital, an inherited capital that has the property of being an *embodied*, and therefore apparently natural, innate, capital. The racism of intelligence is the means through which the members of the dominant class aim to produce a 'theodicy of their own privilege', as Weber puts it, in other words a justification of the social order that they dominate. It is what causes the dominant class to feel justified in being dominant: they feel themselves to be *essentially* superior. Every racism is an essentialism, and the racism of intelligence is the form of sociodicy characteristic of a dominant class whose power is partly based on possession of 'titles' which, like educational qualifications, are presumed to be guarantees of intelligence, and which, in many societies, even for access to positions of economic power, have taken the place of earlier titles such as titles of property and of nobility.

This racism derives some of its properties from the fact that censorship of the crudest and most brutal forms of racism has become stronger, so that the racist impulse can only be expressed in highly euphemized forms, masked by denial (in the psychoanalytic sense). The GRECE[1] uses a language in which it expresses racism but in such a way that it does not express it. When brought in this way to a high degree of euphemization,

Talk given at a Colloquium of the MRAP, UNESCO, May 1978, published in *Cahiers Droit et liberté (Races, sociétés et aptitudes: apports et limites de la science)*, 382, 1978: 67–71 racism becomes virtually *misrecognizable*. The new racists are faced with a problem of optimization: either they increase the overt racist content of their discourse (for example, by coming out in favour of eugenics), at the risk of shocking the audience and losing in communicability, transmissibility, or they decide to say less, in a highly euphemized form, conforming to the norms of the prevailing censorship (by talking about genetics or ecology, for example), and so increase the chance of 'getting the message across' by slipping it through unnoticed.

The most widespread form of euphemization nowadays is obviously the apparent scientificization of language. If scientific discourse is invoked to justify IQ racism, that is not only because science represents the dominant form of legitimate discourse, but also, and more importantly, because a power that believes itself to be based on science, a technocratic type of power, naturally asks science to be the basis of power; because intelligence is what gives the right to govern when government claims to be based on science and on the 'scientific' competence of those who govern (I'm thinking of the role of the sciences in educational selection, where mathematics has become the measure of all intelligence). Science is bound up with what it is asked to justify.

Having said that, I think one should purely and simply refuse to accept the problem of the biological or social foundations of 'intelligence', in which psychologists have allowed themselves to be trapped. Rather than trying to decide the question scientifically, one should to try to look scientifically at the question itself – and try to analyse the social conditions of the emergence of this kind of enquiry and of the class racism to which it points the way. In fact, the arguments of the GRECE are simply the extreme form of the arguments that have come for many years from some *grande école* alumni associations; it is the language of 'leaders' who feel themselves to be legitimized by 'intelligence' and who dominate a society founded on discrimination based on 'intelligence', that is, founded on what the educational system measures under the term 'intelligence'. Intelligence is what is measured by intelligence tests, that is, what the educational system measures. That is all there is to be said in a debate which cannot be decided so long as one remains on the terrain of psychology, because psychology itself (or IQ testing, at least) is the product of the social determinations which are the source of IQ racism, the kind of racism specific to 'élites' whose position is bound up with educational success, a dominant class deriving its legitimacy from educational classification.

Educational classification is a euphemized version of social classification, a social classification that has become natural and absolute, having been censored and alchemically transmuted in such a way that class differences turn into differences of 'intelligence', 'talent', and therefore differences of nature. Religions were never so successful. In educational classification, a social discrimination is legitimized and given the sanction of science. And there we again find psychology and the reinforcement it has brought from the very beginning to the functioning of the educational system. The invention of intelligence tests like the Binet-Simon test is linked to the arrival in the educational system, due to compulsory schooling, of pupils that the system could not cope with, because they were not 'predisposed', 'gifted', that is, endowed by their home background with the predispositions assumed by the ordinary functioning of the school system – cultural capital and a positive attitude towards academic rewards and punishments. Tests which measure the social predisposition required by the school – hence their capacity to predict scholastic success – are a perfect instrument for legitimizing in advance the academic verdicts which in turn legitimize the tests.

Why now this new upsurge of IQ racism? Perhaps a good number of teachers and intellectuals – who have been hit head-on by the crisis of the educational system – are more inclined to express or tolerate the expression in the crudest forms of what was previously a discreet high-table élitism. But we also need to ask why the impulse that leads to IQ racism has also increased. I think it's largely due to the fact that fairly recently the educational system found itself confronted with almost unprecedented problems due to the arrival of people who lacked the socially constituted dispositions that it tacitly demands. Above all, these were people who, by their number, devalued academic qualifications and even devalued the posts they would occupy thanks to those qualifications. Hence the dream (already a reality in some disciplines, like medicine) of the *numerus clausus*. All racisms resemble one another. The *numerus clausus* is a kind of protectionist measure, analogous to immigration restrictions, a riposte to 'overcrowding' provoked by the fear of being 'overwhelmed' by invading hordes.

One is always ready to stigmatize the stigmatizer, to denounce the elementary, 'vulgar' racism of petit-bourgeois resentment. But that's too easy. We must turn the tables and ask what contribution intellectuals make to IQ racism. We should study the role that doctors play in the medicalizing, that is, the naturalizing, of social differences, social stigmata, and the role of psychologists, psychiatrists and psychoanalysts in producing euphemisms that make it possible to refer to the children of sub-proletarians or immigrants in such a way that social cases become psychological cases, and social deficiencies mental deficiencies, etc. In other words, we need to analyse all the forms of second-degree legitimation which reinforce educational legitimation as legitimate discrimination, not forgetting would-be scientific arguments, psychological discourse, and the very remarks we make ourselves.

Note

1   A group of right-wing intellectuals purporting to research on 'European civilization', flourishing in the 1980s [translator].

Further reading

For further discussion, see Bourdieu, P. (1978) *The Inheritors: French Students and Their Relation to Culture*, Chicago and London: Chicago University Press, 77–97.

INDEX